The Honey of Souls

Cassiodorus and the Interpretation
of the Psalms in the Early Medieval West

Derek A. Olsen

A Michael Glazier Book

LITURGICAL PRESS
Collegeville, Minnesota
www.litpress.org

A Michael Glazier Book published by Liturgical Press

Cover design by Jodi Hendrickson. Cover illustration: St. Albans Psalter. Dombibliothek Hildesheim, HS St. God. 1 (Property of the Basilica of St. Godehard, Hildesheim), p. 119.

Unless otherwise noted, Scripture texts in this work are taken from the *New Revised Standard Version Bible*, © 1989, Division of Christian Education of the National Council of the Churches of Christ in the United States of America. Used by permission. All rights reserved.

© 2017 by Order of Saint Benedict, Collegeville, Minnesota. All rights reserved. No part of this book may be reproduced in any form, by print, microfilm, microfiche, mechanical recording, photocopying, translation, or by any other means, known or yet unknown, for any purpose except brief quotations in reviews, without the previous written permission of Liturgical Press, Saint John's Abbey, PO Box 7500, Collegeville, Minnesota 56321-7500. Printed in the United States of America.

Library of Congress Cataloging-in-Publication Data

Names: Olsen, Derek A., author.
Title: The honey of souls : Cassiodorus and the interpretation of the Psalms in the early Medieval West / Derek A. Olson.
Description: Collegeville, Minnesota : Liturgical Press, [2017] | "A Michael Glazier Book." | Includes bibliographical references.
Identifiers: LCCN 2017023548 (print) | LCCN 2017039285 (ebook) | ISBN 9780814684382 (ebook) | ISBN 9780814684146
Subjects: LCSH: Cassiodorus, Senator, approximately 487–approximately 580. Expositio Psalmorum. | Bible. Psalms—Commentaries—Early works to 1800. | Bible. Psalms—Criticism, interpretation, etc.—History—Middle Ages, 600–1500.
Classification: LCC BS1429.C373 (ebook) | LCC BS1429.C373 O47 2017 (print) | DDC 223.2070902—dc23
LC record available at https://lccn.loc.gov/2017023548

Contents

List of Abbreviations   vii

Introduction   ix

Chapter One: The Psalter, a Bible in Miniature   1

Chapter Two: Technological Challenges   27

Chapter Three: Cassiodorus and His Work   61

Chapter Four: An Initial Glance at the *Explanation of the Psalms*   91

Chapter Five: Cassiodorus and the Interpretive Framework   114

Chapter Six: The Preface to the Commentary   147

Chapter Seven: Editing Augustine and Reading the Scriptures   181

Chapter Eight: A Thorough Reading of Psalm 87   220

Chapter Nine: Five Psalms—Short Takes   232

Chapter Ten: The Legacy of Cassiodorus   274

Bibliography   305

Index   309

Abbreviations

ChrDoc — Augustine, *On Christian Doctrine*, trans. D. W. Robertson Jr., Library of Liberal Arts (Upper Saddle River, NJ: Prentice-Hall, 1958)

Conferences — John Cassian, *John Cassian: The Conferences*, trans. Boniface Ramsey, Ancient Christian Writers 57 (Mahwah, NJ: Paulist Press, 1997)

Enarrations — Augustine, *Expositions on the Psalms*, 6 vols., trans. Maria Boulding (New York: New City Press, 2000–2004)

ExplPs — Cassiodorus, *Cassiodorus: Explanation of the Psalms*, 3 vols., trans. P. G. Walsh, Ancient Christian Writers 51–53 (Mahwah, NJ: Paulist Press, 1990)

Institutions — Cassiodorus, *Institutions of Divine and Secular Learning and On the Soul*, trans. James W. Halporn with an introduction by Mark Vessey, Translated Texts for Historians 42 (Liverpool: Liverpool University Press, 2004)

NPNF[1] — *The Nicene and Post-Nicene Fathers, Series 1*, ed. Philip Schaff, 14 vols. (1886–1889; repr. Grand Rapids, MI: Eerdmans)

NPNF[2] — *The Nicene and Post-Nicene Fathers, Series 2*, ed. Philip Schaff and Henry Wace, 14 vols. (1887–1900; repr. Grand Rapids, MI: Eerdmans, 1996)

PL	Patrologia Latina, ed. J.-P. Migne, 217 vols. (Paris, 1844–1864)
Variae	Cassiodorus, *The* Variae *of Magnus Aurelius Cassiodorus Senator*, trans. S. J. B. Barnish, Translated Texts for Historians 12 (Liverpool: Liverpool University Press, 1992)
Wars	Procopius, *The Wars of Justinian*, trans. H. B. Dewing, rev. Anthony Kaldellis (Indianapolis: Hackett Publishing, 2014)

Introduction

There is a sense in which this book is the investigation of a single work, the *Explanation of the Psalms*, by Flavius Magnus Aurelius Cassiodorus Senator, written in Latin at Constantinople between the years 540 and 555 and subsequently finished in his family estates in Italy. This could be a tidy book that would examine the textual tradition of the earliest and most important manuscripts and then devolve into technical terminology about how the interpretive work was done, chiefly with reference to source study and tracing the history of ideas found within the text. Such a work would be a dry and dusty tome, useful only to scholars of the history of the interpretation of the Old Testament. Thankfully, this is not that book.

It can't be that book, because the story of Cassiodorus and his Psalms commentary is bigger, broader, and much more exciting than the treatment usually reserved for late patristic biblical commentaries. This book can't restrict itself to one man in one decade or even to a single text. Because to do so would be to not tell the whole truth about this commentary and what it witnesses to.

This commentary is the book that taught the Middle Ages how to read.

Okay—that's an exaggeration. But not by much.

In order to tell the story of this book and why it is important, we have to deal with the first thousand years of Christianity in the West. We have to talk not just about this book but about books as things, as physical objects with dimension and heft. We have to talk about the Psalms, what it is about this one book of the Bible that gives it such an important place in the history, theology, and spirituality of the church. We have to talk about a whole movement of people and ideas from which this commentary proceeds and that would be shaped by it ever after. But even more than those things, we have to talk about people, fascinating and flawed people, who through the checkered stories of their lives bear witness to faith, to seeking after God, and to the transformation of their lives through encounters with the psalms and the gospels. This commentary matters because those stories reveal why it is interesting and important.

Cassiodorus would insist to you that there is nothing new or unusual or original about his book at all. Naturally, he'd be lying to you. But we have to explore *why* he would choose to lie, what makes that lie interesting to him, how it's not totally a lie, and how the truth behind it would change the way that people would encounter the psalms for the next five hundred years and arguably much longer.

As a child I loved a story attributed to the Hodja Nasreddin, the wise fool of medieval Muslim folktales. He was searching under a streetlight for a valuable ring he had lost and some companions assisted him in the search. After some time, they grew frustrated and asked him exactly where he had lost it. He replied, "Down the road a way." Exasperated, they asked him why he was searching in a different place. "Well, that's simple," he replied. "This is where the light is!"

Anyone who studies the ancient or medieval world knows exactly what the Hodja means. The evidence that has survived is partial and fragmentary. Rarely do we find good material from the time and places that interest us, so we must go searching for the little dots of light that might serve to illuminate the shape of the whole to better understand what we are looking at. Although some aspects of sixth-century Italy are lit by a remarkable array of histories and letters, so much more of it remains in shadow. In order to tell the story of this commentary correctly, then, we will wander almost the breadth of Europe and look as far forward as eleventh-century Ireland to understand what was going on in a different place and at a different time.

Cassiodorus sits near the root of the dominant tradition of Western monasticism. St. Benedict of Nursia, author of the rule that would define monasticism for much of the Western Church, was a contemporary of Cassiodorus. While Benedict and Cassiodorus have been compared as rivals, they are far better seen as complementary, each revealing more about the other that history hides. As a result, the commentary of Cassiodorus and its afterlife is deeply tied to the history, theology, and spirituality of the monastic movement as it was received, profoundly shaped, and distributed from sixth-century Italy. Sometimes contemporary Italian texts—like the Rule of the Master—will shed some light on the subject, but far more frequently we will have to look abroad at other, later, evidence as it trickles down through centuries of Western monastic practice. Only then will we get a true picture of this commentary, why it was necessary, what problems it was addressing, and what its legacy was. We'll know the degree to which we can truly say that this *Explanation of the Psalms* was the book that taught the Middle Ages how to read.

Despite having taken a number of classes on Scripture interpretation, the history of Christian thought, and monasticism in both college and seminary, my first introduction to Cassiodorus occurred in a music class. If that seems a bit incongruous, for me it neatly encapsulates the challenge of his work: it transcends modern attempts to fit things into categories that align with our educational schematizations. Over the course of two semesters studying plainchant with Dr. William Flynn, I was schooled in the sound track of the medieval monastic life. In addition to Guido of Arezzo and Notker Balbus, Dr. Flynn introduced the class to Cassiodorus and his methods of interpreting the psalms as well as teaching the fundamentals of classical learning to the post-classical world. It was Dr. Flynn's own work, *Medieval Music as Medieval Exegesis*, that opened my mind to see Scripture interpretation not only in commentaries (where I expected to find it) but in monastic music, art, and living.

Like the later Saint Bede, Cassiodorus is chiefly known as a historian rather than as a scholar of Scripture. (Both men would be shocked and dismayed at this, seeing their scriptural studies as more important than their historical writings.) Most of the modern scholarly work on Cassiodorus, however, focuses on his historical materials as transmitted in his collection of letters, the *Variae*, or his place in the intellectual history of the West as communicated in book 2 of his *Institutions*. As a result, not much intellectual effort has been expended on his Psalms commentary. In fact, the critical edition in Latin was not produced until 1958 when Marc Adriaen edited the work for Corpus Christianorum Series Latina. All references to the Latin edited text will be to this edition. The first—and only—English translation of the Psalms commentary was published by P. G. Walsh in three volumes as part of the Ancient Christian Writers series. Quotations in English usually come from Walsh's translation; a few I have amended with reference to the Latin text in order to draw out some point that Walsh does not.

One final note on the numbering of the psalms—the numbering systems used in the Latin Psalter used by Cassiodorus and in modern Bibles based on the Hebrew text differs. As I will explain below, the numbering diverges at Psalm 9/10, does an odd little jog in the low hundreds, and remains off by a number until Psalm 148. Because most readers will be following along in modern Bibles that have embraced the Hebrew numbering system, I have referenced all psalm numbers according to the Hebrew numbering system except when I have specifically stated otherwise. This also holds true for my citations of Walsh's commentary! That is, I have adjusted the numbering to match the Hebrew numbering even though Walsh follows Cassiodorus's Latin numbering. Thus, should you choose to go back and look at Walsh's translation, go by the page number rather than the psalm number.

A final word of thanks is due not only to Bill Flynn and the others who have taught and inspired me over the years but also to those who have assisted me in work on this book. A large debt of gratitude goes to Hans Christoffersen and the whole staff at Liturgical Press who have been patient with my delays. Thanks are due to my wife, Meredith, and my daughters; writing is always a family effort, even when only one is writing the words. Finally, my friends Barbara Snyder and William MacKaye read and argued over every section of this book, to its vast improvement.

CHAPTER ONE

The Psalter, a Bible in Miniature

The Wrath of Radegund

Radegund was furious. Of this, there can be no doubt. Her husband had crossed her for the last time, and she set a plan in motion to free herself from him once and for all. Within a short time she had the two letters that she needed: the one giving her leverage and the one that confirmed her spiritual path.

Sixth-century France was a hard place to be a woman. The land was in turmoil; Franks, Burgundians, and Lombards struggled for power; and violence spilled out from Italy as the Roman emperor in the East tried to reassert his authority over his lost lands in the West. In addition to the perennial dangers of sickness and death in childbirth, war brought increased threat of rape and violent death along with its constant companions, famine and pestilence; the Plague of Justinian, one of the first recorded worldwide pandemics, swept through the Mediterranean world in the 540s, devastating Constantinople and Italy and ravaging Gaul. While war and its effects are always hardest on the poor, nobility was no guarantee of safety: Radegund's life was proof of that.

Radegund was born a Thuringian princess; her uncle betrayed and slaughtered her father and took her into his household while she was yet a small child. But her uncle's betrayals bore bitter fruit as spurned allies, the four sons of the Frankish king Clovis, sacked Thuringia, and Radegund—now eleven—was carried off, fated to be the wife of one of the victorious brothers, Chlothar. Imprisoned in a villa in the north of modern France, Radegund learned reading, writing, and religion before she was married in the year 540 to Chlothar as his sixth wife at the age of twenty.

By all accounts, the marriage was not a happy one. And, indeed, why would it be? Chlothar had been part of the original alliance that had killed her father, and he was marrying her primarily to legitimate his claim to Thuringia. While Clothar was an indifferent Christian at best, Radegund was fiercely devoted to her faith and ascetic ideals—including virginity. While Chlothar's wives and concubines bore him seven legitimate children and there were rumors of many more unacknowledged offspring, Radegund remained childless. The joke around the palace was that Chlothar's latest wife was a nun, not a queen.

The last straw came right around the year 550. Chlothar's men murdered the last surviving male member of the Thuringian royal line: Radegund's brother. Radegund was furious and refused to put up with it any more. She fled the palace, triggering a set of events that she had apparently thought through beforehand and cultivated strategically as she suffered through her unhappy marriage.

In the years leading up to this incident she had made the habit of visiting cathedrals, churches, and monasteries in the area and made a reputation for herself. Wearing costly clothing and jewelry, she would walk to the main altar and strip down to her simple day-shift, piling the wealth on the altar as a donation; needless to say, bishops and abbots were always eager to receive her and cultivated her friendship. Upon leaving the court, it was time to call in some favors.

She proposed the establishment of the first religious community for women in the Frankish Empire where she would live according to the Rule of Caesarius of Arles. In a short time, she was able to produce a letter signed by a host of prelates, all supporting her plan. It included the most dire threats for any woman who took religious vows and then wished to forsake the community and return to the world and marriage. Conversely (and more to the point), it likewise threatened anathema and damnation to any man who would attempt to remove any of the women from the religious enclosure.

The other letter that Radegund had been looking for was the blessing of Caesaria II of Arles. Caesaria, abbess of a convent in the Visigothic city of Arles, was the successor of the first Caesaria, sister of the influential bishop and theologian Caesarius of Arles. Caesarius had written a monastic rule of life for his sister's community, and in this letter, Caesaria II not only sends her community's rule to Radegund as the queen had requested but also gives her advice based on her experience. In commending the rule, Caesaria wrote this line, which neatly captures three central themes, not just of Caesaria's and Radegund's lives and spirituality, but of the time and place that we will be considering. She wrote: "Let none of those [women] entering [the community] not learn letters; let all hold the psalter in memory and, as I have said, be zealous to carry out in all things what you read in the gospel."[1]

The first key element here is the emphasis on the psalms. This phrasing here—"hold the psalter in memory"—could simply mean something like "don't forget about the psalms" or "don't forget to say the psalms," but it doesn't. Instead, it means "make sure that everybody has all of the psalms memorized." Looking back over the rest of Caesaria's letter it is quite obvious that she was following her own advice. The letter is littered with Scripture quotations; over half of these come from one book of the Bible: the Psalms. Likewise, she wasn't telling Radegund anything new either. The brief "Life of Radegund," written by her friend and correspondent Venantius Fortunatus, mentions the psalms early and often as a part of her spiritual life as well as her devotion to singing the "hours," a form of liturgical prayer grounded in recitation of the psalms. Fortunatus gives us glimpses of Radegund's future, describing how, as a child, she would organize the other children and lead them into the chapel in a procession singing the psalms.[2] As an adult, she would duck out of royal banquets to attend worship of the hours, singing psalms as she left and only pausing to make sure leftovers from the feasts would be given to the poor.

You can only imagine how the psalms would have spoken to Radegund and sustained her as she endured her situation, married to the man responsible for the deaths of her father, uncle (however traitorous),

---

[1] "A Letter from Caesaria, Abbess of Arles (c. 550), Epistolae," accessed January 30, 2017; https://epistolae.ccnmtl.columbia.edu/letter/915.html.

[2] Fortunatus, Vita 2 (http://mw.mcmaster.ca/scriptorium/radegund.html). "St. Radegund," in *Sainted Women of the Dark Ages*, ed. and trans. Jo Ann McNamara, John E. Halborg, with E. Gordon Whatley (Durham, NC: Duke University Press, 1992), 70–86.

and brother. How many times might Psalm 94 ("O Lord God of vengeance, O God of vengeance show yourself. Rise up, O Judge of the world; give the arrogant their just deserts") have passed through her head as she lay in bed next to her husband?

The second key element in Caesaria's letter was the emphasis on literacy. While the phrasing sounds a bit odd in English, "Let none of those [women] entering [the community] not learn letters," the double negatives have an emphatic sense in Latin, underscoring the importance that everyone—no matter what their origin or social station—be taught how to read. As we continue, we'll explore the close connection between the psalms and literacy in the early medieval world. Indeed, one of the terms for being literate was to be *psalteratus*: knowing the psalms. In a world where literacy was not common, and where women's literacy in particular was not prized, the insistence on making sure that women of all classes within the community are able to read is a fascinating one.

The third key element is the mention of the gospels in relation to the psalms. Modern Protestants in particular may have a number of assumptions about the early medieval church, one of which is that the Bible was rarely read and even more rarely understood. Yet Caesaria makes it plain that she expects Radegund and all of the women to be reading the gospels as their most fundamental source for instruction:

> Though it be holy and good and laudable that you desire to live by the Rule, there is no greater, better, more precious nor more splendid doctrine than the reading of the gospel. See this, hold this, which our Lord and master Christ taught by words and fulfilled by example, who made so many miracles in the world that they can not be counted, and sustained so many ills from his persecutors through patience, that can scarcely be believed.[3]

The words and examples of Jesus are central to the ideal this holy woman lifts up.

Out of all of Scripture, these two sections—the psalms and the gospels—are given special attention. Coming from a liturgical perspective this is hardly surprising because in commending these texts to Radegund, Caesaria is highlighting the two central texts of the two

---

[3] "A Letter from Caesaria, Abbess of Arles (c.550) Epistolae," accessed January 30, 2017, https://epistolae.ccnmtl.columbia.edu/letter/915.html.

central forms of worship in the church of that time. The Liturgy of the Hours (also called the Divine Office) centered around the psalms; the Eucharist (or the Mass) centered around the gospels. But, coming from a spiritual perspective, Caesaria and Radegund would have both deeply believed that the two sections of Scripture were inextricably bound together: the heart and soul of Jesus was not just laid plain by the gospels but was complemented and completed by the psalms. The gospels made manifest his outward words and deeds; the psalms made manifest his inward thoughts and feelings. We will see how this logic works as we go, but understanding and appreciating this link is crucial for grasping the medieval perspective on Jesus.

And Radegund? She got her community. In fact, her husband even donated the land for it (even if it did take the threat of excommunication from one of Radegund's bishop friends). Originally named the Abbey of St. Mary, one of the songs celebrating its name change can still be heard today. In 567, Radegund and her abbey received a relic of the True Cross from the emperor in the East. In honor of the event the name of the community was changed to the Abbey of the Holy Cross, and Radegund's friend Fortunatus wrote a hymn for the occasion, *Vexilla regis prodeunt*, translated in many hymnals as "The royal banners forward go." When Radegund died in 587, she was buried in a chapel near the abbey. When she became venerated as a saint, the chapel was renamed the Church of St. Radegund and remains a parish church today in Poitiers.

Despite the hardships of her life—perhaps because of the hardships of her life—Radegund's faith remained strong and powerful. Her life story recounts episode after episode focused on care for the sick, the poor, the hungry, and the neglected. She used her power to create a safe space for herself and other women—rigorous and not without its own challenges to be sure—but a place where learning and faith and female authority would be respected for centuries to come. And her experience of the psalms lies at the center of it all.

What Jerome Wrote

Radegund and Caesaria were part of a larger movement sweeping through the church, a movement that would shape the contours of the Western Church for several centuries: cenobitic monasticism—vowed men or women living together in set-apart communities for the purposes of prayer and spiritual growth.

The principles of this monastic movement were forged in the deserts of the East, in Egypt and Palestine. Their communication to the Latin-speaking West begins with the great translator Jerome. Jerome is one of those teachers known as the "church fathers"; from this term, "fathers" (*pater* in Latin), we derive the label for both the kind of theology that they did and the period in which they wrote: patristic. The patristic period is usually defined as the first five or six centuries after Christ, and these writers receive special emphasis in certain church circles because they lived within the same fundamental thought-world as the very first Christians. They existed within that Greco-Roman milieu that brought the church to birth and were native inhabitants of the languages and customs in which the church arose. For centuries, then, especially since the rise of historical consciousness in the seventeenth and eighteenth centuries, the church fathers have held a special status because they still lived on the far side of the great ditch of history that separates our present age from the time of Jesus, his disciples, and the first generations of the church.

One of the questions that has arisen in recent years, though, asks the very obvious question: where were the women? If we revere the writing and thinking of the church fathers—where were the church mothers? What were they writing or thinking or doing? Despite some of our conceptions about the place of women in the world of Late Antiquity, there were women writing works of theology and spirituality; one of them—Proba—will appear later within the circle of Cassiodorus. What we learn from Jerome and his letters, though, is that large sections of the work of the church fathers would never have been accomplished if it were not for the encouragement, support, and considerable financial assistance of the church mothers.

In particular, Jerome lived and worked in close relationship with a set of interrelated families guided by wealthy Roman matriarchs. While we have letters that Jerome wrote to popes and theologians, most of his letters were written to these women and their relatives. He served them as a spiritual adviser and as a translator. Most of the biblical commentaries for which Jerome is known were either written by him or translated from Greek sources at the behest of three women in particular, Paula, Eustochium, and Marcella. Paula was, at that time, the great matriarch of the ancient Furia clan. Widowed in middle age after bearing five children, she embraced the new ascetic spirituality coming from the East, fostering it among her children and grandchildren, before embracing it wholeheartedly to the point where she moved to Bethlehem to build and then rule the women in the double monastery where Jerome would also live and work.

One of our best windows into the lives of the church mothers are the letters of Jerome, where he described how they served God. Some of his many letters are explicitly formational. In these works he lays out a vision for how exemplary members of the various roles within the church ought to be educated and behave. Other letters are encomia, letters of praise written to grieving family members on the death of a loved one, recounting their fame, their virtues, and their qualities. These tend to be somewhat idealized portraits—Jerome is likely exaggerating to a degree—but still provide valuable insights into how the devout women of the period lived and served. Two letters that appear one after the other in modern editions of Jerome's letters neatly encapsulate the advice he gave and what he witnessed in the lives of the great mothers of the church and the emphasis that he and they placed on the psalms. The three themes we found in Caesaria's letter to Radegund—the centrality of the psalms, the importance of literacy, and the connection between the psalms and the gospels—are found within these letters as well. The first is Letter 107, written to Laeta, the daughter-in-law of the matriarch Paula who wishes to raise her daughter (also named Paula, after her grandmother) as a virgin of the church. The second is Letter 108, his encomium of Paula upon her death in the year 404, written to her grieving daughter Eustochium.

Letter 107 is a broadly directive letter, giving Laeta hints and tips in a host of areas about the best way to raise her little daughter for the girl's future role as a virgin within the church. He gives instruction on what sort of friends and maids she is to have, and what kinds of toys she is to be given to play with. In particular, Jerome is very insistent on the importance of literacy—literacy with a clear purpose:

> Get for her a set of letters made of boxwood or of ivory and called each by its proper name. Let her play with these, so that even her play may teach her something. And not only make her grasp the right order of the letters and see that she forms their names into

a rhyme, but constantly disarrange their order and put the last letters in the middle and the middle ones at the beginning that she may know them all by sight as well as by sound. Moreover, so soon as she begins to use the styl[us] upon the wax, and her hand is still faltering, either guide her soft fingers by laying your hand upon hers, or else have simple copies cut upon a tablet; so that her efforts confined within these limits may keep to the lines traced out for her and not stray outside of these. Offer prizes for good spelling and draw her onwards with little gifts such as children of her age delight in. . . . The very words which she tries bit by bit to put together and to pronounce ought not to be chance ones, but names specially fixed upon and heaped together for the purpose, those for example of the prophets or the apostles or the list of patriarchs from Adam downwards as it is given by Matthew and Luke. In this way while her tongue will be well-trained, her memory will be likewise developed.[4]

Jerome advises that the young Paula be taught to read and write from the earliest age and focused on the Scriptures. The training of the memory is important, and Jerome will become even more specific about how that facility ought to be put to use: "And let it be her task daily to bring to you the flowers which she has culled from scripture. Let her learn by heart so many verses in the Greek, but let her be instructed in the Latin also."[5] Because the Scriptures were found in Latin and Greek, Jerome thinks it best for her to have equal command of both languages.

While Jerome wants little Paula to memorize pieces of Scripture every day, this discovery ought to take place within a clear program for biblical knowledge. There is a specific order that Jerome believes best for encountering and understanding the many parts of Scripture:

Let her treasures be not silks or gems but manuscripts of the holy scriptures; and in these let her think less of gilding, and Babylonian parchment, and arabesque patterns, than of correctness and accurate punctuation. Let her begin by learning the psalter, and then let her gather rules of life out of the proverbs of Solomon.

---

[4] Jerome, Letter 107.4 (NPNF[2] 6:191).
[5] Ibid., Letter 107.9 (NPNF[2] 6:193).

> From the Preacher [Ecclesiastes] let her gain the habit of despising the world and its vanities. Let her follow the example set in Job of virtue and of patience. Then let her pass on to the gospels never to be laid aside when once they have been taken in hand. Let her also drink in with a willing heart the Acts of the Apostles and the Epistles. As soon as she has enriched the storehouse of her mind with these treasures, let her commit to memory the prophets, the heptateuch [the first seven books of the Bible], the books of Kings and of Chronicles, the rolls also of Ezra and Esther. When she has done all these she may safely read the Song of Songs but not before: for, were she to read it at the beginning, she would fail to perceive that, though it is written in fleshly words, it is a marriage song of a spiritual bridal. And not understanding this she would suffer hurt from it. Let her avoid all apocryphal writings, and if she is led to read such not by the truth of the doctrines which they contain but out of respect for the miracles contained in them; let her understand that they are not really written by those to whom they are ascribed, that many faulty elements have been introduced into them, and that it requires infinite discretion to look for gold in the midst of dirt. Cyprian's writings let her have always in her hands. The letters of Athanasius and the treatises of Hilary she may go through without fear of stumbling. Let her take pleasure in the works and wits of all in whose books a due regard for the faith is not neglected. But if she reads the works of others let it be rather to judge them than to follow them.[6]

This is nothing less than a full program of instruction, moving through the Scriptures and also through the most important writings of the orthodox church fathers. Many clergy have a worse education than that which Jerome prescribes for this little girl! Note, though, the sequence in which the Bible is studied. Jerome insists that she begin with the Psalms. After the Psalms come the wisdom literature of the Old Testament; immediately thereafter she is presented with the gospels, "never to be laid aside." Let's also note his intention in directing her to these books. As he mentions in connection with the prophets, he is not intending solely that she read them—he expects that large portions (if not the totality) be committed to memory.

---

[6] Jerome, Letter 107.12 (NPNF² 6:194).

Psalms is the first biblical book to be encountered, the first book to be learned. That is because the Psalms will form a central aspect of little Paula's devotions for the rest of her life. Jerome prescribes that she follow the Liturgy of the Hours:

> She ought to rise at night to recite prayers and psalms; to sing hymns in the morning; at the third, sixth, and ninth hours to take her place in the line to do battle for Christ; and, lastly, to kindle her lamp and to offer her evening sacrifice. In these occupations let her pass the day, and when night comes let it find her still engaged in them. Let reading follow prayer with her, and prayer again succeed to reading. Time will seem short when employed on tasks so many and so varied.[7]

All of these hours of prayer are, as the first mention intimates, sessions with the psalms. Every day, at every point of the day, she is to pause and sing psalms to God. This habit will not only form her in worship but also ensure that the psalms become a central vocabulary of both thought and praise.

If Jerome's Letter 107 describes what he thinks the ideal monastic upbringing looks like, Letter 108 is an ideal depiction of the monastic life well-lived. He describes the elder Paula's life in glowing terms and, though no doubt exaggerating a bit, cannot be too far from the mark. After all, he writes to her own daughter who lived with her and succeeded her as head of the women's monastery in Bethlehem. This is a very lengthy letter, not least because he gives a description of Paula's pilgrimage to the Holy Land in excruciating detail. After describing this journey, and the generosity of Paula, he tells how she ordered the double monastery that she built. Although the women were divided into three groups along social-class lines, they all worshiped together: "At dawn, at the third, sixth, and ninth hours, at evening, and at midnight they recited the psalter each in turn. No sister was allowed to be ignorant of the psalms, and all had every day to learn a certain portion of the holy scriptures."[8] The memorization that Jerome enjoined on the younger Paula is affirmed in his depiction of the elder Paula: "The holy scriptures she knew by heart, and said of the history contained in them

---

[7] Ibid. (NPNF[2] 6:193).
[8] Ibid., Letter 108.20 (NPNF[2] 6:206).

that it was the foundation of the truth; but, though she loved even this, she still preferred to seek for the underlying spiritual meaning and made this the keystone of the spiritual building raised within her soul."[9] At the center of these remained the psalms. While the memorization of Scripture in both Latin and Greek is mentioned in Letter 107, both Paula and her daughter Eustochium took it one step further when it came to the psalms. Jerome writes:

> I will mention here another fact which to those who are envious may well seem incredible. While I myself beginning as a young man have with much toil and effort partially acquired the Hebrew tongue and study it now unceasingly lest if I leave it, it also may leave me; Paula, on making up her mind that she too would learn it, succeeded so well that she could chant the psalms in Hebrew and could speak the language without a trace of the pronunciation peculiar to Latin. The same accomplishment can be seen to this day in her daughter Eustochium.[10]

Jerome could hardly be exaggerating here; as he was writing the letter to Eustochium herself (as well as for a larger audience), he could hardly make up the fact that she and her mother both had the psalms memorized in Hebrew!

Jerome's Letters 107 and 108 became important sources for the monastic movement in the West. The educational program and the ideal of the ascetic life that he puts forth in his directions for the younger Paula and the depiction of the life of the elder Paula were to inspire generations of Christians for centuries. It's quite likely that these very letters gave inspiration to Caesaria and Radegund as they administered convents of their own. And, again, at the center is the constant experience of the psalms, the literacy necessary to dig the most out of them, and the connection between the psalms and the person of Jesus revealed in the gospels.

---

[9] Ibid., Letter 108.27 (NPNF[2] 6:209).
[10] Ibid., Letter 108.27 (NPNF[2] 6:209–10).

The Rise of Monasticism

With the letters between Caesaria and Radegund, with the letters between Jerome and Laeta, we see women being pointed to the psalms as important and central texts for their spiritual lives. But the psalms weren't just for women; men were directed to the psalms as much as women were. The real shift here was a new spiritual movement that had arisen in the Eastern Church and that was, in the late patristic and early medieval period, flowing into the Western Church. The deserts of Egypt and Palestine were blossoming with hermits, anchorites, and communities of Christians dedicated to lives of intense prayer, meditation, and austerity.

The first Christian centuries had lionized martyrs. Those individuals who died for the faith under the weight of government oppression of Christianity were heroes and were held up as people who closely imitated Christ. For they, like him, were identified as threats to the order of this world by their proclamation of the Gospel of God, were arrested for crimes despite their innocence, and walked the—very literal—way of the cross as they endured public execution for their unwillingness to bend or compromise their faith in the face of certain death. This martyr narrative was a very powerful one as Christian communities grew and spread around the Mediterranean basin, but it depended on one necessary condition: official oppression. Once oppression lessened or vanished, this narrative—imitating Christ chiefly in imitating his death at the hands of a hostile state—had to be transformed. A new way of imitating Christ had to come to the fore.

Change for the church came in the fourth century. After periodic regional waves of persecution, and the occasional imperial edict against Christianity (it seems the persecution was never quite as total or widespread as the martyrdom narrative made it sound), official state-sponsored persecution ended in 315 with the accession of Constantine as emperor. With his Edict of Milan, Christianity became legal, and although Constantine himself was not baptized until just before his death—a standard practice at the time—its legalization opened the gates to a flood of new converts. This caused a crisis for early Christian spirituality. If the martyrdom paradigm could no longer be relied on, how could the most committed Christians imitate Christ within this new environment? The situation only got worse with the adoption of Christianity as the official religion of the Roman Empire with Theodosius in 380.

Two options came to the fore. The first was a continuation of the martyrdom narrative but with a fantastical twist: if it wasn't possible to achieve martyrdom within the boundaries of the empire, perhaps it was possible to find it outside the boundaries! Thus we have the rise of the evangelizing martyr and the popularization of apocryphal stories of the strange and fantastic lands the apostles visited in their zeal to spread the Gospel and the martyrdoms they suffered there.

The other option took the idea of Christian discipline and intensified it. If a literal martyrdom was not possible, a spiritualization of martyrdom could be enacted by embracing radical lifestyle choices mentioned in the gospels and the writings of Paul, then creating structures to carry these out on a daily basis. If imitation of Christ through state-sponsored execution was no longer a reliable option, then imitation of Christ through prayer, fasting, celibacy, and poverty became the new strategy for Christian spirituality. If the martyrs were the first heroes of the Christian Church, and its first paradigm for Christian spirituality, then the anchorites or desert hermits became the second great example, offering a means of embodying Christian commitment in the face of a tolerant and accepting political institution.

The first great star of the eremitical movement was Saint Antony, who achieved local fame for his holiness in the area around Alexandria, Egypt, but whose story and way of life was popularized by Athanasius, the contentious and crusading bishop of Alexandria, whose *Life of St. Antony* became an instant best seller across the Christian Greek-speaking East.

In the many vignettes and spiritual travails that Athanasius offers us in the *Life of Antony*, the discerning reader soon notices a theme: the constant presence of the psalms on the lips of Antony. A major feature of the life is Antony's nigh constant combat with demons in the wilderness. In his first trial a demon of fornication appears before him, and the saint drives it off with the recitation of Psalm 118:7: "The Lord is on my side to help me; I shall look in triumph on those who hate me."[11] After an encounter when he is beaten almost to death—Athanasius is not entirely clear if the demons did this or whether it was the desert bandits that feature frequently in stories of

---

[11] Athanasius, *Life of Antony* 6, pages 3–70 in *Early Christian Lives*, ed. and trans. Carolinne White (New York: Penguin, 1998), 13.

the Desert Fathers—Antony steels himself to face further onslaughts with the words of Psalm 27:3a: "Though an army encamp against me, my heart shall not fear."[12] When confronted by the malice of those who hope to find him dead, he repeats Psalm 68:1-2 and Psalm 118:10.[13] He advises newer monks to maintain silence against demonic foes as recommended by Psalm 39:1-2 and Psalm 38:13-14.[14] He counsels singing Psalm 20:7: "Some take pride in chariots and some in horses, but our pride is in the name of the Lord our God" to make demons flee.[15] More examples could be listed, but this should be sufficient to make the point and to draw some observations.

The hints we get about the use of the psalms in the *Life of Antony* match what we find elsewhere. In other works by and about the Desert Fathers and Mothers, particularly the gathered sayings, the dialogues of John Cassian, and the works of Evagrius of Pontus, we see this same use of a single verse or two repeated over and over as a mantra. The community would gather together at night for the Vigils office, where a minimum of twelve psalms would be sung aloud by the chanter. Between the psalms was provided time for private prayer before the abbot would say a prayer on behalf of all and signal the chanter to move on to the next psalm. Then, during the day, the monks would meditate on a verse or verses from the psalms. Presumably, this would be a verse that they had heard in the wee hours of the morning and that had caught their ear or stuck with them in some way. Then, as they worked, they could mull over that verse, turning it over and over as a ruminative meditation.

Fourth-Century Psalmody

There was another aspect to the legalization of Christianity aside from the drive to find a more rigorous way to live; it also meant that Christians were allowed to start gathering and worshiping publicly. And so they did. The first evidence that we have of public worship are gatherings in the cathedrals at morning and evening for the sing-

---

[12] Athanasius, *Life of Antony* 9, p. 15.
[13] Athanasius, *Life of Antony* 13, p. 18.
[14] Athanasius, *Life of Antony* 27, p. 26.
[15] Athanasius, *Life of Antony* 39, p. 33.

ing of hymns and especially psalms in the presence of the bishop. The lack of evidence in the days before legalization makes it hard to determine what sort of services they were having—we know that Christians developed a fivefold pattern of private or family prayer: at dawn, the third hour, the sixth hour, the ninth hour, and evening. Were they singing psalms at these times or not? The top scholars in the field continue to argue over exactly what was included within these services. What is clear, though, is that with legalization came a flood of public psalmody.

Despite his agnosticism on the singing of psalms at previous times, liturgical scholar James McKinnon sees the emergence of a "later fourth-century psalmodic movement":

> However one might assess the role of monasticism in the phenomenon, it cannot be denied that the closing decades of the fourth century were a time of unprecedented popularity for the singing of biblical psalms. There is no evidence that anything so pervasive and intense existed before this time, nor that anything quite like it would be witnessed again in the history of Christianity. Its literary manifestation was an extraordinary series of extended encomiums of psalmody from the pens of authors including Athanasius, Basil, John Chrysostom, Ambrose [of Milan] and Niceta of Remesiana. Among the various themes prominent in these texts is the explicit endorsement of the role that musical pleasure plays in the efficacy of psalmody. Thus Niceta, for example, tells us that "a psalm is sweet to the ear when sung, it penetrates the soul when it gives pleasure, it is easily remembered when sung often, and what the harshness of the Law cannot force from the minds of man it excludes by the suavity of song." And John Chrysostom writes: "For nothing so arouses the soul, gives it wing, sets it free from the earth, releases it from the prison of the body . . . as concordant melody and sacred song composed in rhythm."[16]

Singing the psalms at morning and evening was not something that the church just thought up on its own—it was suggested to it by the biblical texts themselves. The legal material of the Old Testament describes sacrifices that were supposed to occur in the temple in the

---

[16] James McKinnon, *The Advent Project: The Late Seventh-Century Creation of the Roman Mass Proper* (Berkeley: University of California Press, 2000), 39.

morning and again at evening.[17] In both cases, lambs, bread, and incense were offered. The full experience of this ceremony appears in Sirach 50:12-21 as part of the encomium on the life of the high priest Simon, son of Onias. An important part of it was music: "Then the singers praised [God] with their voices in sweet and full-toned melody" (Sir 50:18). Christian readers—especially those reading from the Greek translation of the Old Testament—would recognize this as a reference to the Psalms as several psalms have labels indicating on what day of the week they should be sung for the temple sacrifice. Thus, when Christian churches began morning and evening services with the psalms, it is clear they were setting them up to mirror the daily temple sacrifices commanded in Scripture. Since the death of Jesus had done away with the old sacrificial system, this was the church's appropriate sacrifice of praise and thanksgiving.

Not only were psalms the principal libretto for the service of morning and evening praise, this was also when they found their way into the Eucharist as well. We don't get a clear picture of how the Eucharist was celebrated until the seventh century, and by then there were several choral elements: at the entrance, between readings, at the offering of the gifts, and during the reception of the consecrated bread and wine. The text of almost all of these musical pieces was taken from the psalms. Just when these parts—typically referred to as the Minor Propers—were added into the Mass is unknown. Augustine does make references to the practice of singing psalms at the offering and at the distribution in his time at the start of the fifth century. Furthermore, Gennadius, a writer who maintained Jerome's list of important church writers, includes mention of a priest of Marseilles named Musaeus who,

> on the request of St. Venerius the bishop, selected from Holy Scriptures passages suited to the various feast days of the year, also passages from the Psalms for responses suited to the season, and the passages for reading. . . . He also addressed to Saint Eustathius the bishop, successor to the above mentioned man of God, an excellent and sizeable volume, a Sacramentary, divided into various sections, according to the various offices and seasons, Readings and

---

[17] This is described in Numbers 28:1-8 and duplicated in Exodus 29:38–30:8.

Psalms, both for reading and chanting, but also filled throughout
with petitions to the Lord and thanksgivings for his benefits.[18]

Musaeus died before 461, so he was likely writing around the same time as Augustine.

It should come as no surprise that the psalms would find a central place in the Eucharist. As mentioned above, psalms were the most appropriate accompaniment to sacrifice in the Old Testament's system. The presence of the psalms in the church's Liturgy of the Hours replicates this in that the psalms are being sung at the time of the morning and evening sacrifices and were seen in solidarity with them. The use of the psalms in the Eucharist replicate it in yet another: as the church was celebrating the sacrifice of Jesus, the Lamb of God, joining their offering at the altar to his self-offering on the cross, psalms were the most appropriate music to be sung to underscore the connection even further.

Liturgical Affections

As we note the rise of the psalms in public worship spurred by this later fourth-century psalmodic movement, we need to clarify the function of the liturgy and what it was trying to accomplish. Modern Christians may consider Christianity to be a religion founded on doctrine—on specific thoughts and beliefs about God, humanity, the world, and how they all relate—and while these things are important and were in those days too, the public worship of the church was up to something different from that.

Scholar Evelyn Birge Vitz discusses the liturgy as a form of education. She identifies its functions less as teaching concepts and more on communicating three other things: presence, affect, and an active response. The many statues and images of the saints, preeminently the Blessed Virgin Mary, depicted the presence of the blessed in and around the community gathered for worship. The relics of the saints or Christ himself—bones, skulls, or fragments of the true cross—reinforced the reality of sacred presences. The proclamation of the gospel was intended to remind the congregation of Christ's promise to be present with even two or three gathered in his name and to enact his teaching

---

[18] Jerome and Gennadius, *On the Illustrious Men* 3.80 (NPNF² 3:398).

presence. As Christian communities struggled to articulate the spiritual mechanics of the Eucharist, they inevitably chose explanations that insisted that somehow Christ was truly present even while veiled under the appearance of bread and wine. The bottom line was that spiritual realities, the persons proclaimed and invoked in the liturgy, were neither light years away in some remote heaven nor separated by time and space for the worshipers; they were there—they were present—a palpable experience captured so neatly in Tennyson's phrase: "Closer is He than breathing, and nearer than hands and feet."[19] This is the sense that late antiquity and early medieval worshipers were looking for. When investigating the major monotheistic options for conversion in the tenth century, the Russian prince Vladimir of Kiev chose to join with the Eastern Orthodox Church due in large measure to the response of his emissaries to worship in the most beautiful church in the world, the Hagia Sophia: "We no longer knew whether we were in heaven or earth nor seen such beauty, and we know not how to tell of it."[20]

Speaking of affect, Vitz draws a contrast between the emotional and doctrinal perspectives on the faith: "From the liturgy men and women learned religion as involving affect. That is, liturgically grounded Christianity strongly promoted feelings and emotions—of love, trust, fear, sorrow, and the like—toward the members of the Trinity, the Virgin, and the saints, far more than intellectual assent to doctrine or articles of belief. Here again, one could provide dozens of examples."[21] Thus, forming the religious affections—deep patterns of feeling forged from the union between emotion and doctrine—were a central factor in the faith as experienced by Christians in these periods.

Vitz understands the third factor as flowing directly from the first two: "If liturgical religion was about presence and affect, it also called for active response on the part of the believer. This is to say that such feelings as compunction, contrition, love, and so on were linked to the

---

[19] Alfred Tennyson, "The Higher Pantheism," accessed June 26, 2017; https://www.poetryfoundation.org/poems-and-poets/poems/detail/45323.

[20] The Primary Chronicle, year 6495 (987).

[21] Evelyn Birge Vitz, "Liturgy as Education in the Middle Ages," in *Medieval Education*, ed. Ronald Begley and Joseph Koterski, Fordham Series in Medieval Studies 4 (New York: Fordham University Press, 2000), 20–34, at 28.

will and to behavior."[22] The liturgy engaged the feelings but urged the worshipers to go beyond simply the short-term emotional experience. Pilgrimages and works of mercy, as Vitz mentions, were important aspects of this response.

In the times and places when the liturgy was conducted in a language that the majority of worshipers could understand, the psalms were ideal vehicles for all three of these. The pervasive use of direct address to God in the psalms invokes the presence of the deity into the midst of the worshipers. Clearly, the psalms are filled with a wide variety of feeling language; their breadth runs the entire gamut from joy to contentment to repentance to anger to despair. If the Christian faith were looking for an emotional grammar to describe spiritual experience, no better source could be found than the Psalter. The connection between emotion and active response is also a common feature of the psalms. As several interpreters note, the psalms do not just enjoin rejoicing or repentance or contrition; they also provide the ideal template for what this looks like.

Insight from Athanasius

In McKinnon's description of the later fourth-century psalmodic movement, the very first teacher whom he mentions is Athanasius; he put this one first for a reason. One of the important early documents that communicates the late fourth-century perspective on the Psalms is a letter from Athanasius, bishop of Alexandria, to Marcellinus. We don't have very much information about the circumstances around the writing of this letter. We don't know when he wrote it or even who the recipient was. The great Anglican priest and hymnodist John Mason Neale suggested that the text could have been misattributed and that the true author and recipient were Athanasius II, bishop of Antioch, and the Eastern chronicler known as Count Marcellinus. As tempting as that would be for our purposes—it would put the letter just within the lifetime of Cassiodorus—it is unlikely this is the case. (It's more likely that the Marcellinus we're dealing with here is one identified as a deacon in another text by Athanasius.)

---

[22] Ibid., 29.

The letter is cast as a framed narrative. Within the text, Athanasius is recounting a conversation that he had with a certain "studious old man."[23] He never explicitly says this, but the implication is that the old man was one of the Desert Fathers and, indeed, the wisdom on the psalms in the letter does seem to be in close contact with the methods of reading and singing that we see in those sources. Athanasius makes five major arguments about the Psalter and, in the course of making those arguments, skips his way through the Psalms twice, pointing out both groupings and purposes for specific psalms. The five arguments that he puts forward map quite well onto the general themes that we have identified earlier. Not only that, these arguments are worth rehearsing because of the esteem in which Cassiodorus held this particular work.

The first point that Athanasius makes is that while each book of the Old and New Testaments has its own particular message—grows its own particular fruit, in his metaphor—the Psalter is a garden: "which, besides its special fruit, grows also some of those of all the rest." That is, while there are books of laws, of histories, of prophecies, the psalms contain all of these and more. In order to demonstrate this, Athanasius's old man walks the reader in sequence through the principle genres of the Old and New Testaments, pointing out psalms that correspond to various points of these books' proclamation. He starts with the historical materials in this fashion:

> The creation, for instance, of which we read in Genesis is spoken of in Psalm 19, "The heavens declare the glory of God: and the firmament showeth His handiwork," and again in 24, "The earth is the Lord's and the fullness thereof: the inhabited earth and all that dwell therein. He Himself laid the foundations of it on the seas." The exodus from Egypt, which Exodus, Numbers, and Deuteronomy record, is fitly sung in Psalms 87, 105, 106, and 114. . . . You see, then, that all the subjects mentioned in the historical books are mentioned also in one Psalm or another; but when we come to the matters of which the Prophets speak we find that these [topics] occur in almost all [of the psalms].[24]

---

[23] Athanasius, "Letter to Marcellinus," pages 97–119 in *On the Incarnation*, trans. a religious of CSMV (Crestwood, NY: St. Vladimir's Seminary Press, 1996), 97.

[24] Athanasius, "Letter to Marcellinus," 98.

Naturally, the events of which the prophets speak, in the old man's interpretation, are all predictions of the coming of Christ. But there are far more than veiled hints to Christ in the psalms in this reading: "Having thus shown that Christ should come in human form, the Psalter goes on to show that He can suffer in the flesh He has assumed."[25] The narrative identifies several psalms connected to the passion of Christ, then passes on to other events in the life of Christ. Athanasius concludes this point by breaking into his transcription with a summary: "My old friend made rather a point of this, that the things we find in the Psalms about the Saviour are stated in other books of Scripture too; he stressed that fact that one interpretation is common to them all, and that they have but one voice in the Holy Spirit."[26]

The second point the old man makes is that the focus of the Psalter is not just events in the past. Rather, the psalms function as a mirror for the reader:

> Among all of the books [of the Bible], the Psalter has certainly a very special grace, a choiceness of quality to it well worthy to be pondered; for, besides the characteristics which it shares with others, it has this peculiar marvel of its own, that within it are represented and portrayed in all their great variety the movements of the human soul. It is like a picture, in which you see *yourself* portrayed and, seeing, may understand and consequently form yourself upon the pattern given. Elsewhere in the Bible you may read only that the Law commands this or that to be done, you listen to the Prophets to learn about the Saviour's coming or you turn to the historical books to learn the doings of the kings and holy men; but in the Psalter, besides all these things, you learn about *yourself*. You find depicted in it all the movements of your soul, all its changes, its ups and downs, its failures and recoveries.[27]

He is speaking here about the emotional breadth of the psalms. The psalms give words to the feelings of the heart and in those words you are able to identify your own emotions, to name your own feelings and states of being.[28]

---

[25] Athanasius, "Letter to Marcellinus," 100.
[26] Athanasius, "Letter to Marcellinus," 102.
[27] Athanasius, "Letter to Marcellinus," 103. Emphasis in the original.
[28] The image that jumps immediately to my mind is the poignant metaphor of Psalm 102:6-7: "I am like an owl of the wilderness, like a little owl of the waste places. I lie awake; I am like a lonely bird on the housetop."

The third point builds on this second. Not only does the Psalter provide emotional templates; it furthermore invites its readers to inhabit them. The psalms give their readers language with which to express themselves to God:

> For he who reads the other [biblical] books is clearly reading not his own words but those of holy men and other people about whom they write; but the marvel with the Psalter is that, barring those prophecies about the Saviour and some about the Gentiles, the reader takes all its words upon his lips as though they were his own, and each one sings the Psalms as though they had been written for his special benefit, and takes them up and recites them, not as though someone else were speaking or another person's feelings being described, but as himself speaking of himself, offering the words to God as his own heart's utterance, just as though he himself had made them up. Not as the words of the patriarchs or of Moses and the other prophets will he reverence these: no, he is bold to take them as his own and written for his very self. Whether he has kept the Law or whether he has broken it, it is his own doings that the Psalms describe; every one is bound to find his very self in them and, be he faithful soul or be he sinner, each reads in them descriptions of himself.[29]

This point gets at an important truth about the psalms—they are not in impersonal language. Those who read or pray or sing them say "I" and "we," and as the identifications noted in the second point become self-identifications, the words take on more and more significance to the individual. Because of their inherent lack of context, those who pray them regularly become a context for them.

The fourth point moves beyond finding the self in the text and moves to the paradox in the Psalter. Christians understand the Bible to be God's own self-revelation to humanity. If that is so, then what do readers make of the "I" and "we" language directed to God? How can this speech directed to God be an aspect of God's self-revelation? The obvious answer from a trinitarian perspective is that we are hearing one person of the Trinity addressing another. The voice speaking is that of Christ and, as Christ proved with his outward deeds, the

---

[29] Athanasius, "Letter to Marcellinus," 105.

pioneer and perfecter of the faith, so the Psalms provide a pattern for the interior life:

> The Greek legislators had indeed a great command of language; but the Lord, the true Lord of all, Who cares for all His works, did not only lay down precepts but also gave himself as model of how they should be carried out, for all who would to know and imitate. And therefore, *before* He came among us, He sketched the likeness of this perfect life for us in words, in this same book of Psalms; in order that, just as he revealed Himself in flesh to be the perfect, heavenly Man, so in the Psalms also men of goodwill might see the pattern life portrayed, and find therein the healing and correction of their own. Briefly, then, if indeed any more is needed to drive home the point, the whole divine Scripture is the teacher of virtue and true faith, but the Psalter gives a picture of the spiritual life.[30]

As the gospels offer to their readers the outward life of Christ, the psalms—Athanasius's learned friend declares—offer their readers the inward life.

The fifth and final point follows hard on the last. If Christians want to imitate Christ fully, then they will do well to take onto their lips and into their hearts the words that Christ used, to be shaped by it and to use toward God these words from God:

> It is possible for us, therefore, to find in the Psalter not only the reflection of our own soul's state, together with precept and example for all possible conditions, but also a fit form of words wherewith to please the Lord on each of life's occasions, words both of repentance and thankfulness, so that we fall not into sin; for it is not for our actions only that we must give account before the Judge, but also for our every idle word.[31]

This, then, gives the old teacher an opportunity to go through the Psalter once again. Whereas before he was connecting items for other biblical books to specific psalms, this time he moves through the Psalter identifying various circumstances in which the words of the psalm

---

[30] Athanasius, "Letter to Marcellinus," 106–7. Emphasis in the original.
[31] Athanasius, "Letter to Marcellinus," 107.

are particularly appropriate. While he does not touch on every psalm, he comes quite close and offers a drive-by commentary on fit purposes for the majority of the psalms.

The letter concludes with an exhortation to sing the psalms, not merely read them. The old man offers two reasons for this in particular:

> In the first place, it is fitting that the sacred writings should praise God in poetry as well as prose, because the freer, less restricted form of verse, in which the Psalms, together with the Canticles and Odes, are cast, ensures that by them men should express their love to God with all the strength and power they possess. And secondly, the reason lies in the unifying effect which chanting the Psalms has upon the singer. For to sing the Psalms demands such concentration of a man's whole being on them that, in doing it, his usual disharmony of mind and corresponding bodily confusion is resolved, just as the notes of several flutes are brought by harmony to one effect. . . . When, therefore, the Psalms are chanted, it is not from any mere desire for sweet music but as the outward expression of the inward harmony obtaining in the soul, because such harmonious recitation is in itself the index of a peaceful and well-ordered heart.[32]

With an almost Pythagorean appreciation for inward and outward harmonics, the teacher asserts that the efficacy of the Psalms is boosted through their chanting. In the singing, focus is achieved, a focus with the purpose being the soul's transformation in consonance with the lip's words.

Athanasius, writing at the beginning of the later fourth-century psalmodic movement, solidly hits two of the three major themes that we have seen so far in this quick survey of lives and spirituality in the hinge point between late antiquity and the early medieval world. Literacy doesn't seem to be a major theme in his conversation with his teaching friend. Memorization certainly does, as does the connection between Christ and the psalms.

While memorization of the psalms is not discussed explicitly, it seems to be assumed throughout. The fact that the old man—without a text at hand—can run through the entire Psalter not once but twice

---

[32] Athanasius, "Letter to Marcellinus," 114, 115.

(the first time identifying how various psalms connect to the various divisions of the biblical text, the second how they connect with the various life circumstances) assumes memorization. You simply can't do that if you don't know the psalms deeply and intimately with a familiarity born of ceaseless repetition. Furthermore, the second and third points that Athanasius makes are deeply connected with memorization as well. Using the emotional states of the psalms as a mirror to perceive the motion of your own soul and then to claim the words, thoughts, and feelings of the psalms as your own requires an internalization most thoroughly accomplished through memorization.

The connection between Christ and the psalms is more obvious. The first point of Athanasius finds Christ in the psalms in several different modes. That is, it finds references to the coming of Christ, hints about the two natures of Christ, as well as passages directly foretelling events in the incarnation, life, ministry, death, resurrection, and ascension of Christ. The fourth point asserts that Christ himself provided a pattern for godly living in the psalms even before his earthly incarnation. Through the spirit, prophetically through David, Athanasius understands Christ to have laid down a perfect image of his interior life in the words of these songs. The fifth point then enjoins their use on Christians in their own imitation of Christ. Imitation—a form of moral and spiritual argument found throughout the writings of Paul ("Be imitators of me, as I am of Christ" [1 Cor 11:1])—is not just about replicating the deeds or putting into action the teachings of Jesus; it is also taking his own virtues and mind-sets into the hearts of Christians through the words and prayers that he provided.

Summary

From out of the shadows of history, we catch glimpses of extraordinary figures. They emerge as people of their own time and of their own world, deeply committed to principles, philosophies, and faiths that may seem odd or downright strange to us. For instance, a life of voluntary virginity seems like a bizarre life choice in the post-Freud, post–birth control present. As we dig into the stories of women like Radegund, Caesaria, and the church mothers, we come to understand that there's far more at work here than simply an avoidance of sex: issues of family continuance, autonomy, personal safety, and religious piety all play a role and open our eyes to a different kind of experience that belongs to a world we do not inhabit.

In a similar way, we cannot assume that they read the Scriptures in the same way that we do, or that their ways are dogmatic and backward while ours are enlightened. In order to understand why they made the reading choices they did, we need to open our minds to the world they experienced and see what they were trying to achieve and how the Scriptures fit into the goal of a fulfilled life.

In this brief glance at the West at the hinge between late antiquity and the early medieval periods, we see the Psalms rising to the fore as a powerful tool for spiritual growth and flourishing. Radegund lives a strong life of social justice grounded in principles rooted in the Psalms. Jerome offers the Psalms as a chief template for growth, describing how they should shape the young Paula and how they did shape the exemplary life and faith of the elder Paula. Within newly legalized churches, the Psalms burst forth as the soundtrack of a new movement. Athanasius and the wisdom of the desert focus on the Psalms as the gateway to the Mind of Christ.

Throughout these moments we have surveyed, we see threads involving memorization and interiorization, literacy, and steadfast conviction of the deep connection between the psalms and the gospels. As we continue, we will continue to see these threads emerge. Having looked at some moments, some glimpses, some vignettes, let us now turn to consider the world as it stood at this great hinge between two periods and the cultural force—the technological challenge—that faced the church in the West and the role of the Psalms within it.

CHAPTER TWO

Technological Challenges

The Church's Technology Problem

The church in the West, as we make the turn from the world of late antiquity into the early medieval period, had a serious technology problem. A number of things that puzzle modern readers about the medieval church are directly related to this fundamental problem, but we rarely think about it in this way because we are frequently seeing the various symptoms of the problem rather than considering the problem that lays at the root of it all.

To sketch a quick outline before diving into each point, we can identify three big issues in early Christianity that all stem from one central problem of technology. This central problem is literacy. We have to put this in perspective, though, to get at just what the problem is. The church began as a community. It was established as a group of people who were all driven by a common belief: that the God of Israel had decisively intervened in history in the person of Jesus Christ, and that the life, death, resurrection, and ascension of Jesus had ongoing power and ongoing implications for the relationships between God, humanity, and the cosmos. The Scriptures were an important part of this reflection but exist in tension with the community. Because of the church's insistence that the meaning of Jesus could not be understood apart from the God revealed to the people of Israel, it meant that the church had to reflect on the Jewish Scriptures. Furthermore, as the community developed and grew, it recorded its remembrances, its reflections, its communication, and its conflicts in written form, eventually collecting this material in what would become the New Testament and thus relegating the Jewish Scriptures to the category of Old Testament. Old—but not obsolete; Old—but still useful. And it fought some major theological battles in the second and third centuries to be clear on this point.

The key thing here is that the community produced the Christian Bible, not the other way around. The church as an organic body handed down its own teachings, habits, and ritual actions; the Bible was one aspect of this handing down, not the source of it. I realize this cuts against some American Protestant narratives that set the Bible as a completely separate and independent entity, but the community is the true starting place. Within the community we find the historical and theological principles that shaped the development of the church as it grew beyond the circle of women who initially proclaimed the resurrection into a faith that would span the breadth of the Roman Imperium.

So the embodied church community and the Scriptures existed in tension with one another. As the church spread, it identified the Scriptures of the Old and New Testaments as a central point of unity. As wandering teachers spread out across the known world, communicating the faith as they understood what they had received, the Scriptures became a touchstone to control the teaching and keep it within a tolerable range of variations. As the history of church controversies demonstrates, however, the Scriptures alone were not sufficient to maintain readings understood as within the tolerable range. It wasn't enough to read the same books; they had to be read in generally the same way. Thus, as early as the second century, the bishop and theologian Irenaeus of Lyon stated a theological principle in his big book against heresy that there are three interdependent marks of the church: a stable canon of Scripture to be read (that's the Old and New Testaments, including those books referred to as the Apocrypha), the creeds that nail down rules for reading, and the apostolic succession, which is a line of teachers—bishops—who are part of the organic community that goes back to Jesus and the first disciples and who maintain both the faith as taught by that community and the spiritual power of the Holy Spirit communicated by the laying on of hands in an unbroken line back to the apostles.

But the more we move out in time and space from that central founding experience, the more important books become to capture and maintain the experience, the right methods of reading, and the lists that trace the lines of bishops back to the apostles. Specifically, the more the church spreads across the imperium, the more important the Bible becomes.

The Bible arrived in Rome within the first Christian generation. The apostle Paul writes a rather famous letter called Romans to the church community that already exists in Rome. The letter that Paul sent and the Bible that the Roman community is reading are in the same language: Greek. And that shouldn't surprise us—even though it frequently does. One of the lasting legacies of Alexander the Great and his ten-year tear across the Balkans, Northern Africa, the Near East, and as far as western India was linguistic: Greek became the common tongue of commerce. Naturally, ethnic groups and enclaves had their mother tongues, but increasingly Greek was the language in which to get things done and sometimes even overtook native languages. One example that has direct relevance to our story is the translation of the Jewish Scriptures into Greek. In the second and first centuries before Christ, the Jewish enclave in Alexandria translated the Scriptures into Greek, and this version became so popular that we find it in use in Palestine in the first century. Indeed, this Greek text, known as the Septuagint, was the first Bible of the early church. As the church spread, the Greek text went with it too. Thus, the church in Rome—what we tend to think of as a rather Latin-based area—read Greek, spoke Greek, and wrote their own texts in Greek for over a century after its founding.

This sets up what would become the church's big technology problem. But it gets worse too. As pressures on the empire grew, a cultural rift began to open between the predominately Latinate West and the Greek-speaking East, and knowledge of Greek faded in the West. There we have our big issue: How do we get a book that starts in Greek and make it present to people who can't read and, furthermore, don't understand Greek? How the church in the West developed in the next several centuries is illuminated by the ways in which the church tackled this situation.

This is the point where we have to try to enter into the experience of these late antique Christians. There is so much about the Bible and the faith that can be taken for granted if the chief paradigm for thinking about that faith is what we encounter in the modern West—particularly in Protestant America. As a result, we need to shift our mind-set in order to grasp what the difficulties were on the ground then. Until we have accomplished that, we won't understand why these Christians chose the paths they did and how these paths offer solutions to the problems confronting them.

As I break it down, in order to grasp the extent and character of the literacy problem, we need to approach it from four different angles:

- the physicality of faith
- issues inherent in manuscript production
- the language barriers
- rampant illiteracy

In exploring these angles, we will put ourselves in a position to understand the solutions and to appreciate why the psalms emerged as a central answer to the church's big technology problem.

Physicality of Faith

When modern Americans think about the Bible, we take for granted that it has a certain shape. The shape that it has now is not the shape it has always had. When we dive into late antiquity and the early medieval world, we will discover that the Bible had a very different shape, meaning that Christians in those times and places had a very different encounter with the Scriptures. Recognizing and defining the gaps in our experience will give us some important insight into the role of the Bible then and especially the central place given to the psalms.

By my desk I have an edition of the New Oxford Annotated Bible I received in high school. Its rough red cover has faded to a pale burgundy and shows some wear at the top corners. Despite the title, it's no longer "new," showing its age not only on the cover but by the underlines, marginal scrawlings, and torn bits of paper marking various spots—many for reasons I no longer recall. Some are notes from college, others from seminary or legacies of Bible studies past; in some spots a discerning investigator will note a new hand—comments and highlighting from my elder daughter from occasions on which she borrowed my Bible rather than using one of her own.

It's not a large book. Bigger than a novel, but lacking the size and heft of many of the volumes in my collection, the front cover is roughly nine inches by six inches and all 1,904 pages leave it only two inches thick. It's not quite three pounds in weight. Opening it, the paper is thin yet strong, the printing clean and regular, columns marching across the page to be bounded at the bottom by a hefty section of notes and annotations. The text is the Revised Standard Version, one now fallen out of favor and largely replaced by its successor, the New Revised Standard Version. At the head of each book is a short introduction signed by a biblical scholar that locates each writing in its historical context and points out some salient features of its content; the names of the scholars are those of a generation or two before me, and it is their notes I find at the bottom of my pages.

If, for whatever reason, I feel the need to consult a different Bible, I won't have to go very far. Within an arm span of my desk are at least six in a variety of languages: Hebrew, Greek, Latin. I own several English translations and, were I to fire up my computer, would have access to dozens more Bibles, thanks to software on my hard drive. Venturing onto the internet would expand the number, no doubt, into the hundreds if not thousands in myriad tongues. Thanks to the work of missionaries and scholars throughout the nineteenth and twentieth centuries, it is now difficult to find languages into which the Bible has *not* been translated.

Now let's consider the closest analogue to my New Oxford Annotated Bible that a monk in the early medieval period might encounter. The Codex Amiatinus is one of the earliest complete Latin Bibles that has survived to the present day. In fact, it is one of three that was produced by a Northumbrian monastery but is the only one that survives intact. Like my Bible, it contains the Old and New Testaments and the Apocrypha. The first obvious difference, though, is the size. The Codex Amiatinus is over nineteen inches high, more than thirteen inches across, and seven inches thick. Composed not of paper but of wooden boards enclosing 2,058 parchment pages,[1] it weighs in

---

[1] A codicologist would frown on a reference to "pages" and would insist that the codex actually contains 1,029 leaves. She would be absolutely correct in insisting on this, as a parchment leaf is composed of both a front and a back, but in common conversation these days we speak of pages.

at just over seventy-five pounds. Right there, the dimensions of the book communicate some very important principles about how it can and cannot be used. First, this is not a Bible to be carried around! It is a Bible with sufficient heft that not only is it put it in one place, but it also goes a far way in defining a space. Second, and related, this is not a book for one person but rather for a community. This is a central fixture of a room to define the activity that happens in that room, and that room, of course, is an oratory—a church.

A further aspect of the size of the book is the expense in producing it. We tend to think of expense in terms of financial outlay—how much coinage would it cost to produce such a book? The economy of early medieval monasteries did not usually work that way. The monastic tradition placed an emphasis on self-sufficiency; the monastery was a world unto itself, capable of supporting itself and its inhabitants. Each leaf of the manuscript was the size of half of a sheep hide, meaning that the cost of the pages alone for the Codex Amiatinus was 515 sheep.

When we dig into the holdings of early medieval monastic libraries, it becomes evident quite quickly that the model of the Bible as a single volume between two covers was quite rare. In fact, if a monastery had such a thing, it would usually have one to be kept in the oratory; it was communal property. Instead of the one-volume model, the Scriptures were seen less as a holy book than as a sacred library—and referred to as such. The library records from the large and quite wealthy monastery of Reichnau, dating from 822, begin with a listing titled "Of books of the Old and New Testaments":

- one "bibliotheca" (a one-volume Bible)
- another, of Erich (from Erich? by Erich? The Latin is unclear.)
- three volumes of the Heptateuch (the first seven books of the Old Testament)
- three volumes of Kings and Chronicles[2]
- three volumes of the prophets
- Job and Tobit in one book

---

[2] For those wondering about the two books of Samuel, those were traditionally numbered with the Kings. Hence, most medieval sources refer to the four books of Kings whereas modern people will refer to two books of Samuel and two books of Kings.

- another Job in one book
- another Job and Judith in one book
- three volumes of Solomon (Proverbs/Ecclesiastes/Song of Songs/Wisdom of Solomon?)
- Judith, Esther, and Ezra in one book
- Esther and Ezra in one book
- two volumes of the Maccabees
- eight volumes of the four gospels
- four volumes of the letters of Paul the Apostle
- two volumes of the Acts of the Apostles, the General Epistles, and Revelation
- one volume of the Acts of the Apostles

Four things jump out from this collection. First, there are only two one-volume Bibles. "Pandects" is the term used by modern scholars (which may well have been coined by Cassiodorus), but the cataloger of this collection chose to use the term "bibliotheca," a Latin word that has moved into modern Spanish, French, and Italian as "library." Second, the biblical books were separated into several volumes. Gathering a complete Bible from these scriptural volumes was literally the task of pulling together a library of different books. There appear to have been three different multivolume Bible sets; hence most sections of the Bible had three volumes. Third, apart from these three multivolume Bibles, note that there were five extra copies of the gospels, bringing the total up to eight. The number of volumes demonstrates the extra attention given to the four gospels in the community. Fourth—and perhaps most pertinent for the sake of this investigation—there are no volumes of the Psalms in the list.

This is not because the monastery did not own any volumes of the Psalms. Rather, they were collected in a different place. After scrolling through a long list of theological works and commentaries by the church fathers, we will come to the list of books used in the liturgical worship of the monastery:

- fifty-three volumes of sacramentaries (the books used by priests for the celebration of the Mass)
- twelve volumes of lectionaries (the books that contained the excerpted scriptural readings for Mass)

- ten antiphonaries (books that contained chants for Mass)
- eight Office books (books that likely contained the chants used in the Daily Prayer offices)
- fifty Psalters

This statistic more than anything else should convey the perspective on the psalms held by the church within the early medieval monastic movement, but there are some other interesting things going on here as well. Remember this point—we're going to come back to it in a little bit.

The Bible then was experienced in a physically different way from the Bible now. If we wanted to experience the Bible as a one-volume collection, then we'd better hope that we lived near a wealthy monastery or cathedral so that we could go look at it in the sanctuary, likely perusing it as it sat chained to a reading desk in a central location. It is much more likely, though, that we would have experienced it as a multivolume set of books. Again, if we lived near a wealthy monastery we might have one or more full sets. However, if we were in a village, there's a good chance that the priest might only have one or two volumes out of the full collection of nine that made up a typical early medieval set.

This leads us to a concrete question: How do we get a sense of the whole if the Bible is—literally—split up into parts? How do we get a handle on the big picture?

There's one more aspect of the physicality of faith that we need to consider as well: light. I have in my head an image from a film of a line of monks processing from their dormitory into the oratory for the wee early hours of the morning prayer time variously referred to as Vigils, Matins, or the Night Office. Think three o'clock in the morning here. In this movie memory, each one of these monks is carrying a candle as they move from one space into the other, and the implication is that they are going to be using them as they pray.

But candles were expensive. Consider some back-of-the-envelope math: the average beeswax taper (which is the candle in the image in my head) is about twelve inches long and contains four ounces of wax. It burns about an inch an hour, assuming no major drafts. If it needs to burn for only three hours of darkness, that's a new candle every four days and therefore ninety-two candles a year containing twenty-three pounds of wax. If a medieval skep beehive produces five pounds of wax per year, that's roughly five hives per monk per year solely dedicated to lighting the Night Office, not counting any other purposes. In a monastery of fifty monks, they would be completely overrun with bees!

Of course, beeswax candles were usually reserved for altars; tallow candles and oil lamps were far more common for regular lighting. But even these were not cheap. These days we consider those who "burn the midnight oil" to be studious; in antiquity this activity would indicate not studiousness but conspicuous wealth: they are the kind of people who can afford to provide hours of artificial light for themselves. This raises a very practical question. If monks and clergy attached to cathedral chapters are rising to pray in the middle of the night—which they were—how do they make these activities as economical as possible, given the financial and agricultural constraints around artificial lighting?

Manuscript Production Issues

"This work is written; Lord, give me a drink! My right hand is killing me." So wrote an anonymous scribe at the end of a manuscript. Even though it was penned in the late fourteenth century—almost a thousand years distant from the time we are considering here—nothing about the technology of producing manuscripts had changed from the earlier period. Our English word "manuscript" is the Latin term "handwritten." The work of copying entire books by hand has never been and never will be easy. Or, in the words scribbled by another medieval scribe, "Three fingers write, two eyes see, one tongue speaks, the whole body suffers."

Copying manuscripts by hand has several drawbacks. Perhaps the most obvious is that such books cannot be mass-produced. Books could only be copied from an exemplar. That is, a scribe had to have a source text to copy from. There were two ways to accomplish this: a scribe could either look at the source text or listen to it. The most common method as we see it represented in manuscript images was to look directly at the book and write out what the scribe saw. Thus, one scribe was taking visual reference and working on one book at a time. Aside from illustrations, we know that many books were produced this way because of the kinds of errors that we find in them—some are inherently visual. Skipping a line because of the way an eye travels across a page, losing a chunk of text because the eye skipped from one occurrence of a word to another one and omitting the words in between, or copying out incorrect letters because the scribe misunderstood the script that he saw are all signals of books copied visually.

Within the visual method, there were two ways to speed up the work. One was to exchange scribes. While there was one manuscript being copied from one exemplum, scribes could take turns to keep the work going and to have fresh eyes and a fresh right hand on it. The other, possible only when the work was planned to a high degree and parchment space carefully calculated, was to assign different scribes to different sections of the same book. Thus, in some gospel books, the gospels were planned so that each would begin on a new quire or sheaf of folded pages. In this way four scribes could be working on each of the four gospels in order to complete the volume faster.

The other method for copying was to listen to the text being read by a lector and copy down what was heard. This method would be practical if several scribes were all making copies of the same text at the same time. Despite what might be expected, studies have shown that transcribing a text from an aural source takes just as much time as using a visual source. The only advantage of this method is that multiple copies can be made at the same time from a single exemplum—it's like setting a photocopier to make five copies when we push the button, rather than just one. Just as there are typical visual errors, there are a variety of common aural errors as well, spelling mistakes or incorrect words written based on what scribes thought they heard caused sometimes by poor pronunciation or even an accent. This copying method seems to have been less common than the visual method.

The bottom line is that there was no such thing as mass production on the scale that we are used to. Producing a legible text takes time, and it takes work. Unlike modern print runs that produce hundreds or thousands of identical books at a time, ancient and medieval scribes were producing one at a time. The closest the early medieval West got to a Bible factory was the monastery of St. Martin in Tours at the height of its powers in the first half of the ninth century. Modern scholar David Ganz has produced a fascinating picture of the work accomplished there. Under Charlemagne, the great English scholar

Alcuin was made abbot and granted vast resources. He and his successor, Fridugisus, took the art of copying pandects of the Bible to a whole new level. Through careful planning, calculation, and scribal efficiencies, they reduced the size of the Bible (only 450 leaves, meaning only half as many sheep hides as the Codex Amiatinus) developed new variations of scripts to write smaller while still maintaining legibility, and used anywhere from two to twenty-four scribes on each work. The result was the closest thing to mass production the early Middle Ages would see: forty-six Bibles and eighteen gospel books have survived that were produced in the period from around 800 to 853. (The year 853 begins a crushing series of Viking raids that devastated the abbey's ability to produce much of anything.) Making an educated guess on how many may have been lost, Ganz estimates that at full production in its heyday, the abbey of St. Martin was producing two Bibles a year for more than a half-century.[3] Now, to be fair, they were producing other books as well—patristic texts and Carolingian texts as well as Bibles—but think about that and what it means for how few Bibles, whether one-volume pandects or the much more common multivolume collections, were in circulation.

Consider just the Christianization of England following the successful mission of Augustine of Canterbury in the late sixth century. Based on the number of churches we know existed, for each to have a Bible would have meant more than the three hundred books produced within two centuries.[4] Then consider how many would have been needed on the continent and you realize just how much of a problem production was. How do you deal with the problem of supply?

Not only that, manuscripts are infamous for a lack of editorial control. If I compare the text of my Revised Standard Version Bible with any other Revised Standard Version, I can count on seeing the same words in the same verses and chapters. That's part of the beauty

---

[3] David Ganz, "Mass Production of Early Medieval Manuscripts: The Carolingian Bibles from Tours," in *The Early Medieval Bible: Its Production, Decoration, and Use*, ed. Richard Gameson (Cambridge: Cambridge University Press, 1994), 53–62, at 53.

[4] Richard Gameson, "The Royal 1. B. Vii Gospels and English Book Production in the Seventh and Eighth Centuries," in Gameson, *The Early Medieval Bible*, 24–52, at 45.

of mechanized mass production: not only does it produce books on a vastly greater scale, but they are identical. Not so with manuscripts. What was produced was based on what the scribe saw and heard. If they were copying from a faulty or poorly written manuscript, their best production was only as good as their source. And, sometimes it was worse than that. Another error we see, particularly in gospel books, is memory inserting itself into the present. A scribe copying a familiar story might start writing the words he remembers rather than the words that he sees; it's not uncommon to find verses from the Gospel of Matthew stuck in the Gospel of Luke, based on scribal memory playing tricks on the copying hand.

Thus, one aspect of the church's technology problem was the means of textual production and reproduction. Manuscripts can be produced only so quickly and will inevitably contain errors. This complicates the problem of availability.

Language

The next difficulty that we identified is language. Not only was there an issue with grappling with the books themselves and getting them copied accurately, but then there was the language problem. And this problem has more facets than we typically appreciate. When we consider the Bible in the early medieval West, the first hurdle to cross was the initial problem of getting the text from its original language (Greek) into the dominant language of the West: Latin.

As our lightning sketch of early church history at the beginning of the chapter indicated, the first Bibles of the church were all in Greek. The Old Testament was the Septuagint, the Greek translation of the Jewish Scriptures done by Jewish scribes in Alexandria in the two centuries before the Christian era. The name "Septuagint" comes from the well-circulated advertising campaign that accompanied this version in the so-called Letter of Aristeas. This text breathlessly explains that this translation of the Jewish Scriptures into Greek is the best because, when the Great Library at Alexandria realized it needed a copy of the Jewish Scriptures, they imported seventy wise elders (*septuaginta* in Latin, also sometimes referred to in shorthand by the Roman numerals for seventy, LXX), locked them all in separate rooms, and set them to work translating. At the end of their work, when all of the manuscripts were compared, all seventy translations were identical—thereby proving that this edition was crafted not by men but by the Spirit of God, which inspired all seventy elders to write exactly the same thing. However fantastic this story seems to us, it made sure that this edition became the most circulated version of the Greek Old Testament. There were earlier versions that scholars now refer to as the Old Greek, and later editions by writers like Theodotion, Aquila, and Symmachus, which are superior in many respects to the Septuagint, but they never achieved the market share that the Septuagint did.

The texts of the New Testament were all composed in Greek, frequently with reference specifically to the text of the Old Testament in Greek. Thus, we can tell that the authors of Matthew, Hebrews, and Revelation were making reference to the text of the Septuagint in Greek where they quoted Old Testament passages because there are small but noticeable differences between the Hebrew readings and what are found in the Greek. Indeed, one of the explanations for the odd dialect of Greek found in the book of Revelation is that it is self-consciously adopting a Septuagint style in order to sound more biblical—just as some preachers today will offer prayers in Jacobean English in order to conform to biblical style found in the King James Version.

As facility with Greek faded in the West and those who were literate only in Latin demanded copies of the Scriptures, the result was chaos. The first center of Latin-language Christianity was North Africa; Tertullian and Cyprian, writing in Roman Carthage, were the first major theologians writing in the tongue. Latin Christianity spread from Africa to Rome in the third century, and by the fourth Augustine of Hippo was complaining about the sorry state of biblical translations from Latin into Greek. Although a learned and cultured man—even a teacher of rhetoric before his conversion—Augustine could not work in Greek. In his treatise *On Christian Teaching*, he spends five chapters discussing the problems of language and how a Latin-speaking audience should work with and correct problematic Latin texts.[5] Augustine

---

[5] Augustine discusses this in book 2, chapters 11–15. This work goes by various English names, based on how scholars interpret the Latin title *De Doctrine Christiana*. "On Christian Doctrine" is likely one of the worst options, but common nonetheless for obvious reasons.

starts by grousing about the many different translations and their varying quality: "We can enumerate those who have translated the Scriptures from Hebrew into Greek, but those who have translated them into Latin is innumerable. In the early times of the faith when anyone found a Greek codex, and he thought that he had some facility in both languages, he attempted to translate it."[6] He then explains that one of the strategies for handling the multiplicity of renderings is to compare them with one another and, by seeing the different translation options, to triangulate on the true meaning of a text. The danger here is that not all readings are equal.

Augustine reminds his readers that sometimes a varying translation is produced by bad translation:

> Many translators are deceived by ambiguity in the original language which they do not understand, so that they transfer the meaning to something completely alien to the writer's intention. Thus some codices have "their feet are sharp to shed blood," for the word *oxus* in Greek means both "sharp" and "swift." But he sees the meaning who translates "their feet swift to shed blood"; the other, drawn in another direction by an ambiguous sign, erred. And such translations are not obscure, they are false, and when this is the situation the codices are to be emended rather than interpreted.[7]

In recommending emendation rather than interpretation Augustine is trying to be helpful—but he's not. The problem is that this discussion comes as part of a larger conversation around "ambiguous signs" and the place and importance of figurative language in Scripture (we'll dig into this discussion more in a later chapter). How is a Latin speaker to know what is ambiguous against what is bad? Augustine's response is to check the Greek—but if the reader's Greek is no better than the translator's (assuming he can even get his hands on a Greek text!) how is this correction supposed to occur?

The best Augustine can do at this point is to commend one particular version of the Latin text which he refers to as "the Itala."[8] Other

---

[6] Augustine, *Christian Instruction* 2.11.16 (ChrDoc, p. 44).
[7] Augustine, *Christian Instruction* 2.12.18 (ChrDoc, p. 45).
[8] Augustine, *Christian Instruction* 2.15.22 (ChrDoc, p. 48).

than dropping this tantalizing hint, we know nothing further about it except that he clarifies that it has been emended with reference to the Greek text. Augustine wrote these comments in North Africa in the year 396. It turns out that he wasn't the only one to have noticed the problems with the Latin Bible, though, because in 382, Pope Damasus asked his secretary, a short-tempered fellow named Jerome with a sharp wit and an even sharper tongue (whom we encountered in the first chapter), to produce a trustworthy edition of the gospels and the psalms. Jerome framed the task thus:

> You urge me to revise the old Latin version, and, as it were, to sit in judgment on the copies of the Scriptures which are now scattered throughout the world; and, inasmuch as they differ from one another, you would have me decide which of them agree with the Greek original. . . . For if we are to pin our faith to the Latin texts, it is for our opponents to tell us which; for there are almost as many forms of texts as there are copies. If, on the other hand, we are to glean the truth from a comparison of many, why not go back to the original Greek and correct the mistakes introduced by inaccurate translators, and the blundering alterations of confident but ignorant critics, and, further, all that has been inserted or changed by copyists more asleep than awake? . . . We must confess that as we have [the New Testament] in our language it is marked by discrepancies, and now that stream is distributed into various channels we must go back to the fountainhead. . . . I therefore promise in this short Preface the four Gospels only, which are to be taken in the following order, Matthew, Mark, Luke, and John, as they have been revised by a comparison of the Greek manuscripts. Only early ones have been used. But to avoid any great divergences from the Latin which we are accustomed to read, I have used my pen with some restraint, and while I have corrected only such passages as seemed to convey a different meaning, I have allowed the rest to remain as they are.[9]

This preface, written to Pope Damasus in 383, contains within it several points that need to be highlighted. First, Jerome is showing broad agreement with Augustine. There are a lot of different versions, most of them bad. Second, Jerome is very clear here that he is not doing a

---

[9] Jerome, "Preface to the Four Gospels" (NPNF[2] 6:487–88).

new translation. He seems to be pressing for one ("why not go back to the original Greek?"), but he does not go that route. Third, he has deliberately carried out a very conservative revision. As acerbic as his tongue was, even he quailed at the thought of the flood of opprobrium that would pour upon him if he changed too much. The problem is that humans tend to be a very conservative species when it comes to our treasured words, especially our religious words.[10] Jerome knew that there was only so much he could get away with.

Jerome was an exceedingly well-educated man and his writings are replete with citations from Cicero and Virgil, the greatest of Latin stylists. The gospels that he revised show little trace of this style. The Greek of the New Testament is *Koine* Greek, the common Greek used as a common language among people with different mother tongues. While there is a simple elegance to the Greek of John and some classical pretensions in the constructions of Hebrews, most of it is basic and largely unconcerned with classical grammatical canons. The Greek of the Septuagint is even less so and betrays translators working in a second language; it is littered with Hebraic words and constructions. The Latin texts that Jerome adjusted for meaning were likewise in a popular vernacular, often betraying through stilted constructions and lots of loan words their thoroughly Greek origin. They are not the text we would expect Jerome to produce had he felt the freedom to do it his own way.

Shortly thereafter Jerome also finished his first run through the Psalms. This edition, produced at Rome, stayed there with one exception. As a result, it is known as the *Romanum*. It too was a light-handed revision.

We're not sure what Damasus thought of these—and he died shortly after receiving them. Jerome, who had managed to make enemies with a number of influential Roman clergymen, headed off to Bethlehem to spend the rest of his life as a monk, accompanied by Paula and Eustochium (whom we met in the previous chapter). Once ensconced in his new home, he did another revision of the Psalter that we date to about 388. This one spread quickly throughout Gaul and was referred to as the *Gallicanum*; it became the standard Psalter

---

[10] If you don't believe me, just take a look at the controversies surrounding prayer book revision in the American Episcopal Church or arguments over recent changes to the English edition of the Roman Catholic Mass!

throughout the Latin West with the exception of Rome, where the *Romanum* was retained. (Because the subsequent invasions of the Angles, Saxons, and Jutes gutted the British church, fresh missionaries had to be sent to the newly settled English. As they were sent from Rome by Gregory the Great, they took with them the *Romanum*, which became the Psalter used throughout England.)

Jerome did a fresh translation of the Old Testament from the Septuagint but quickly became dissatisfied with it. After learning Hebrew in the Holy Land, he could not ignore the differences that he found between the Greek and Hebrew texts and determined that the Hebrew texts were superior. Accordingly, he did not release his translation of the Septuagint and instead did an entirely new translation from the Hebrew, which was finally completed around 405. This, then, was the final shape of Jerome's work on the biblical text. He translated the Hebrew text of the Old Testament, ignored the Apocrypha (those Old Testament books found in Greek, not Hebrew), and revised the Old Latin of the gospels. The rest of the New Testament he did not touch, and a version of the Old Latin for the Epistles, Acts, and Revelation was attached to Jerome's work to round things out.

The response to his work was predictable: people hated it. Augustine took him to task for using the Hebrew as a base text rather than the Septuagint. There were differences between the two texts, but Augustine—convinced by the tale of the Seventy shut up in their separate cells—argued that if there were differences the Septuagint represented an additional revelation from God that ought to be used. As part of his argument, he recounted the story of a riot that broke out in a church when Jerome's version of Job was read—they hated the change from what they were used to. But, whatever its faults, Jerome's text did gain acceptance, and after several centuries of existing alongside the surviving Old Latin versions it emerged out of the early Middle Ages as the *de facto* text of the Bible.

Modern people often wonder why the Bible was not translated into the languages of the people in late antiquity and the early Middle Ages. Here is one factor: consider how long it took for a stable, reliable version of the Bible to become available in Latin! In the time period that we are considering, though, there's another factor as well.

Looking back at the collapse of the Roman system in the West we see lots and lots of barbarians. It's easy to imagine them all milling about in an undifferentiated fur-clad mass. But that's not the way it worked then. Jerome spoke of a flood of "Quadi, Vandals, Sarmatians, Alans, Gepids, Herules, Saxons, Burgundians, Allemanni, and Pannonians."[11] And that's to leave aside the Goths, Ostrogoths, Huns, and Lombards who would feature in the later parts of this tale. It's hard to know much about their languages because most of what survives is from the Roman side. We can only guess how accurate they were about the names of the groups, let alone whether the chroniclers understood how the various groups organized themselves. From what we can determine, most of these groups spoke their own mother tongues, and even within groupings there were dialects. To translate the Bible into the language of the people, which people would be chosen? Which of the languages, dialects, or subdialects would get picked?

Thus, the problem of language was a major factor in the church's technology problem. And, when we speak of the West, we must do so remembering that Latin was not the original tongue of the Christian Church: it was Greek. Just getting the Bible into acceptable, reliable Latin was a major hurdle, let alone the challenge of getting it into other languages from there.

Literacy

Literacy is a hard thing to measure well when we are speaking of a bygone age. In our own day, literacy is widespread. Modern America is a broadly literate nation; we can count on the fact that most of the people we will interact with day by day can both read and write English at least at a basic level. Some assessments for literacy in the ancient world set the bar as low as being able to write our name. Others include basic facility in written texts. After surveying many relevant studies and focusing on one by William Harris, in a discussion of the milieu of early Christianity, scholar Harry Gamble concludes that "granting regional and temporal variations, throughout the entire period of classical Greek, Hellenistic, and Roman imperial civilization, the extent of literacy was about 10 percent and never exceeded 15 to 20 percent

---

[11] Jerome, Letter 123.16 (NPNF[2] 6:237).

of the population as a whole."[12] Harris's study defines literacy here at its lowest common denominator, "the ability to read or write at any level."[13] As the period we are focusing on lands at the very end of Imperial Rome, this can generally be assumed for late antiquity as well.

As we cross the nebulous border into the early medieval period, we would do well to heed Frans van Liere's admonition, though:

> Full literacy in the Early Middle Ages, meaning the ability to read and write in Latin, was mainly confined to a narrow group in society, the clergy, or ever more narrowly, the monks. But mainly does not mean exclusively. Many people, clergy and laity alike, may have been able to read but not write, and even those who could not were not entirely cut off from the written word, because they could have others read it to them. Recent research has added many shades of gray to a black-and-white image. There was both more illiteracy among the clergy, and more literacy among the laity, than is often supposed.[14]

While we normally think of the clergy as fully literate in Latin, works of social history like Karen Jolly's work on the distribution of Anglo-Saxon churches reminds us that social and educational stratification existed within clerical ranks too. Rather than thinking of the average village priest as being fully literate in Latin, it's likely closer to reality to see him as equivalent to a singer who has been trained to pronounce Latin properly but has the level of understanding of someone with a year or two of high-school Latin—good enough to get through basic narratives and texts he already knows well, but hopeless in the face of Virgil's *Aeneid* or Augustine's *Confessions*.

There's another aspect of literacy too that combines with the earlier point about language brought to our attention by a wondrous text that is a complete anomaly. On permanent display in the Carolina Rediviva library in Uppsala, Sweden, sits the Codex Argentus (the Silver Book). It is a sixth-century manuscript commissioned by the Gothic king

---

[12] Harry Y. Gamble, *Books and Readers in the Early Church: A History of Early Christian Texts* (New Haven, CT: Yale University Press, 1995), 4.
[13] Ibid.
[14] Frans van Liere, *An Introduction to the Medieval Bible* (New York: Cambridge University Press, 2014), 179. Emphasis in original.

Theoderic the Great and likely a sister text to the Codex Veronensis, commissioned at the same time and in the same style. Both books are deluxe manuscripts written on purple parchment with silver and gold ink. While the Codex Veronensis contains the gospels in an Old Latin text, the Codex Argentus contains the gospels written in Gothic, likely the translation done by the Gothic Arian bishop and missionary Ulfias (or Wulfias) in the fourth century.

According to the ninth-century epitome of the *Ecclesiastical History* of the Arian Philostorgius, Ulfias was responsible for quite a lot of work among his people:

> Accordingly [Ulfias] took the greatest care of [the Goths] in many ways, and amongst others, he reduced their language to a written form, and translated into their vulgar tongue all the books of holy Scripture, with the exception of the Books of Kings, which he omitted, because they are a mere narrative of military exploits, and the Gothic tribes were especially fond of war, and were in more need of restraints to check their military passions than of spurs to urge them on to deeds of war. But those books have the greatest influence in exciting the minds of readers, inasmuch as they are regarded with great veneration, and are adapted to lead the hearts of believers to the worship of God.[15]

This is quite a career; Ulfias both created a written language for Gothic and used it to write most of the Bible into his own language. But here's what makes this an anomaly: despite his hard work to create a written language for Gothic (based chiefly on the Greek alphabet) the Bible is the only text we possess in Gothic aside from a few inscriptions, and this codex is one of the few surviving witnesses to it. Written Gothic was a blip on the screen and vanished virtually without a trace. The reason likely comes back to literacy. The door to literacy was one of the two main languages of the time; anyone who wanted to read Gothic already knew how to read either Latin or Greek (or both). Why go to the time and trouble of writing down the translation of a text if its content was already preserved in a language that one could already read and understand?

---

[15] Edward Walford, *Epitome of the Ecclesiastical History of Philostorgius, Compiled by Photius, Pariarch of Constantinople* (London: Henry G. Bohn, 1855). Accessed online at www.tertullian.org/fathers/philostorgius.htm on 10/28/16.

Thus, massive illiteracy was the fourth major aspect of the church's technology problem that it had to grapple with in late antiquity and the early medieval period. For the words of Scripture to be encountered and treasured, for important thoughts to be transmitted in a stable form across time and space as the faith spread, this bottleneck of knowledge had to be solved.

Liturgy Is the Answer

The church dealt with its technology problem in many different ways, but I am going to argue that the chief means of addressing all of these different aspects of the technology problem in late antiquity and the early medieval West was the liturgy. It is not a complete solution, nor the only solution; rather, it was one of an array of strategies, but it was the central one, and a key aspect of how and why it was able to be the chief means rests on the psalms.

Keeping in mind the four chief aspects of the technological problem (the physicality of the faith, manuscript culture, language barriers, and massive illiteracy), deployment of the liturgy as it became standardized and stable in the Latin West was able to address each of these. Let me lay out the case in a big-picture format, then come back and tease out the various elements, showing how they addressed the issues faced by the church: the liturgies of the Mass and the Office enabled the church to return the texts of Scripture into an oral medium that could be broadly received by the faithful whether literate or not (mostly not). The clergy were trained specifically to function as "scribes of/for the Kingdom of God"[16] who could convert the texts of Scripture into oral performance. As the liturgy was not able to bear the full volume of Scripture, the two kinds of liturgies centered on three portions of texts that conveyed the most essential material, condensing the scope of the Bible into a set of selections that could be easily contained in three manageable volumes rather than in nine volumes (as with the multivolume Bibles) or one unmanageable volume (the pandects). As a result, the Mass transmitted the gospels containing the outward words and works of Jesus, supplemented by the epistle which excerpted the letters of Paul, the General Epistles, and some of the Old Testament

---

[16] I'm riffing here on Matthew 13:52.

Prophets; the Office focused on the transmission of the psalms which contained simultaneously the essence of Scripture but also the inner thoughts and feelings of Jesus. Since the psalms were understood as a microcosm of Scripture, to learn them was to learn the scope of Scripture. Constant repetition of the psalms moved them from the realm of textual manuscript culture into the communal memory of an oral culture. As possessions of communal oral memory, they also served as the gateway into spoken and written Latin language acquisition.

That's a lot of stuff; now let's unpack it and see how the liturgy and the psalms addressed the church's tech problem.

The first problematic aspect that we took up was the physicality of the faith. Talking specifically about the issue of big heavy books and the expense of artificial light, the liturgical answer to this challenge was twofold: strategically limit the necessary texts and leverage memory over lighting.

Recall again that library list we looked at. The Bible section had two biblical pandects and three multivolume Bibles. The Liturgy section had twelve lectionaries and fifty Psalters. The term "lectionary" is a little ambiguous. In one sense, the term "lectionary" refers to a list of readings and in this case there were two such lists to account for two kinds of readings. The Mass in the church at Rome had two readings at the time, a gospel and an epistle. The gospel reading represented a story or episode-sized selection of material usually around eight to ten modern verses in length. The epistle was usually a selection from one of the Pauline letters, but usually on fasting days a reading from the Old Testament appeared. Isaiah or Wisdom books, like the Wisdom of Solomon, Ben Sirach (Ecclesiasticus), or Proverbs, were common. These readings tended to be a bit shorter and were around four to five modern verses in length (although some could be as long as ten). As the passage about the priest Musaeus indicates, gospel readings and epistle readings appropriate to the liturgical season were appointed first for all Sundays of the year and eventually for the Wednesdays, Fridays, and Saturdays as well in a repeating one-year cycle. By means of this system, most of the gospels of Matthew and John and the majority of Luke were appointed every year; Mark appears occasionally, which is not a surprise as much of its material is duplicated in both Matthew and Luke. No such coverage obtained in the epistle reading; there are marginally more readings from the books of Romans and

Isaiah than other books, but generally these selections are hitting the high points and not trying to present the contents of whole books like we get in the gospels.

As lists, these lectionaries were helpful because they told the clergy what to prepare and to present at each service; where they truly came into their own as an answer to the technology problem is when they became books in their own right. In a lectionary book, the readings themselves were excerpted and copied in the order in which they appeared throughout the liturgical year. Thus, a gospel lectionary (or Evangelary) would not start with Matthew 1, the beginning of the first chapter of the first gospel; rather, it would begin with the reading for the first Sunday in the yearly cycle. Ironically, this was frequently Matthew 1:18-21, but that's because this was the appointed text for the Vigil of Christmas, the first liturgical occasion in the book, not because it was the beginning of Matthew.[17] Accordingly, it would be followed immediately by Luke 2:1-14, the reading for the first Mass of Christmas.

As helpful as it is for the gospel lectionary, it was even more so for the epistle lectionary (or Epistolary). A gospel book already contains all four gospels. All we need is a list or even a good set of marginal notations and we're good to go. Not so with the epistles. Since these readings spanned Paul's Epistles, the General Epistles, Acts, Revelation, Isaiah, and the Wisdom literature, we would need at least four volumes of a multipart Bible or a full-on pandect to gather this material together. An epistolary, a dedicated book with the epistle lessons copied out in order, could replace a costly set or a massive tome with one efficient volume.

In this way, the Mass—a central service of the church that was expected that all the faithful would attend on Sundays and major feast days—became the locus for communicating the content of the four gospels: the narratives that present the words and works of Jesus Christ whom the church regards as God incarnate.

---

[17] While the modern liturgical year begins with the First Sunday of Advent, the liturgical season prior to Christmas, the lectionaries from the earliest period don't start there. One reason for this is because the season of Advent was still in the process of coming together.

The Office—the eight prayer services appointed throughout the day, every day—focused itself on the psalms. The lay faithful were encouraged to attend at least the main morning Office, Lauds, and the main evening service, Vespers, on Saturday evening and Sunday, but for the most part these services were relegated to the religious professionals: monks, nuns, and clerics of the various ranks. St. Benedict in his rule outlines the norm: "For those monks show themselves too lazy in the service to which they are vowed, who chant less than the psalter with the customary canticles in the course of a week, whereas we read that our holy Fathers strenuously fulfilled that task in a single day. May we, lukewarm as we are, perform it at least in a whole week!" (RB 18.25). Thus, all 150 psalms were sung every week. However, some were also sung much more frequently than others. As additional devotions multiplied, certain psalms were chanted much more frequently than the rest to the degree that under a particular English monastic customary the monks would pray Psalm 51 six times a day during the season of Lent!

This repetition, all the psalms every single week, many more frequently than that, would lead naturally to the memorization of the psalms even if memorization was not encouraged. But it was encouraged! Not only was it encouraged, it was explicitly legislated in the more fulsome monastic rules. The Rule of the Master, the basic text from which Benedict adapted his rule, goes into great detail about exactly how the psalms get memorized:

> In winter from the winter equinox, which is September 24, until Easter, because it is cold and the brothers cannot do any work in the morning, they are to devote the time from Prime [the prayer office that ends around daybreak] to Terce [the prayer office in the mid-morning] to reading, with the various deaneries [groups of ten under an older leader] in places separated from one another to avoid having the entire community crowded together and disturbing one another with their voices; let one of the ten in each place do the reading while the rest of his group listen. During these three hours the boys, in their deanery, are to learn letters on their tablets from someone who is literate. Moreover, we also exhort illiterate adults up to the age of fifty to learn letters. Again, we wish it kept in mind that during these same periods the psalms are to be studied by those who do not know them, directed by the deans in their respective deanery. So during these three hours they are to read and listen to one another, and take turns teaching letters and the psalms to those who do not know them. (RM 50.9-15)

And throughout the summer season, whether the meal is at the sixth hour or the ninth, for whatever time remains after None [the prayer office in mid-afternoon] until time for Vespers [the prayer office at sundown] to begin, the various deaneries having been separated from one another in different places, some as directed by their deans are to read, others listen, others learn and teach letters, others study psalms which they have transcribed. When they have mastered and memorized them perfectly, let their deans take them to the abbot to recite by heart the psalm or canticle or lesson of any kind. And as soon as he has recited it in its entirety, let him ask prayers for himself. Then when those present have prayed for him, the abbot concludes and the one who has done the reciting kisses the abbot's knees. Either the abbot or the deans immediately order something new to be transcribed [to be learned], and after anything has been transcribed, before he studies it, let him again ask those present to pray for him; and in this way the learning of it is to be undertaken. (RM 50.62-69)

While this is one description from one rule, it is broadly representative of the monastic tradition in the West. While this text was written in the first half of the sixth century in Italy (the exact time and place we will discuss further in the next chapter), we can see the same energy and devotion given to these same activities for the next five hundred years across the continent.

Liturgical scholar Susan Boynton describes how the memorization of the psalms and other liturgical materials was a central activity in the process of forming child oblates into adult monks. She begins by listing the daunting number of liturgical roles for boys in both the Office and the Mass from a twelfth-century customary: "[They] pronounce the versicles of each psalm at all the canonical hours, intone the antiphons on ferial [non-feast] days, and intone whatever is sung at the morning mass, unless it is a major feast day; at Lauds and Vespers, they sing a responsory and say the versicles; in the summer at Matins they say the single short lesson; they always read in chapter, never in refectory."[18] Naturally, this is in addition to knowing all of

---

[18] Susan Boynton, "Training for the Liturgy as a Form of Monastic Education," in *The Practice of the Bible in the Middle Ages: Production, Reception, and Performance in Western Christianity*, ed. Susan Boynton and Diane J. Reilly (New York: Columbia University Press, 2011), 7–20, at 8, quoting from the Cluniac customary of Bernard.

the psalms. Continuing, she emphasizes the continuity of these duties and the material that had to be learned:

> Learning these chants and readings, as well as many others, seems to have occupied every free moment of the day. The training process necessarily constituted a monk's entire education, at least until he mastered the most essential liturgical material. The first chants learned were the psalms, canticles and hymns. The Murbach Statutes of 816 mention these chants first in a programme of elementary learning, and the same items in the same order, were apparently assigned to beginners in the twelfth century by the Augustinian canons of St Victor of Paris, whose customary states that "when a novice sits in the cloister, he should learn his psalter, and repeat it literally by heart, and afterwards the hymnary."[19]

Again, this is not a matter of observing this kind of activity in a few scattered sources; rather, they bear witness to the great tradition of life and formation in the intentional liturgical communities in the medieval West, the monasteries and cathedrals, and the formation for most clergy in the days before seminaries. Her point is that the liturgy was the central activity of life in these communities and that education for serving and for singing was the central form of monastic education: the performance of Scripture and ritual in the liturgy was the central task of these communities.

Let's take a step back and consider what the act of memorizing the psalms does. By memorizing all of the psalms, the technological challenge of books, manuscripts, and literacy is transcended. When the psalms are learned primarily in choir, the psalms are taken out of the realm of textual technology and become part of an oral, communal tradition. As an oral tradition, it is no longer limited by the problems of literacy. The challenges caused by the physicality of faith evaporate. It doesn't matter what kind of books they are, how large or heavy or expensive, if they are rendered no longer necessary. Further, the challenge and expense of artificial lighting is removed—or certainly reduced—through memorization. If everyone knows the psalms, only one person with one book and one lamp is needed: the ruler of the choir who knows which psalm needs to be sung at which part in the

---

[19] Ibid.

service and can lead off with the correct starting chant for the correct psalm (called the incipit).

As a communal tradition, the problem of textual errors is reduced. As we saw in the material from the Rule of the Master, the deans and abbot certified the memorization of each psalm by each oblate. It doesn't matter what kind of text the oblate was working from or how bad of a copy it might have been, the oral memory of the elders would correct the oblate at this point of certification, and the entire choir would function as a mechanism of self-correction as they sang the psalms together. As an ongoing mechanism for correction, monks and oblates alike were required as part of Chapter—the daily monastic business meeting—to confess publicly before the community any errors they made in singing the psalms and to receive punishment or correction for it. In this way, attention to the text of the psalms, their continual re-presentation and repetition, ingrained them deeply into the collective memory of the monastic communities, as well as cathedrals and larger churches that contained intentional liturgical communities of clergy.

Thus, the principle of selecting readings according to a lectionary, repeating the same readings for the same services every year, and the constant repetition of the psalms were powerful answers to the problems of the physicality of the faith and the complications of manuscript culture.

Again, the text from the Rule of the Master and the work of Susan Boynton underscore the means by which the language barrier and illiteracy were overcome—at least in monastic establishments. In the turn from late antiquity into the early medieval period, the broad mass of barbarians frequently hailed from a variety of regions and spoke in a host of tongues. A major force in their formation, though, was economic and the greatest sources of jobs were the two halves of the Roman Empire. Whether fighting for them or against them, learning at least the rudiments of Greek or Latin was a useful commercial skill; from the sources that discuss such matters, it seems that many of the tribesmen who fought knew either Greek, Latin, or both. Hence, at the start of the period, language seems not to have been a large issue. As time went on, as barbarian populations settled and intermingled, they assimilated linguistically, but linguistic drift also occurred due to the interaction between Latin and their mother tongues. What we refer to now as the "Romance languages"—Spanish, Portuguese, French, Italian, and Romanian—are all derivatives from the Vulgar Latin learned by these groups. It looks like the Romance languages started diverging enough from Latin that they were not fully intelligible at some point in the eighth century. We know this from two chief sources: first, we start seeing Romance glosses in Latin texts that translate unfamiliar or unintelligible Latin words into familiar Romance words. Second, as part of Charlemagne's religious reforms, the Council of Tours declared in 813 that clergy needed to preach in the common Romance languages of the region (*rusticam Romanam linguam*) or in the Germanic language (*Theodiscam*—from the German term that simply means "the people's [*Theod*-] language [*-isc*]").

This does not mean that this was the first accommodation to non-Latin speakers; several local church councils had decreed that a minimum level of knowledge for lay Christians was the ability to recite the creed, the Ten Commandments, and the Lord's Prayer in their own language.

Even while the church lost Latin as a native language and expanded into peoples who spoke Germanic languages, Latin remained the language of the liturgies and the Scriptures. Without making a formal decision of it, the church continued to work on the old paradigm—that barbarians who wished to do business with Rome needed to learn Latin—even while the world shifted around them. Decrees like those of the Council of Tours at least acknowledged this reality and attempted to accommodate for those who were not able to learn Latin. For those who did need to learn Latin, the memorization of the Psalter became the key to both literacy and Latin alike. Because the psalms were taught primarily orally in the choir week after week, they provided students with a ready-made base of Latin when it came time both to learn how to read and to understand the Latin language and how it worked. The 150 psalms in Latin contain 30,000 words—roughly the number of words in the first three chapters of this book. However, the psalms are composed of only some 2,100 unique words, not a burdensome number for a young mind to wrap itself around. When it came time to learn grammar—parts of speech, verb tenses, how the endings of words determine how they are being used in a sentence—students already had a host of examples that a teacher could draw on.

Moreover, monks were—increasingly as we move through the period—people who sang, and the psalms were the foundation of their libretto. Not only did they sing through all of the psalms every week in the seven prayer offices; most of the changeable chants in the Mass were drawn from the psalms as well.

The memorized store of psalms became the key to literacy, and the process of clerical or monastic formation was the key to solving the massive illiteracy around them. We must remember, illiteracy was not an anomaly in the ancient world. Neither, for that matter, were language barriers. For those who didn't know how to read, didn't want to know how, or couldn't be bothered to read whether they knew how or not, there was an easy solution: the scribe. Someone who couldn't or didn't want to read could find a specialist who did. One of the stock characters of the Roman Imperium was the Greek scribe. A man, whether slave or free, with rhetorical and philosophical training and the ability to read both Greek and Latin fluently was a staple of wealthy Roman households. If someone wasn't wealthy, a scribe could be hired in the marketplace; for a few coins he could read a letter or write one as it was dictated, confident that the person to whom it was sent would be able to find a scribe at the other end. A trustworthy scribe could do all of the reading and writing—and produce it in whichever language most suitable for the correspondence. As the church sought to establish households of faith across the imperium and even beyond its borders, it also needed scribes trained for the kingdom of God. The clergy—along with and through their sacramental and pastoral duties—were the professional readers who could transform the sacred texts of Scripture and rite into spoken word and ritual action. As the decrees from the Council of Tours clarify, the job of translating the sacred texts into the language of the people was an expected part of the scribe's task. Thus, it didn't matter what language the books were in. The responsibility of the clergy was to teach their meaning regardless of the language in which they were written.

Basic literacy started—as we see in the Rule of the Master and in other representatives of the tradition—with the learning of the psalms, canticles, and hymns. It didn't stop there, though, and, as Boynton notes, virtually all free time could be absorbed in learning either chant or readings. Which texts were learned at which times depended on clerical grades. In these days before seminaries, clergy were trained in the midst of these communities. Ordination was a process, not an event, and was conceived as movement up a ladder of learning and formation through a set of nine ordered grades. Each grade had its functions (liturgical and otherwise), and as a boy was formed in each grade he would learn the parts proper to it. In particular, two of the later grades had specific responsibilities for sets of material in the services: subdeacons read or chanted the epistle reading in the Mass while deacons chanted the gospel reading. Typically, the older boys would reach the subdeacon grade, and learning the epistle texts is mentioned in the tenth-century colloquy of Aelfric Bata and also in the Murbach Statutes mentioned before. This text mentions these liturgical selections specifically. After memorizing the psalms, hymns, and canticles, the students were to memorize the Rule of St Benedict, and after that, the *liber comitis*—a term that could apply strictly to the Epistolary or more broadly to both Mass lectionaries, the epistle and the gospel texts, combined in a single book.

Thus, training for the liturgy—the memorization of the psalms, the epistles, and the gospels, learning to sing the chants and hymns—was the chief training ground that taught the clergy how to read and understand the scriptural texts in their own tongues, enabling them to read them and explain them in their people's mother tongues.

We may wonder how well this actually worked. All indications suggest that it actually worked pretty well. We see signs of it in literary works from across late antiquity and the early medieval period. A great example is the Confession of St. Patrick. Written by Patrick, the famous apostle to Ireland, at some point in the fifth century, it is littered with allusions to the Scriptures. When we think of Patrick sitting down to write, however, it's unlikely he did so with a Bible next to him. Of the almost three hundred references, citations, or allusions to the Scriptures in this brief document, almost one-sixth are from the Psalms; the rest are mostly from the four gospels, the epistles, Isaiah, and the Wisdom literature. My hunch is that, if these references were compared with the contents of the gospel and epistle lectionaries, the correspondence between the two would be remarkable. Furthermore, based on what we know from the more credible portions of the Life of St. Patrick by Muirchu, he was deeply committed to this pattern of life:

> Of [Patrick's] diligence in prayer, we shall try to write down only a few details out of the many things that might be said about Patrick. Daily, whether he was staying in one place or traveling along the road, he used to sing all the psalms and hymns and the Apocalypse of John and all the spiritual songs of the scriptures. No less than a hundred times in each hour of the day and each hour of the night he made the sign of the triumphant cross upon himself; and at every cross he saw as he traveled, he used to get down from his chariot and turn towards it in order to pray.[20]

While the frequency of his crossings is undoubtedly an exaggeration, the repetition of the psalms, canticles, and hymns is probably not. This is a glimpse of authentic Celtic spirituality—a rigorous, monastic-based spirituality rooted in the Psalms and the Scriptures!

A Love Song to a Psalter

The Irish monk Mael Isu O Brolchain died in 1086 in a monastery in Armagh, having received the title "chief sage of Ireland." At some point, he wrote a poem that for many years was assumed to be about an elderly nun in a kind of ascetic marriage. However, James Carney, a specialist in medieval Irish poetry, recognized the true object of the poet's affections:

> The problem lay upon my mind for many years before the easy and natural solution suggested itself: it was a poem written by a religious in his old age to an old and tattered copy of the Psalms which had been his first lesson book. The solution, which has found general acceptance by scholars, emerged quite clearly when I noted that in early Ireland a boy destined for the Church began his education at the age of seven, and that the Psalter, from which he learned Latin, reading, singing and religion, was his first lesson book. This book which he had used in his youth in its virgin freshness passed through four generations of young scholars before by some chance it came back into the old priest's hands again.[21]

---

[20] Muirchu, "Life of Patrick," pages 91–117 in *Celtic Spirituality*, trans. Oliver Davies, Classics of Western Spirituality (Mahwah, NJ: Paulist Press, 1999), 112.

[21] James Carney, *Medieval Irish Lyrics* (Berkeley: University of California Press, 1967), xxviii.

We have talked at some length in these two chapters about the Psalter and about when and how a student would have encountered it. What this poem reveals, though, is what they felt about it. Here, we see the thoughts of an old man taking in his hands again the book of his youth:

> Crinóc, lady of measured melody,
> not young, but with modest maiden mind,
> together once in Niall's northern land
> we slept, we two, as man and womankind.
>
> You came and slept with me for that first time,
> skilled wise amazon annihilating fears
> and I a fresh-faced boy, not bent as now,
> a gentle lad of seven melodious years.
>
> There we were then on that firm Irish earth
> Desirous, but in pure and mystic sense;
> Burning with love my flesh, still free from fault
> As fool of God in smitten innocence.
>
> Your counsel is ever there to hand,
> we choose it, following you in everything:
> love of your word is the best of loves,
> our gentle conversation with the King.
>
> Guiltless you are of any sin with man,
> Fair is your name, and bright, and without stain,
> Although I know that when you went from me
> Each in his turn, four lay where I had lain.
>
> And now you come, your final pilgrimage,
> Wearied with toil and travel, grimed with dust,
> Wise still but body not immaculate:
> Time it is that ravished you, not lust.
>
> Again I offer you a faultless love,
> A love unfettered for which surely we
> Will not be punished in the depths of hell
> But together ever walk in piety.
>
> Seeking the presence of elusive God
> wandering we stray, but the way is found,
> following the mighty melodies that with you
> throughout the pathways of the world resound.

> Not ever silent, you bring the word of God
> to all who in the present world abide,
> and then through you, through finest mesh,
> man's earnest prayer to God is purified.
>
> May the King give us beauty back again
> Who ever did his will with eager mind,
> May he look on us with eagerness and love,
> Our old and perished bodies left behind.[22]

In Mael Isu's poem, Lady Wisdom—the beautiful, the desirable, the beloved—is none other than the Psalter itself. Images of fleshly intimacy are cooled with a spiritual admonition, but the monk paints with exquisite colors a lover who initiates him into the arts of love and directs him to ultimate love in God: the Psalter is his Diotima.

Of course, this is one look at the Psalter from the far end of the learning process. Undoubtedly other young Irish lads did not feel this way while slowly learning the text. The second earliest evidence of the psalms we have in Ireland is a student's tablet, wooden boards covered with a layer of wax, into which has been scratched with a stylus Psalms 29–31 in the Gallican translation. This artifact is known as the Springmont Bog Tablets because that is where they were recovered. While we will never know how they came to be in Springmont Bog, I like to imagine a particularly willful student hurling his tablet into the bog in a fit of pique after a difficult time with his lesson!

Summary

The technological challenge facing the church as it spread into the West was a tricky one: How are insights communicated from the Greek Scriptures into an illiterate, Latinate culture? How does one crack the literacy nut? I argue that the liturgy and the psalms were central strategies for solving these problems. Obviously, that's not the only reason why the church used them, but I do think that part of the importance placed on them was the way they addressed this major issue.

The liturgy transformed the text of Scripture into an oral experience. Clergy were the literate scribes for the kingdom of God who

---

[22] Ibid., 75–79.

could turn static marks on parchment into words—either Latin or the hearers' mother tongue—that allowed them to grasp the content of the otherwise silent books. The liturgical services themselves focused the church's gaze onto the gospels and psalms, supplementing them with tastes of the epistles, prophecy, and wisdom. But more than data downloads, the services were places where the presence of God was felt, where religious affect was encouraged, and motivations for active deeds of faith were planted. The psalms played an important part in all of this.

As a microcosm of Scripture, they were short enough to be memorized yet broad enough to convey a sense of the whole span of Scripture in condensed form. As memorized prayers, they provided a template for the interior life and a guide for learning how to pray. As communal oral performance, they ensured word-for-word retention through their constant repetition and intentional practices in the communities to recognize and correct faults. Finally, this memorized store of information was a central pathway for learning both literacy and Latin.

Armed with this perspective, we are now equipped to appreciate the place of the psalms in both the educational life and devotional life of late antiquity and the early medieval period. The Psalms were not simply one book of Scripture out of many; rather, they were the fundamental starting place from which all else sprang. Singing the psalms, learning the psalms, meditating on the psalms was at the center of the monastic vocation and experience. Now we know the backstory of the Psalms. Now we know why it is not an exaggeration to say that how monks and clergy viewed the Psalms had an impact on everything else that they read and thought. And so, finally, we're ready to appreciate the pivotal place of an introductory commentary on the Psalms. We're getting a sense of how odd and unusual it must be that there were only two complete commentaries on the Psalms that came out of the patristic period to the early medieval West—Augustine and Cassiodorus—and why they are so important for understanding how the Middle Ages learned to read.

CHAPTER THREE

Cassiodorus and His Work

An Age Goes Dark

Historians like the term "Dark Ages" even less than they like the term "Middle Ages." Both of these terms were invented as value judgments so that writers of the Renaissance and the Enlightenment could look down on the age that came before them and that separated them from the luster of classical antiquity. Conventionally speaking, the term "Dark Ages" usually gets applied to the general time period that we're looking at. One end of the period is bounded by the loss of central authority in the Roman West at some point in the fifth century (usually referred to as the Fall of Rome); the other end is conveniently anchored by the Norman conquest of England in 1066. The term "early medieval" is a better way to refer to this span of time because, even though the word "medieval" is simply a Latin translation of "middle ages," it does not carry the same overt value judgment with it. Migration Period is another term for the fourth through the eighth centuries that focuses on the mass movements of tribal peoples around and into Europe, basing the title on a description of events.

All that having been said, there are some times and places that have earned the label "Dark Age" due to the amount of destruction, devastation, and death focused in a particular place at a particular time. By any reckoning the Italian sixth century earns that label due to the amount of mayhem and human misery that occurred there. If the four horsemen of the apocalypse are rightly reckoned as War, Famine, Plague, and Death, all four were certainly present then.

The central figure of our story, Cassiodorus Senator, played a pivotal role in the events that shaped the sixth century. Furthermore, he is one of our most important sources for what was going on at the highest levels of government in the West. Throughout his career in government, he was—essentially—a ghostwriter for the Amal kings, writing letters explaining the law, appointing officials, chastising others, and sending formal proclamations to the Senate and foreign powers. As we will discuss, he collected these into twelve books called the *Variae*, which give us a fascinating insight into what was going on at the time. Through his eyes and his pen, we see a vision of Gothic-held Italy at its best, but we also see the turn into chaos that will define the middle and end of the sixth century. Cassiodorus's famous contemporary, the philosopher Boethius, envisioned fortune like a wheel: while God's providence (the big picture of history) might be fixed, fortune itself (the day-to-day progress of events) was fickle and ever-changing. Just as Boethius's career path followed an arc from the highest of public offices to execution, the path of Cassiodorus was quite similar. He started life as a wealthy scion of one of Italy's great families and ended it as a simple monk. This arc lies behind the *Explanation of the Psalms*; the Psalms commentary is not fully understood without grasping the changes to the world that Cassiodorus experienced as the tottering structure of the state in the West collapsed thunderously around him from the pressure of centuries, internal rot, and the hubris of mighty men.

The Rise of Cassiodorus

The fifth century opened with a massive influx of barbarians across the Rhine River and an angry federate army led by Alaric sacking Rome, partly as recompense for a slaughter of thousands of Gothic hostages—mostly women and children—by Roman mobs. The mobs had themselves been angered by the apparent inaction of the army against a large Gothic force led by Radagaisus plundering northern Italy. Thus, the barbarian sack of Rome in 410 was more about an epic failure of internal affairs than the usual conventional narrative of barbarians hating civilization. By the middle of the fifth century, the power of the western Roman Empire was largely limited to Italy itself as migrating tribes took over Spain and Roman Gaul, and tribes clashed with the eastern Roman Empire in the Balkans and Greece. The capital of the

West had been moved out of Rome to the more defensible Ravenna, and by the end of the fifth century Rome was but a pale shadow of itself; it had started the fifth century with a population around eight hundred thousand souls and ended it with a count somewhere around one hundred thousand. That's the numerical equivalent of the population of San Francisco dropping to that of Billings, Montana, over the course of a century.

A turning point that set up the horrors of the sixth century was the deposition of the last emperor of the West in 476 by Odoacer. To call the deposed Romulus August the last Roman emperor of the West would be a little misleading if by Roman we mean born of Italian stock; that ship had sailed as early as AD 193 when the Libyan-born Septimius Severus had emerged victorious from the disaster of succession known to history as the Year of Five Emperors. From that point on, the emperors tended to be descended from North African or Syrian stock until the rise of powers in Pannonia and Moesia, the provinces on the Danube that were a hotbed of motion as tribes from Asia moved into Europe and north European tribes migrated into southern Europe.

In 476 Odoacer did something different and proclaimed himself king (*rex*) rather than emperor. The Roman Senate at his behest sent the imperial regalia back to Zeno, the emperor of the eastern Roman Empire centered in Constantinople, requesting that the empire be unified and that Odoacer be formally recognized as the empire's regent in the West. Zeno, despite his Greek name, was himself a borderland barbarian of the Isuarian people; he recognized Odoacer but never trusted him. Zeno had his own Gothic problem as two warlords named Theoderic warred against each other and him in the East. However, after Theoderic the Amal came out victorious, Zeno persuaded him that his true future lay in the West. Agreeing, Theoderic swept into Italy and in 493 personally killed Odoacer at a banquet that was supposed to have celebrated a peace treaty between the two.

Despite this rocky start, the rise of Theoderic the Amal was a bright spot in an otherwise troublesome time, and he earned himself the name "Theoderic the Great." Theoderic inherited an Italy that had suffered decades of invasion and depredation but that still had a Roman bureaucratic system intact. As he settled into his new position, three different groups emerged as power players in the new order. The first group was, clearly, the barbarian might of the military. The Gothic nobility retained control of the military. Then there was the old aristocracy of Rome. Most of the senatorial families had either died out or fled, and in the sixth century there were two great clans, the Decii and the Anicii, who wielded the ancient authority of the Roman Senate. The third group consisted of provincial nobles, large landholders outside of Rome, some of whom had come into Italy relatively recently and were disdained as *nouveau riche* newcomers by the ancient Roman clans. Theoderic gave these provincial nobles important places in his Ravenna-centered government, giving himself leverage against the old Roman aristocracy by playing the two off one another and these two against the Gothic military.

In the opening years of the sixth century, a young law clerk at the court of King Theoderic was promoted into the role of quaestor, a bureaucratic position that had been in use since the time of the Roman Republic. At this point in time quaestor was the third most powerful position in the civil government, behind the master of offices and the praetorian prefect. A host of petitions to the king flowed through the quaestor's office, especially those coming from the Senate in Rome and any disputes between Gothic warriors. While not technically a legislator, he would send out letters in the king's name that would state and interpret the law.

The young man's name was Flavius Magnus Aurelius Cassiodorus Senator. Known to his contemporaries as Senator (as a name rather than a title), he is known to history as Cassiodorus. This promotion was neither by chance nor unexpected as the young man's father currently served as praetorian prefect and his grandfather had served at court before him. Members of the Cassiodori family were among the most important of the provincial nobles, and they served Theoderic well as foils to the rich ancient families of Rome. The Cassiodori held lands in Squillace, a town in the southern region of Calabria, nestled right in the ball of the foot of Italy's boot.

There was more behind the appointment than rank nepotism, however. The young man had a gift, and beginning in 507, the letters issuing forth from the quaestor's office under the name of Theoderic were well-written and redolent of classical learning and panache. On the one hand, they communicated clearly the needs of the government; on the other, they communicated a sophistication and polish appropriate for a government peopled by wise rulers and educated men.

The shape of the career of the youngest Cassiodorus demonstrates not only his family's power and riches but also his own personal qualities. He served as quaestor for four or five years, from his appointment in 507 to 511 or 512. From there he became consul at Rome in 514. Back in the Roman Republic, the consul was the highest office; two men would serve each year and make decisions for the city. By this time, the chief functions of the consul were quite different. Rather than ruling the city, the primary responsibility of the consul lay in providing funds for the great public entertainments—feasts and games—for the enjoyment of the citizens. Because the empire was divided into two administrative regions, one in the West and the other in the East centered in Constantinople, one consul was selected from the West to pay for the games in Rome, and one was picked from the East to pay for the games in Constantinople. For whatever reason, Cassiodorus served as sole consul in his year. Between chariot races, gladiatorial contests, and theatrical extravaganzas in Rome (and maybe also Milan), serving as a popular and memorable consul was a costly proposition. The consul had to spend enough money to put on a spectacular show, bringing honor to himself, his family, and the ruling powers—but not enough to bankrupt himself and his family. It was a tightrope that some failed to walk successfully, and accounts from the time tell of consuls who overspent themselves into deep debt.

After serving as consul, Cassiodorus disappears from the record for a few years. Whether he returned to his family lands or assisted with administration in Rome is not clear. He does seem to have served as governor of his home province for the typical year term at some point in this span. Between collecting taxes and the customary bribes, serving as governor was a time-honored way for an ex-consul to recoup his losses and plump the family purse.

All the while, Theoderic held sway from Ravenna. The game of statecraft in the fifth and sixth centuries was a rough-and-tumble combination of poker, Russian roulette, and whack-a-mole: Theoderic had to balance the two groups of Italian nobles off one another, credibly maintain the fiction that he was the servant of the emperor in the East while dissuading said emperor from trying to usurp his authority and taxes, beat down rival claimants within the ranks of the Gothic nobles, and curb the power of other barbarians attempting to replicate his success. Theoderic was a master of the game.

The delicate balancing act was disrupted, however, by events in the East. Emperor Zeno's successor, Anastasius, died in 518, and on the death of his successor the imperial purple was seized by Justin, a career military man who had started life as a Thracian swineherd. But he was old and power quickly passed to his nephew Justinian. An ambitious man, Justinian—the last Latin-speaking emperor of the East—proclaimed his presence on the world stage as a recovery of *Romanitas*. At his direction, his skillful generals Belisarius and Narses began great campaigns against the Persians and Vandal-held North Africa, seeking to recapture what Justinian considered the proper extent of the Roman Empire. The senators of Rome began casting hopeful eyes East.

Around this time, Cassiodorus returns to the historical stage. His return to political life was connected with a series of tragic events that would lead to the Gothic succession crisis. It is once again his skill in writing that earns him another look; he publishes his *Chronica* and possibly a first draft of his *Gothic History* in 519 in honor of, and as flattery to, Eutharic, the Visigothic warlord who had married Theoderic's only daughter, who held the consulship that year alongside Justin, emperor in the East. The purpose of these works was to remind the Gothic rulers that he was available for service, ready to assist them loyally in their work, and willing to rise up through the ranks of government and power. Rise Cassiodorus would, but at the expense of another.

Interlude: A Cautionary Tale

In 522, another great Roman aristocrat was showered with honors: Anicius Manlius Severinus Boethius. Theoderic in Ravenna selected one of Boethius's sons to be the consul of Rome, representing the West, while Justin in Constantinople selected Boethius's other son to be the consul representing the East; Boethius himself was tapped for the high position of master of offices. Boethius, a scion of one of the two great Roman senatorial families, the Anicii, was a philosopher as well as a public servant. As far as we know, he was the single greater intellect in the West than Cassiodorus—certainly the only one from whom we have writings. He wrote treatises on music, theology, arithmetic, and geometry. As fluent in Greek as he was in Latin (an achievement becoming more and more rare in this time), he translated the only texts of Aristotle from Greek into Latin that the medieval West would know until the Crusades brought the Arabic editions of Ibn Rushd and Ibn Sina to light. In the introduction to his *Commentary on Aristotle's De Interpretatione*, Boethius lays out a plan for how his philosophical work would unfold:

> I wish to translate the whole work of Aristotle, so far as it is accessible to me, into the Roman idiom and conscientiously offer his complete utterances in the Latin tongue. Everything Aristotle wrote on the difficult art of logic, on the important realm of moral experience, and on the exact comprehension of natural objects, I shall translate in the correct order. Moreover, I shall make all this comprehensible by interpretive explanations. I should also like to translate all Plato's Dialogues, and likewise explain them, and thus present them in a Latin version. When this is accomplished, I will furthermore not shrink from proving that the Aristotelian and Platonic conceptions in every way harmonize, and do not, as is widely supposed, completely contradict one another. I will show, moreover, that they are in agreement with one another at the philosophically decisive points. This is the task to which I dedicate myself, so far as life and leisure for work are vouchsafed to me.[1]

Unfortunately for Boethius and for the unfolding of Western philosophical tradition, the leisurely fulfillment of this ambitious plan of work was not to be, for philosophy was not his only ambition. Somewhere in the year 522 or 523 also came the death of Eutharic, the strong and appointed heir of Theoderic, the presumptive next king in the West.

The master of offices was one of the two highest civil posts in the empire, just below the praetorian prefect. The master of offices received his title because his position oversaw four offices that handled all the imperial correspondence and all foreign envoys who came to address the emperor. All information about doings in the empire and relations with its neighbors flowed through this office. If a wealthy, intelligent, well-connected man of ancient birth steeped in Plato's *Republic* and its vision of philosopher-kings wanted to subvert the empire, this was the perfect place from which to do it.

---

[1] Boethius, *The Consolation of Philosophy*, rev. ed., trans. Victor Watts (London: Penguin, 1999), xv–xvi.

We do not have clear visibility into what happened next. Cassiodorus's collection of official letters is silent on the matter; there is one Eastern-leaning history by an anonymous hand that gives one take on events, and then there is Boethius's side of the story. In short, Boethius was arrested on a charge of treason in 524 or 525. He was accused of conspiring with other members of the senatorial class and of holding treasonous correspondence with the emperor in the East. Imprisoned within a church in Pavia—a city in northern Italy—Boethius embedded his side of the story in a book that would become the most important work of philosophy for the early medieval West behind the Bible, the *Consolation of Philosophy*.

The story of Boethius does not end well. Both he and his father-in-law, Symmachus, were executed at the order of Theoderic. The brilliance of Boethius's *Consolation* ensures that his side of the story is never forgotten, though; it's easy to buy the caricature of the noble Roman philosopher unjustly accused and killed by a thuggish barbarian ruler. We'll probably never really know the true story, and Cassiodorus never tells us. But, then, he's not entirely a neutral observer.

Attaining the Heights

The death of Boethius created a hole in the Gothic administration; Cassiodorus fit nicely into the space and was appointed the new master of offices. If he had any role in the fall of Boethius, it has been muffled by the passing of centuries. He does not refer to it. The histories say nothing. Boethius himself never mentions Cassiodorus. We do know that Cassiodorus will be succeeded in his post by Cyprian—one of the chief accusers of Boethius—and the only words from Cassiodorus about his successor are favorable.

Whatever circumstances enabled it, Cassiodorus was appointed in 523 by Theoderic to wield an enormous amount of control in his new job. The master of offices had a rather large and unruly set of tasks. He managed the four great offices of imperial correspondence that communicated to foreign dignitaries, to the Senate, and to any others outside of the quaestor's duties. He also managed the messengers who sped the letters on their way and the household troops. He did not have to collect money but did spend it in collecting provisions for the capitol and ensuring that suitable ministers were attending to these provisions. In the midst of these duties, we know that Cassiodorus was also writing the letters that the quaestor ought to have been writing. Whether the incumbents were incompetent, Cassiodorus was prevailed upon to aid as the situation arose, or Cassiodorus requested the additional task for himself, we will never know. He does not hesitate to let us know of his opinion and informs history that he was always happy to help the quaestors beneath him: "For, when refined eloquence was needed, the case was straightaway entrusted to [my] genius."[2]

The great cloud on the horizon was the Gothic succession. Theoderic's only legitimate daughter, Amalasuntha, was married to the Visigoth Eutharic who was proclaimed Theoderic's successor. But disaster struck with Eutharic's death in 522. He had only one son, the young Athalaric who became the heir of the aging Theoderic. The great warlord died in 526, and Athalaric took the throne under the watchful eye of his mother, Theoderic's widowed daughter, Amalasuntha. Cassiodorus remained in office long enough to manage the tricky transition between one ruler and another. He then retired his post in 527 once the transition had fully occurred. While we might consider four years to be a rather short shift, Roman political terms historically worked on one- or two- year increments. By these standards, Cassiodorus held high positions for relatively long lengths of time.

What Cassiodorus did for the next six years is unclear. He returns to the stage again in dramatic fashion, though. We have two letters dated September 1, 533, one from King Athalaric to Cassiodorus, informing him of his appointment to the highest civilian job in the kingdom, praetorian prefect, and another letter from Athalaric to the Roman Senate, informing them of the same thing. Both letters go into great detail about the past political career of Cassiodorus, describing his rise at a young age, his close friendship and wise counsel showered on Theoderic, of the trust and goodwill of the entire populace gained by his many virtues, and a thoroughgoing denial of any shade of corruption or avarice upon him in sharp contrast to all of the other politicians of the time. The letter to the Senate concludes with a particular commendation of his religious virtues. It is his reading of the Scriptures, the letter informs us, that has so gifted him with the humility, modesty, and benevolence that he possesses.[3]

---

[2] Cassiodorus, *Variae* IX.24.6, p. 125.
[3] Cassiodorus, *Variae* IX.25.11, p. 130.

Needless to say, Cassiodorus wrote both letters himself at the direction of Athalaric.

Serving as praetorian prefect was tantamount to being a king in all but name. Or, perhaps the better way to say it is that the praetorian prefect was responsible for everything that a king ought to be doing whether he was or not. He collected taxes and spent them. He disciplined all civil government officials. His word was law to be contradicted only by his military counterpart or the king himself. After years of writing letters in the name of others (which he still continued to do), Cassiodorus had now arrived at the point where he could send letters under his own name.

Cassiodorus remains in this office through a very rough political ride. King Athalaric dies roughly a year after appointing Cassiodorus praetorian prefect. Cassiodorus then writes a few letters in the name of Athalaric's mother, Amalasuntha, before she disappears from the record, imprisoned and murdered by her kinsman Theodahad, who seized the throne in 535. These instabilities provided the perfect pretext for the ambitious Emperor Justinian, waiting in the wings in the East, and he commanded his best general, Belisarius, to recapture Rome from the barbarians.

The stage was now set, and hell itself was unleashed on Italy.

For the next five years, armies trampled the length of Italy, killing, burning, and pillaging. Two different Eastern armies were in the field against the Gothic forces while forces of Franks and Burgundians intermittently popped over the Alps to aid one side or the other, each time sating their own appetites for plunder. Several Gothic kings rose and fell over the course of the war until Ravenna, the Gothic capital in the north, fell to Belisarius in 540. The latest Gothic king, Witiges, and his immediate court were sent to Constantinople where he died shortly thereafter.

Wars bring famine. Growing fields are trampled by marching boots and drenched in blood; supplies are horded, stolen, or burned as armies seek to feed themselves and deny food to their enemies. The peasantry is conscripted as cannon fodder and put to the sword. War on its own is bad enough, but a strange weather event—likely caused by the eruption of one or more volcanoes in the Americas—devastated harvests across the globe in 536. Procopius, the Eastern chronicler of the Gothic Wars, recounts that the sun's brightness was dimmed and it seemed like a constant state of eclipse. Irish chronicles report failure of the harvests from 536 until 539. Chinese chronicles report not only crop failures but snow falling in August. In Italy, food already scarce, thanks to continuing violence, became even more scarce. But worse even than the famine was a virulence somehow aided by the unseasonal weather.

As the Eastern reconquest of Italy seemed complete, the situation destabilized further. Plague swept across the known world in a toxic wave. Starting from rats in China, the first recorded transcontinental pandemic swept across the Eurasian continent initially killing somewhere around 25 million people, roughly 13 percent of the global population. Constantinople was hammered, and Justinian himself fell ill but recovered. The bacterial culprit, *Yersina pestis*, is the very same bug responsible for the Black Death in fourteenth-century Europe and the English Plague Year of 1666. Just as the Black Death upended European society and set a new course for the late Middle Ages, so the Plague of Justinian (as it came to be known) caused similar repercussions across the early medieval world.

The plague swept through Italy in 542; the Eastern armies were hit hard. This event, combined with renewed hostilities with Persians on their Eastern borders drawing off troops and generals, inspired a Gothic revolt. The war in Italy rekindled and would continue to burn for another twelve years. Eastern armies returned to tramp the length of Italy, devastation reigned unchecked, and the Italian aristocracy largely fled to Constantinople for safety. Finally, in 554 Justinian issued his Pragmatic Sanction, restoring lands in Italy to the Roman aristocracy, displacing barbarian landholders, and in 555 the final fighting force of Goths surrendered.

At one point in the renewed fighting, during a Gothic recapture of the city, Procopius gives us another glimpse of the population of Rome: "Among the common people, however, it so fell out that only five hundred men were left in the whole city, and these with difficulty found refuge in sanctuaries. The rest of the population was gone, some having departed to other lands and some having been carried off by the famine, as I explained."[4] That's a drop from eight hundred thousand people in the fourth century to just five hundred in the middle of the sixth century.

---

[4] Procopius, *Wars* 7.20.19-20, p. 421.

Italy was once again in Roman hands. The empire, though now securely centered in the East, once more claimed Rome, its ancestral home. But what a cost! The death toll has been estimated to be as high as five million souls. In terms of resources, one estimate puts the cost of the war on the Eastern treasury at 300,000 pounds of gold. James O'Donnell offers a look at the financial cost from another direction: Justinian inherited a treasury containing 28 million solidi; his wars cost about 36 million solidi with 21.5 million of that going to the war in Italy. Indeed, the final two years cost roughly half of the full amount. And this account doesn't even factor in his spending on building campaigns back in Constantinople. Since, in a good year, the empire would bring in 5 million solidi, his warlike pretensions left the East deeply in debt.[5] A veritable fortune in finances but even more so in human lives was squandered in this largely symbolic recapturing of the Roman homeland. And the last indignity was yet to be suffered.

Only three years after the death of Justinian, in 568, the Germanic Lombards moved south *en masse* and stripped Italy from its nominally Roman masters. A new flood of pillaging and killing undid any reconstruction since the end of the Gothic War. While Eastern control would linger in some regions for hundreds of years, the Lombard conquest permanently finished the Eastern dream of a renewed Roman Empire around the Mediterranean basin. Weakened by fighting in Italy and by ravages on its northern and eastern borders by barbarians and Persians alike, the Eastern Empire never attempted to retake Italy and focused on its own survival.

Truly, the Italian sixth century deserves the label of "Dark Age" as misery upon misery swept through the peninsula.

Finding Cassiodorus

Somehow, in the midst of this press of history, though, we have lost sight of our central character. Cassiodorus is playing a part in some of the major events of the age up through the usurpation of Theodahad. Cassiodorus preserves some letters from him and a few letters in the

---

[5] James J. O'Donnell, *The Ruin of the Roman Empire: A New History* (New York: Ecco, 2009), 289.

name of his queen, Gudelina, and then a few in the name of Witigis, the Gothic general promoted to king. The first of these is a testosterone-drenched proclamation of his reign to the Goths; the other four refer to a peace embassy sent to Justinian. And then—silence.

At some point after the year 538, Cassiodorus begins pulling together what will become an incredible witness to history. Going to the archives where copies of the many letters that he has written over the past three decades are stored, he begins to put together a collection of correspondences that spans the years in which he served the Gothic government. The letters fill twelve books under the title of *Variae Epistolae*, usually just referred to as *Variae*. The first five books contain 235 letters written by Cassiodorus in the name of King Theoderic. The next two books contain seventy-two templates for official correspondence announcing promotions or orders frequently sent from one official to another. The next two books contain fifty-eight letters written on behalf of Theoderic's successor, Athalaric. Book 10 silently illustrates the complications around the succession as it contains letters from Amalasuntha, her betrayer Theodahad, his wife, Gudelina, and their successor, Witigis, for a total of thirty-five letters. Finally, the last two books contain sixty-seven letters that Cassiodorus wrote under his own name as praetorian prefect. He creates with judicious selections of letters an idealized image of a Gothic kingdom that was—especially under Theoderic and even under his successor, Athalaric—stable, possessed of a solid amount of *Romanitas* in both its governance and correspondence, and was on good terms with the East.

We can pause here and take stock of things—because that's just what Cassiodorus did. Sometime just after 538, he wrote a brief text called the *Order of the House of the Cassiodori*. In it, he describes his accomplishments so far in life:

> Cassiodorus Senator was a man of great learning, and distinguished by his many honours. While still a young man, when he was legal adviser [*consilarius*] to his father, the Patrician and Praetorian Prefect Cassiodorus, and delivered a most eloquent speech in praise of Theoderic king of the Goths, he was appointed Quaestor by him, also Patrician and Ordinary Consul, and, at a later date, Master of the Offices and <Praetorian Prefect. He submitted> formulae for official documents, which he arranged in twelve books, and entitled *Variae*. At the command of King

Theoderic, he wrote a history of the Goths, setting out their origin, habitations, and character in twelve books.[6]

At this moment we have a snapshot of Cassiodorus at the top of the political heap. Confidant of kings, political wonder of the West, scholar, diplomat, and historian. As Boethius reminds us, however, the only constant thing about Lady Luck is change: it is the one stable feature of her character.

Despite the portrayal of the state of things in the *Variae*, good terms with the East were a fantasy rather than the reality. At the point when Cassiodorus was assembling these letters, Justinian's invasion was well under way and the reconquest of Italy was in progress. In some of the final letters of the *Variae*, Cassiodorus mentions the presence of foreign armies, which refers either to the armies of the East in the field or to their proxies. We don't know where Cassiodorus was during this time, but the most likely location was in Ravenna with the rest of the royal court, carrying out his duties as best he could. With the fall of Ravenna in 540, the capture of Witigis, and his deportation to Constantinople, we would do well to assume that Cassiodorus went with him, either as a member of his court or as a private citizen fleeing the ruin of Italy. He had risen high, seen far, done much, but his time in the spotlight was now over.

The Fall of Cassiodorus

We lose sight of Cassiodorus after the publication of the *Variae*. Exactly when and how long he was in Constantinople isn't entirely clear. We catch brief glimpses of him in the Eastern capital in 550 and again in 551. O'Donnell, whose reconstruction seems the best to me, argues that he arrived with Witigis in 540 and remained until the Pragmatic Sanction in 554 that declared the Gothic War over and sent many of the exiled Italians back to their home estates. This is an important period for us, because this is most likely when and where *The Explanation of the Psalms* was written.

Constantinople in the mid-sixth century was a bustling imperial city. Rome was a city of ancient splendor and dignity. Having grown up as a powerful Italian city-state, it had eased into its region-

---

[6] Cassiodorus, *Variae*, xxxvi.

commanding role with the growth of the republic, and had accidentally become an imperial center as the republic gave way to the imperium. Constantinople, on the other hand, had been planned as an imperial city from the start. Susceptible to fire as all ancient cities were, Constantinople had suffered two major ones in recent years: one hit the city in 475, burning large areas of it to the ground (including the imperial library that had lost 120,000 volumes in the blaze), while the recent Nika riots in 532 had burned roughly half the city. Justinian took the opportunity to rebuild in style, the centerpiece being the great Church of Holy Wisdom—the Hagia Sophia—which would become the greatest architectural wonder of the age. While Rome was crumbling and under siege, Constantinople was building and growing.

As an imperial city, it was also the center of a great bureaucracy. Just as Cassiodorus had overseen offices full of scribes, envoys, and planners in Ravenna and Rome, the government offices of the East were all located in Constantinople. Furthermore, familiar names populate the lists of high-ranking officials. The Anicii and the Decii were the leading senatorial families of Old Rome, but their clans had spread to and extended their power in New Rome as well. In some of the surviving copies of his *Order of the House of the Cassiodori*, Cassiodorus appears to claim family connections with the ill-fated Boethius and his father-in-law, Symmachus, and therefore with some branch of the Anicii clan. At some point after the collation of the *Variae*, Cassiodorus wrote a thirteenth chapter titled "On the Soul." Cleaving closely to material from Augustine's *City of God*, he discourses about the nature of the soul and its qualities and its virtues then—in a section with no parallel in Augustine—describes how a wise soul can distinguish between evil men and good men. M. Shane Bjornlie makes the suggestion that the *Variae*, particularly with this extra chapter, can be seen as a portfolio of his former work, demonstrating his rhetorical capabilities and his philosophical suitability in choosing good employees.[7] In a bureaucratic center, especially after the massive depopulation caused by the plague of 542, could we not see the former praetorian prefect of the West recommending himself for a new job in the East?

---

[7] M. Shane Bjornlie, *Politics and Tradition Between Rome, Ravenna and Constantinople: A Study of Cassiodorus and the Variae, 527–554* (Cambridge: Cambridge University Press, 2013).

As intriguing and plausible as this possibility may be, we have no clear visibility into whether or not it was the case. What we can say is that there is no record of Cassiodorus ever holding a position in Constantinople. Cassiodorus does, however, go to Constantinople and comes out again with his head and neck still connected. Remember—he was the civil head of government for a state in arms against the emperor and may well have been brought to the city in captivity along with King Witigis. His survival was not a foregone conclusion.

The first glimpse that we have of him in the city is in the midst of a theological dispute. Theology was one of the great preoccupations of the city and was by no means a spectator sport. Opinions were held and shared by everyone. Gregory of Nyssa reports in 381 on the eve of the First Council of Constantinople: "Garment sellers, money changers, food vendors—they are all at it. If you ask for change, they philosophize about the Begotten and the Unbegotten. If you inquire about the price of bread, the answer is that the Father is greater and the Son inferior. If you say to the attendant, 'Is my bath ready?' he tells you that the Son was made out of nothing."[8] The educated also participated even if they ended up throwing up their hands in frustration—at least in public. The historian Procopius, for his part, writes:

> As for the [theological] points in dispute, although I know them well, I will by no means mention them for I consider it a sort of insane stupidity to investigate the nature of God, asking what sort it is. For man cannot, I think, accurately understand even human affairs, much less those pertaining to the nature of God. I will therefore maintain a safe silence concerning these matters, simply for the sake of not discrediting old and venerable beliefs. For my part, I will say nothing whatever about God save that he is altogether good and has all things in his power. But let each one say what he thinks about these matters, both priest and layman.[9]

One of the reasons theology was such a matter of corporate concerns to the capital was because of the political implications. While the four major ecumenical councils had already met in attempts to wrap human language and understanding around the church's lived experience of

---

[8] Jonathan Hill, *The History of Christian Thought* (Downers Grove, IL: IVP, 2003), 67.
[9] Procopius, *Wars* 5.3.6-9, loc. 6934.

the Holy Trinity, different theological opinions persisted in certain regions of the empire and among certain peoples. For instance, the Goths were Arians; many of the bishops of the Levant were Monophysites. More was at stake here than just theological opinions. As the empire and the church negotiated questions of authority and status with one another, bishops held important positions of political control. Since the Goths were Arians, their bishops stood outside of the hierarchy focused on Rome and Constantinople; their bishops could not be swayed to put political pressure on them with threats of excommunication or other forms of church discipline. While these theological matters will come up later with reference to the psalm commentary, we'll leave technical discussions of the differences for later, noting only that these were politically sensitive discussions. Nowhere was this more clear than around the person of Pope Vigilius.

When the Eastern forces took Rome, they installed a new pope, Vigilius, whom they expected to behave in predictable ways—favoring Justinian's attempts to mollify restive Monophysite provinces in the East. On being consecrated, though, he refused. Angered by a churchman who refused to stay bought, they brought him back to Constantinople for a serious talking-to. The chronicle of the popes recalls how he was kidnapped and hustled off in the midst of celebrating Mass at the church of St. Cecilia in Rome.

At issue was a controversy about the so-called Three Chapters. Justinian was attempting to coerce a common faith by condemning Origen, the great Alexandrian teacher of the second century, and also three teachers from the Antiochene camp. While the bishops in the East had no problem with the second condemnation, the West refused. Vigilius stood strong, for at least a time, in resisting what must have been increasing pressure on him. After three years of resisting, he folded in 548. He would later recant this position, but in the meantime, he wrote a letter in 550 excommunicating two of his followers, Rusticus and Sebastianus. Procopius tells us that Pope Vigilius was accompanied by "very many notable men" from Italy and mentions the patrician Cethegus by name.[10] Vigilius's letter also mentions two notable men with him: Cethegus, a *gloriosus vir* (a "glorious man")

---

[10] Procopius, *Wars* 7.35.9-10, loc. 11794.

and *patricius* (a "patrician"), and Cassiodorus, *religiosus vir* (a "religious man") and *filius noster* ("our son"). Thus, Cassiodorus was, at this point, certainly in Constantinople within the expatriate community surrounding the captive pontiff. Indeed, we can securely date the *Explanation of the Psalms* to this period due to its dedication to Pope Vigilius.

The second note regarding the presence of Cassiodorus comes thanks to a work now lost. In the *Order of the House of the Cassiodori*, mention is made of the *History of the Goths* in twelve books. This book is lost to history—at least directly. There is, however, an indirect copy of it. The Byzantine scholar Jordanes wrote his *Getica* as a summary of the work by Cassiodorus and, in doing so, borrowed a copy of it for three days from the steward of Cassiodorus's household in early 551. From this evidence it seems likely that Cassiodorus was part of the Latinate literary circles of Constantinople. The combination of his former position, his ranking among the Italian exiles, and his friendship with literary figures in Constantinople would certainly have opened to him the doors of the imperial library, a likely resource if not location for the writing of the *Explanation of the Psalms*.

Founded in 357 by Constantius II, the library was initially intended to collect the great works of Greek authors to be copied by scribes working at government expense. The scope expanded under Emperor Valens; not content with Greek authors alone, he provided money for four scribes copying Greek works and another three to copy Latin texts as well as some assistants to maintain it. Theodosius II established a school of higher studies around it in 425. Gamble describes it this way:

> The imperial library was not a Christian library in the strict sense, although it must have contained Christian literature along with non-Christian. The comment of Nicephorus [H.E. 4.3] that Theodosius II collected texts of Christian scripture and commentaries on them from far and wide may well signify their presence in the library. It is not clear who made use of the library. At first it must chiefly have served the imperial family, the civil servants who worked in the palace precincts, and a select group of scholars, but after the academy of literary and philosophical studies was reorganized by Theodosius II it would also have served as the library of the academy. The library was restored after the fire of

475 but was apparently destroyed when Leo the Isaurian dissolved the school in 726.[11]

One thing that we know about Cassiodorus's *Explanation of the Psalms* was that he wrote it with reference to Augustine's great commentary on the Psalms. Furthermore, Cassiodorus explicitly tells us in the *Institutes* that he has managed to acquire only two decades (that is, commentary on twenty psalms) of Augustine's commentary for his monastery Vivarium.[12] Thus, the imperial library in Constantinople is the most likely location for the commentary's composition.

Turn to the Religious Life

Just as Cassiodorus took stock of things when he wrote his *Order of the House of the Cassiodori*, he paused one other time in his life to look over his works. This time, however, he was writing as an old man and surveying the second half of his life's work.

> After the *Explanation of the Psalms*, on which by the Lord's favour I expended my first labour in the time of my conversion; and after the *Institutions* on how to understand divine and human texts, in two books of (I think) ample size, wherein you will find more of utility than of elegance; after the *Explanation of the Epistle to the Romans*, from which I removed the perversities of the Pelagian heresy, urging others to do the same for the remainder of the commentary [on the Pauline epistles]; after the collection which by the Lord's favour I made of the *Arts* of Donatus with their commentaries, a book of etymologies, and another book by Sacerdos on figures of speech and thought, so that the simpler brethren, being instructed, might be able to make sense of texts of this kind without confusion; after the book of headings (*tituli*) collected from Scripture, which I called the *Reminder*, because it allows those who have no appetite for long readings quickly to review the contents; after the *Summaries* of the Apostolic Epistles, Acts, and Revelation, in which those texts are expounded as briefly as

---

[11] Gamble, *Books and Readers*, 169.
[12] Cassiodorus, *Institutions* 1.4.1, p. 120. James Halporn disagrees with O'Donnell's conclusions here and asserts that Cassiodorus is speaking about some other collection of commentaries rather than Augustine's.

possible; finally in my ninety-third year and with the Lord's help, I have come to the excerpting of my beloved orthographers, and if I have succeeded in gathering their flowers—of those, that is, that I undertook to abridge—into a single work, then, unless I am mistaken, the corrector and scribe will no longer suffer confusion.[13]

This catalog of seven works—a theologically significant number to Cassiodorus—represents his postconversion employment, the bulk of which was completed at Vivarium.

Clearly, Cassiodorus's life has taken a turn. While the first half of his life was spent in politics and government, the second half was spent in theological reflection and writing. While we might be forgiven for thinking that his work would end at the respectable age of fifty to fifty-five with the fall of Ravenna in 540, the surprisingly long-lived patrician gave an entire second career over to the church, writing up until the end. (There is no record of any works after his book on orthography.)

What motivated this turn to religion? One piece of historical data may be helpful here. Emperor Justinian had many ways of dealing with those who flouted his authority. Various modes of execution were open to him, but another was the imposition of monastic discipline. If there were a bureaucrat who might be dangerous to kill, but you needed him out of the way and without any more children, imprisonment in a monastery was a live option, and one that Justinian seems to have preferred progressively through his reign.[14] Of the things we know about the Vivarium, the monastery where Cassiodorus lived out his days, we know that it would remain in an Eastern-held region for the rest of his life and that the two men named as abbots in the *Institutions*, Chacedonius and Gerontius, both have Greek names.[15] The modern town of Squillace is based on the foundations of a Byzantine-era fortress. Did Justinian pardon Cassiodorus provided that he become a monk and live out the rest of his days in seclusion under the watchful eye of men faithful to the East? The historical-fiction writer in me wants to believe it; the historian in me thinks it unlikely.

---

[13] Cassiodorus, *Institutions*, Introduction, pp. 15–16.
[14] See Julia Hilner, "Monastic Imprisonment in Justinian's Novels," *Journal of Early Christian Studies* 15, no. 2 (Summer 2007): 205–37.
[15] Cassiodorus, *Institutions* 1.32.1, p. 166.

A much more likely turn of events would be to see a religious vocation progressively growing in Cassiodorus as he moved through the last cycles of his political career. O'Donnell rightly asks when it was that Vivarium was established. Just because Cassiodorus goes to live there after he leaves Constantinople does not mean that this was when it was founded. Pointing to the example of the Cassiodorian contemporary Liberius, O'Donnell notes that he founded a monastery on his estates in Campania without ever living in it. In an age where founding institutions was a well-regarded patrician activity, we do not need to suppose that it required the physical presence of the founder. Indeed, the fact that the Vivarium had two abbots, neither of whom were Cassiodorus, suggests that it had been organized to function perfectly well apart from his presence. (Recall too that Queen Radegund did exactly the same thing in 550—established a convent, selected an abbess, and lived there in retirement, technically outside of the convent's jurisdiction as a married and ordained deaconess.)

Three other pieces of evidence prior to his journey to Constantinople suggest that Cassiodorus had been planning a move of this sort for a while. First, we noted above the proclamation of humility flowing from his own pen in the letter ostensibly from King Athalaric to the Senate announcing his appointment as praetorian prefect. Cassiodorus claims, however, that all of these virtues had been established in him by means of his study of Scripture. The phrase he uses is an interesting one: *Hos igitur mores lectio diuina solidauit* ("Therefore these habits have been established through sacred reading"). As the period moves on, this particular phrase, *lectio divina* (sacred reading), will acquire a technical meaning deeply connected to monastic spirituality. This is the first signal that Cassiodorus himself might already have been heading toward a more reflective theological mode.

The second is a discussion that he had with Pope Agapetus. He records both the attempt and its failure in the first words of the *Institutes*:

> When I realized that there was such a zealous and eager pursuit of secular learning, by which the majority of mankind hopes to obtain knowledge of this world, I was deeply grieved, I admit, that Holy Scripture should so lack public teachers, whereas secular authors certainly flourish in widespread teaching. Together with blessed Pope Agapetus of Rome, I made efforts to collect money so that it should rather be the Christian schools in the city of Rome

that should employ learned teachers—the money having been collected—from whom the faithful might gain eternal salvation for their souls and the adornment of sober and pure eloquence for their speech. They say that such a system existed for a long time at Alexandria and that the Hebrews are now using it enthusiastically in Nisibis, a city of Syria. But since I could not accomplish this task because of raging wars and violent struggles in the Kingdom of Italy—for a peaceful endeavour has no place in a time of unrest—I was moved by divine love to devise for you, with God's help, these introductory books to take the place of a teacher.[16]

Pope Agapetus was pope for only a short time. Elected in 535, he died in 536. While the school never came to pass, the two men at least got a start on things. In Rome, opposite a fifth-century church stands the ruins of a library from roughly the same period. At one point, there was a line of poetry running along the top of an interior wall describing the contents of a fresco below it. The poetry, though gone now, was preserved; of the fresco itself, nothing is known. The poetry says this:

> A venerable company of saints is seated in a long row,
> Teaching the mystical sayings of the divine law
> Among them, as is right, sits bishop Agapit,
> Who by art founded this beautiful place for books.
> All partake of the same grace, all share in the same holy labour;
> Their words may vary, but in faith they are one.[17]

Whether the school ever existed, a library to support it was at least created, even though it seems that Cassiodorus—whisked off to Ravenna by political affairs—likely never knew of its existence.[18] It is usually assumed that the school was an idea in the mind of Cassiodorus before the notion of a monastery and that this joint effort must have predated the founding of Vivarium. But we're assuming what the text never says: a publicly funded school in Rome is a different animal altogether from a community of prayer down in Squillace. Whether or not the school came to fruition is immaterial. Rather, this is another piece of

---

[16] Cassiodorus, *Institutions* 1.1.1, p. 105.

[17] Cassiodorus, *Institutions*, Introduction, pp. 25–26.

[18] O'Donnell argues convincingly that Cassiodorus had no knowledge of the fate of the project, including this initial success.

evidence that Cassiodorus was already moving in thought toward a religious legacy in addition to his political one.

The final note comes from the opening of the *Explanation of the Psalms* itself. Cassiodorus recognizes the need for a commentary on the Psalms based on his own experience of study:

> Some time ago at Ravenna I thrust aside the anxieties of official positions and the flavour of secular cares with their harmful taste. Once I had sampled that honey of souls, the divine psalter, I did what longing souls often do, and plunged eagerly in to examine and to drink in sweet draughts of the words of salvation after the deep bitterness of my active life.[19]

We have evidence from the *Variae* that Cassiodorus served as praetorian prefect into 538, but the record stops there. Was the study of the Psalms a respite from the cares of government or a rejection of them? Was Scripture his evening reading once he got home from the job, or does this study of the Psalms reflect a turn away from the public and the secular to the private and the sacred? The second interpretation seems more likely, but the phrasing does not exclude the first option. An even deeper question is why he was engaging in an intensive study of the Psalms to begin with.

Augustine's spiritual autobiography, *The Confessions*, relates a period in the theologian's life when he leaves his secular career as a teacher of rhetoric and receives baptism. At this point in the late fourth century, baptism was frequently put off until later in life. Baptism washed away the sins committed before baptism, but theologians were unclear as to how baptismal purity could be maintained or restored. (The practice of private confession would not arise for several more centuries.) Augustine and several friends journeyed to a villa at Cassiciacum, and Augustine recalls a devotion to the Psalms that resulted in some particularly intense spiritual experiences.[20] While Cassiodorus had probably been baptized as a child (this became the norm by the mid-fifth century in the West), he does seem to be following Augustine's steps with an intensive study of the Psalms in preparation for a shift from a secular to a sacred calling.

---

[19] Cassiodorus, *ExplPs* Pref., p. 23.
[20] Augustine, *Confessions* 9.3-4, pp. 184–85.

Most signs, then, point to a movement of spirit at some point in the early years of the 530s, when Cassiodorus began to seriously consider the religious life. While there's no smoking gun of spirituality, this would seem to be the most logical progression in his movement from statesman to monk.

Life in Vivarium

One of the features of the early medieval period was the repurposing of buildings and especially villas from late antiquity. Cassiodorus's Vivarium is a perfect example of that trend. Indeed, it would not have required much renovation at all to turn the home of a country gentleman into a serviceable monastic enclosure. Cassiodorus describes the site in classic pastoral terms and informs his monks why it will be eagerly sought by outsiders:

> In fact, the location of the monastery of Vivarium encourages you to prepare many things for pilgrims and the needy since you have irrigated gardens and the fish-filled stream of Pellena that flows nearby. The stream is neither dangerous from big waves nor negligible because of slight flow. Directed skillfully it flows wherever you consider it necessary and provides enough water for your gardens and mills. It is available when needed and when it satisfies your needs it recedes to a distance; when turned to a specific purpose, its sudden appearance does not frighten nor does it fail to appear when required. The sea also lies before you for various kinds of fishing and the captured fish can be closed up in fish ponds when you wish. For with God's aid I have constructed pleasant pools here in which many fish meander safely in pens. It is so like a mountain cave that the fish does not feel at all captive since it has freedom both to get its food and to hide in hollows as usual. I have also had baths constructed to benefit the afflictions of the body. Clear streams, known to be pleasant for drinking and washing, flow nicely into the baths. So, far from you having any reason to long for other places, your monastery is sought by outsiders.[21]

---

[21] Cassiodorus, *Institutions* 1.29.1, p. 162.

You could be forgiven for feeling a little jealous of the monks—Cassiodorus seems to have forgotten that he was writing a manual for monks rather than an advertisement for a vacation villa! This is the place where Cassiodorus will spend the rest of his life and labors. Consider for a moment, though, the world in which this pleasant villa was set.

Squillace was about as far on the margins of Italy as one can go. It was nowhere near Rome or Ravenna. If there were a place in the country farthest from the seats of power, this was it. While this might have been a radical shift for a man used to walking the halls of power, on the flip side it meant that devastation had not focused on his region. The great population centers of Italy had suffered dreadfully between the wars, famines, and plague. The old trade connections that linked urban areas with villages or villa-centered economies completely collapsed. (Barnish does note, though, that Squillace is not too far from the main shipping routes from Constantinople to Sicily.) Populations retreated into themselves, becoming distrustful of outsiders and fortifying the structures they decided to retain. The broader social network between regions was functionally dissolved. The notion of monastic self-sufficiency was less a theologically driven ideal and much more a basic fact of economic reality: for those who were not able to grow or catch the food needed, starvation was a real possibility.

Of the works that Cassiodorus composed here, the most significant is surely the *Institutes*. On the one hand, this is a fascinating text because it lays bare the mind of a learned early medieval Christian bibliophile like no other. On the other hand, it reveals the mind-set of a man who sees a culture in free-fall, no longer capable of creating suitable teachers. In place of a learned class, he offers a self-teaching text. The proper title of the work is *Institutions of Divine and Secular Learning*, and the two parts of the title refer to material clustered into two books. The first book focuses on divine learning—books about Scripture and theology as well as some general reflection about the monastery and what goes on there. The second book lays out a scheme for secular learning and provides a whirlwind tour of the seven liberal arts: grammar, rhetoric, dialectic (the arts for reading), arithmetic, music, geometry, and astronomy (the mathematical arts).

Classifying the *Institutions* is tricky because it is not a monastic rule. While it does touch on monastic matters, it is not interested in

86 *The Honey of Souls*

legislating the shape of the Christian life or the communal structures that will establish monastic worship and practice. This is no Rule of Benedict or even *Institutes* of John Cassian—both of which are much more legislative than this. Rather, the *Institutions* of Cassiodorus is a plan for study, a structure to form and shape a Christian intellect, thoroughly grounding it in the knowledge needed by a Christian thinker. It is this focus on the intellect and thinking that draws the ire of modern monastic authors like Jean Leclercq, who holds Cassiodorus and Benedict up next to each other and finds Cassiodorus wanting. Leclercq charges that "the director of Vivarium, although he shares the life of the monks, organizes and even directs it, is not a monk and does not think like a monk."[22] The problem for Leclercq is the both/and: the monastic life cannot focus both on divine and on secular studies; the secular must be clearly subordinate, a tool useful only for approaching and accessing the divine. Monasticism is less about the head and what goes in it than the heart and how it is shaped and formed.

The first book of the *Institutions* is part library tour, part wish list. Cassiodorus introduces the nine divisions of the Bible that we have encountered earlier that make up the multivolume Bibles:

- the Octateuch (the first eight books of the Old Testament from Genesis through Ruth that describe the early history of God's people)
- Kings (the later historical books, including the books of Samuel, Kings, and Chronicles)
- Prophets
- Psalter
- Solomon (the Wisdom literature: Proverbs, Ecclesiastes, Song of Songs, the book of Wisdom, and Sirach)
- Hagiographa (Job, Tobit, Esther, Judith, Maccabees)
- Gospels
- Apostolic Letters
- Acts of the Apostles and Revelation

---

[22] Jean Leclercq, *The Love of Learning and the Desire for God: A Study of Monastic Culture*, trans. Catharine Misrahi (New York: Fordham University Press, 1982), 19.

For each of these books, Cassiodorus lists the commentaries that he recommends. In most cases they are in the library at Vivarium, and he will even make reference to specific volumes that he has assembled. In the case of a Greek commentary by John Chrysostom, he notes that it is "in the eighth bookcase I spoke of, which houses the Greek books."[23] He also refers to books that he does not own, however, and mentions collections that he is in the midst of acquiring. For instance, he says of Jeremiah, "Jerome is also said to have written a commentary in twenty books on Jeremiah of which I have been able to find only six but I am, with the Lord's aid, looking for the rest."[24] Generally speaking, the commentaries that he recommends can be divided into three groups: the vast majority are commentaries from the Latin Fathers or their translations of Origen, but he also refers to several commentaries by Greek authors (including John Chrysostom and Didymus the Blind) translated into Latin by his contemporaries, and he mentions a few commentaries by his contemporaries. Of the contemporaries Cassiodorus mentions, Bellator the priest, appears to be one of his in-house translators and commentators.

After discussing the book divisions themselves, Cassiodorus provides some general use handbooks on interpreting the Scriptures (which we'll look at in chapter 5), talks about the four councils that defined christological doctrine, ways that other people group the Scriptures, and then rounds off his discussion with how to correct the text of Scripture and how wonderful Scripture is.

Moving on to Christian authors, he notes a set of patristic texts to read, leading it off with a number of selections from Augustine. After recommending the Jewish historian Josephus, he lays out a number of Christian historians before recommending the diligent reading of the church fathers, specifically calling out Hilary of Poitiers, Cyprian of Carthage, Ambrose of Milan, Jerome, and Augustine. He brings the list up to his own time by mentioning his near contemporaries Eugippius and Dionysius Exiguus. At this point he offers a general summary of what he has said.

Generally the last section of the *Institutions* focuses on monastic life in Vivarium, but he does stick in a few chapters he evidently forgot

---

[23] Cassiodorus, *Institutions* 1.8.15, pp. 130–31.
[24] Cassiodorus, *Institutions* 1.3.3, p. 118.

from the earlier part. Thus, he begins with listing geographers who will help give a sense of the holy places in Palestine to people who will never leave southern Italy. Then he discusses texts a bit more before speaking of those who cannot read or are not made for study. By discussing their work, he segues into the work around the monastery. While "it is quite appropriate for monks to cultivate gardens, to plough fields, and to rejoice in the harvest of fruits," he does have a different idea in mind for those with more literary skills.[25] He reminds them:

> Of all the tasks that can be achieved among you by physical labour, what pleases me most (perhaps not unjustifiably) is the work of scribes if they write correctly. By repeated reading of Scripture they instruct their minds and by writing they spread the beneficial teachings of the Lord far and wide. A blessed purpose, a praiseworthy zeal, to preach to men with the hand, to set tongues free with one's fingers and in silence to give mankind salvation and to fight with pen and ink against the unlawful snares of the devil.[26]

From his perspective, copying books is the proper employment for monks, and many would follow that advice for centuries to come. After reminding them to read some medical writers and passing along some advice to the abbots and monks, he concludes book 1 with a prayer.

Book 2 is both easier and harder to describe. Easier because it only has seven chapters. Harder because in these seven chapters he attempts to give a crash course of an entire educational program. He goes through the seven liberal arts: grammar, rhetoric, dialectic, arithmetic, music, geometry, and astronomy. For each, he offers a survey of the key points, usually cribbing them from the central classical authors on the topics. For instance, grammar offers a relatively quick run through the high points of Donatus; at the end, Cassiodorus recommends the volume of Donatus bundled with some other texts, including Sacerdos, that can be found in the library. The section on rhetoric is brief and lifted from Cicero and Fortunatianus. Dialectic, on the other hand, is a very long chapter that relies heavily on the Aristotelian translations of Boethius, the works of Marcus Victorinus, and Cicero, treating things like syllogisms and definitions at great length.

---

[25] Cassiodorus, *Institutions* 1.28.5, p. 161.
[26] Cassiodorus, *Institutions* 1.30.1, p. 163.

In short, the *Institutions* is a package designed to convey fundamental data on classical learning to any literate monk without need of a teacher. Cassiodorus was not trying to gather together all the information that was out there; that would have to wait a few more decades for Isidore of Seville's *Etymologies*. Instead, he was trying to give them the skills he thought they needed to know to properly understand the Scriptures and the faith.

Apart from the look back in his book on orthography (the principles of spelling, capitalization, punctuation, and such), we know nothing else about the life of Cassiodorus in Vivarium. We assume that he died shortly after drafting this book on orthography; ninety-three is quite old even for us in an age of increasing medical science, let alone the Italian sixth century. His monastery does not seem to have survived him very long, either. As O'Donnell recounts, Italian workmen building a summer home on a pleasant stretch of the Italian coast near modern Squillace in 1952 uncovered a sixth-century sarcophagus in the ruins of an ancient church.[27] Two Greek inscriptions indicate that the unnamed occupant was revered as a saint by the locals. There's no proof, but the location, dating, and circumstances certainly suggest that this stone box is the last mortal resting place of Cassiodorus.

Summary

Flavius Magnus Aurelius Cassiodorus Senator is one of the most fascinating figures of his age. Born into a wealthy provincial family, he witnessed the turbulence of sixth-century Italy firsthand. Progressively climbing the ranks of the civil service through his writing talents, he received a thorough education and moved through the ranks of quaestor and consul before being named master of offices and eventually praetorian prefect. The first half of his life is characterized by political successes as a trusted aide to the Gothic kings and queens. Our knowledge of this tumultuous time is greatly enhanced by the *Variae*, his collected letters in twelve volumes. With the Eastern Empire's attempt to recapture Italy and the West, though, his opportunities evaporated before his eyes. After fleeing—or forced—to

---

[27] James J. O'Donnell, *Cassiodorus* (Berkeley: University of California Press, 1979), 197.

Constantinople, he lived with the exile community and gave comfort to the captive pope while he wrote his magnum opus, the *Explanation of the Psalms*. Returning to Italy after Justinian's Pragmatic Sanction, he spent the rest of his life at Vivarium, a monastic community housed in his country estate. There, he wrote, among other things, the *Institutions*, a work that tries to communicate the essentials of a classical Latin education to the monks and those who would come after him. From successful civil servant to monastic recluse, Cassiodorus embodies in his own story a turn from bureaucratic late antiquity into an early medieval world of faith.

CHAPTER FOUR

An Initial Glance at the *Explanation of the Psalms*

Encountering the Commentary

If we were to go into the Bavarian State Library, enter into their special collections area, and search the shelves for Cassiodorus's writing, we'd find him. Tucked between a twelfth-century commentary on the Gospel of Matthew and a ninth-century volume of the major prophets, we'd locate an incomplete copy of Cassiodorus's *Explanation of the Psalms*. I say incomplete because there is a volume missing. There are only two here: the first volume, which contains the introductory key, the prefaces, and Psalms 1 through 50, and also the third volume with Psalms 101 through 150 in it. The second volume is gone. It's had plenty of time to go missing, of course, since this set was transcribed in the second quarter of the ninth century: sometime between the years 825 and 850.

Its first home was the monastery where it was written, St. Emmeram's Abbey in Regensburg, Germany. The monastery was founded in 739 at the same time that the Diocese of Regensburg became an official diocese of the church, but it was named after the itinerant St. Emmerman, a Frankish bishop. The monastery didn't have an official library until St. Wolfgang ordered one constructed on his arrival as bishop of Regensburg in 972. Shortly thereafter a catalog was drawn up that lists among its holdings two volumes on the Psalms by

Cassiodorus. Apparently the second volume had already walked off at some point in the intervening century and a half.

Let's take a look at the first volume of the Psalms commentary. The book is large and thick. It's heavy, due partly to the weight of the leather-covered oak boards binding it and due partly to the 304 leaves of parchment that required the heavy wooden covers to hold it closed. Five impressed and discolored circles with nail holes in the center on the cover of the codex mark the places where five metal bosses had added to the weight.

If we take the heavy volume down from the shelf—or more likely, an archivist wearing white gloves to keep finger oils off the ancient leather takes it down and brings it to our foam book rest in the reading room—we can turn it to the front side of leaf 101 to take a glimpse inside this ancient work. The leaves were each numbered with pencil in the top corner at some point in the past—likely the nineteenth century—and archivists still prefer to speak of the *recto* (the front side) and *verso* (the back side) of leaves rather than calling it page 202 as we would today.

Of course, the likelihood of going to the Bavarian State Library and getting access to study this manuscript is not that great. Thanks to

Folio 101, recto, of BSB Clm 14077

modern technology, that's not a problem anymore. Starting in 1997, the library began digitizing its holdings and, a decade later, partnered with Google to expand the project; at some point, this volume was painstakingly photographed and put online in its entirety in the public domain. Thanks to this arrangement, we can see the page here, check it out in living color online, or download the whole volume as a PDF.[1]

As we gaze at the recto of folio 101 (or "f. 101r"), we'll see two columns of twenty-seven lines of mostly black lowercase script. It's Latin. On the plus side, there are spaces between the words that make it a bit easier to read; we won't have to sound it out to figure out where words begin and end. On the minus side, squiggles over letters, lines crossing through the descending parts of the letter *p*, and some unusual looking loops let us know that there is a fair amount of abbreviation in the text that does make it hard to read until we learn what the various lines mean. What will catch our attention is the red. In the middle of the left-hand column is a block of writing in red uppercase letters, and there's another line in red in the middle of the right-hand column as well. In addition, the text under both of these red lines starts with large red letters that poke out into the left margin. As we scan down, we notice that every once in a while a black initial will also poke out into that margin, signaling the start of something.

As we look closer, we can see how the initials in the margins and the lines themselves are so regular; the scribe used a drypoint stylus (that is, one with no ink on it) to score lines on the parchment to make out where the columns, lines, and initials ought to go, a regular grid to keep the writing nice and tidy.

Drypoint lines and initials, f.101v

---

[1] This page can be seen at: http://daten.digitale-sammlungen.de/bsb00035046/image_205.

Flipping the leaf over (now we're on "f. 101v"), we see that the same drypoint guidelines used on the front can be seen and felt on the back as well. This page looks much like the other, but it has an uppercase line started with a red initial at the top of the right-hand column, and there are two unusual marks in the margin. The higher one looks like the letters "ETH" slammed together with a line over the top; the lower one is a P with part of a circle going through the staff.

Returning to the front (f. 101r), let's take a look at what some of these things mean.

The red block in the middle of the right-hand column lets us know that one psalm has ended and another begun; expanding the abbreviations it would read *Explicit Psalmus XVI; Incipit Psalmus XVII* ("The end of Psalm 16; the beginning of Psalm 17"). Pulling out a modern English Bible to follow along, we'd want to turn to Psalm 18, rather than Psalm 17. Both the Greek Septuagint and the Latin Vulgate Psalters combine Psalms 9 and 10, throwing off the numbering by one. Then there's an odd jog between Psalms 113 and 115 where psalms are divided differently again until the Vulgate Psalm 116 and the Hebrew Psalm 117. The numbers don't converge again until Psalm 148 so that both schemes end up with 150 by the end. To avoid confusion, I've chosen to use the modern psalm numbers and also the verses as found in the New Revised Standard Version (NRSV) throughout this book unless indicated otherwise.

Marginal markings

Interpreting the Title

After noting the end of one psalm and the beginning of the next, the other red uppercase letters are the superscription or title of Psalm 18: "Unto the end, a psalm of David the boy [*puero*] of the Lord, who spoke to the Lord the words of this canticle on the day that the Lord delivered him from the hands of all his enemies, and from the hand of Saul, and said . . ."[2] The NRSV has something a bit different for the title ("To the Leader. A Psalm of David the servant of the LORD . . ."). We'll notice that these two versions start differently: "unto the end" versus "to the leader." This is a translation issue. The Hebrew word has a range of meanings that goes somewhere between "inspect" and "permanent"; when the translators of the Septuagint rendered it in Greek, they chose the latter end of the scale (something permanent is fixed and finished and therefore the end) whereas modern scholarship prefers the former sense of the term (the person who does the inspecting is the overseer or the leader). As a result "To the end" shows up quite a lot in the Latin text whereas modern scholars think that this line was intended to give some directions to whoever was leading the singing.

Cassiodorus uses a four-part structure for the interpretation of each psalm. This is the first, exploration of the title of the psalms. He begins his analysis of the title by noticing that three items here line up in a coherent interpretive direction: "The three expressions, *unto the end, of David, the boy*, can undoubtedly be applied to the King our Saviour."[3] Right off, then, he sees these three phrases pointing to Jesus. That in itself is a pretty large interpretive move and is something that we are going to want to look at closer. But how do these three phrases do this? He's already explained the first two earlier in the commentary. Indeed, these two items are common enough that he devotes two of his short chapters in the introduction to answering these questions before the commentary proper even gets underway.

Chapter 3 of the introduction is titled "The Meaning of 'Unto the End' Which Often Appears in Headings." He explains that the word "end [*finis*]" can refer either to the common meaning where something

---

[2] Cassiodorus, *ExplPs* 18.title, p. 1.176.
[3] Ibid.

reaches a point beyond which it cannot go or to an ultimate goal: a "perfect and abiding end."[4] He cites Paul's words in Romans 10:4 ("For Christ is the end [*finis*] of the law so that there may be righteousness for everyone who believes") and asserts, "So the end [*finis*] and fullness of the law is our Lord Christ."[5] The chapter ends with an admonition: "So whenever you find the phrase, Unto the end, in psalm-headings, concentrate your mind keenly on the Lord Saviour, who is the End without end, and the full perfection of all blessings."[6] Thus, the phrase "To the end" is a reference to Jesus.

David is of great significance for two reasons. The first is the biological connection between David and Jesus; David is found in both of the genealogies of Jesus, the one provided at the opening of the Gospel of Matthew (titled "The Genealogy of Jesus, Christ, the son of David, the son of Abraham" [Matt 1:1]) and the one in Luke's version (see Luke 3:31). Second, "Son of David" appears in the New Testament as a title for the expected messianic king who was to come and deliver the Jewish people from their oppressors, which the New Testament uniformly applies to Jesus. Both the biological and scriptural components are captured as Cassiodorus discusses the singing of the psalms in the preface: "In company with the divine angels whom we cannot hear, we mingle words of praise through Him who came from the seed of David, the Lord Christ. As He Himself says in the Apocalypse: I am the root and source of David (Rev 22:16)."[7] Hence, Cassiodorus will read references to David as pointing through him to Christ as well.

The third phrase in the title that points to Jesus is "the boy [*puero*]." Cassiodorus explains this with reference to the prophet Isaiah: "For we read in the prophet also the word boy [*puer*]: A boy is born to us [*puer natus est nobis*]."[8] The reference is to Isaiah 9:6. The only problem is that's not what the text says. The Vulgate text of Isaiah reads: "For a child has been born for us [*parvulus enim natus est nobis*]" (Isa 9:6); *parvulus* means literally "a little one" in the Latin. Cassiodorus has the right sense but a different word. Nevertheless, the earliest surviving

---

[4] Cassiodorus, *ExplPs* Intro.5, p. 1.30.
[5] Ibid.
[6] Ibid.
[7] Cassiodorus, *ExplPs* Intro.Pref, p. 1.25.
[8] Cassiodorus, *ExplPs* 18.title, p. 1.176.

An Initial Glance at the Explanation of the Psalms   97

liturgical chants for Christmas use the phrase *Puer natus est nobis* constantly. It's quite likely that Cassiodorus is remembering the prophet through the Christmas liturgies, which unmistakably consider this particular *puer* to be Jesus.

Moving to the next section in the title, Cassiodorus finds a special meaning in one of the words that gets used:

> After these words what follows: *Who spoke to the Lord the words of this canticle*, are to be added so that a fuller and total context appears. *Canticle* clearly means a meditation [*contemplationem*] on heavenly things, so that our gaze may not rest merely on the history of king David.[9]

Elsewhere, in chapter 10 of the introduction, he warns us to be alert for such hidden meanings concealed in the psalm headings:

> Some psalm-headings where they make similar allusions must clearly be understood in the spiritual [*spiritualiter*] sense, for if you ponder the literal [*litteram*] meaning the heading is irrelevant, since you do not find in the psalms the content indicated by the headings. But if a figurative [*tropicum*][10] interpretation is applied to them, they seem totally appropriate.[11]

Each allusion should be checked to see if they may be indicating a spiritual meaning as well as an historical or literal meaning.

Finally, the last section of the title is addressed:

> *On the day that the Lord delivered him from the hands of all his enemies, and from the hand of Saul, and said.* This event is very well known from our reading of Kings, where there is a more extended description of how David was freed from subjection to his enemies. [This is a similitude (*similitudinem*) of] the Lord's resurrection and the deliverance of [the members of] His body from the devil's power [is] proclaimed.[12]

---

[9] Ibid.
[10] That is, one pertaining to literary tropes or turns of phrase. We'll talk more about these in chapter 6.
[11] Cassiodorus, *ExplPs* Intro.10, p. 1.32.
[12] Cassiodorus, *ExplPs* 18.title, p. 1.176. Material in brackets was adapted to clear up difficulties in Walsh's translation.

Cassiodorus makes the connection to the historical books as recommended by the title. (While David's story is found in our books of 1 and 2 Samuel and followed by 1 and 2 Kings, the Vulgate refers to all of these as the books of 1 Kings through 4 Kings.) But there is more to the reference than just the histories; Cassiodorus notes a spiritual significance here as well. A "similitude" in Latin rhetoric is an extended illustrative example. He is saying that there is something fundamentally similar between David's deliverance and the resurrection of Jesus. The first foreshadows and finds its ultimate meaning in the second.

One of the interpretive rules passed on by Augustine states that references to Christ can also be read of the church—his Body—and vice versa. The use of *membrorum* here does not indicate that the similitude is just about saving the physical, resurrected body of Jesus from the devil, but that the resurrection has profound implications for the church and has broken the devil's power over the multitude of members baptized into the Body and gathered into the church.

Dividing the Psalm

Division of the psalm

Having made it from the middle of the left-hand column of f.101r to the middle of the right-hand column, we have now arrived at the next red uppercase line. This one says simply *Divisio Psalmi* ("The Division of the Psalm"). If an analysis of the title is the first part of Cassiodorus's four-part scheme for interpreting each psalm, the second part is the division. Here's how he describes this section from the introduction: "Secondly, every psalm must be divided according to its nature, so that our understanding may not be confused either by a sudden change of subject, or by the introduction of different speakers."[13] Drawing on the principles of

---

[13] Cassiodorus, *ExplPs* Pref.10, p. 1.35.

classical drama, Cassiodorus pays careful attention to verb endings and pronouns to determine who or what person or group is talking to whom. Correctly differentiating between speakers is an important part of reading a classical oration or tragedy correctly; Cassiodorus believes it only appropriate that the same techniques be applied to the psalms.

His section on the division into the various speakers is rather lengthy but is quite instructive. Because of the way it lays out such an important aspect of Cassiodorus's work, I shall quote this whole section in full:

> This psalm cannot be allotted to a single spokesman [*personae*]. In the first section, the prophet speaks, giving thanks because God's devotion has deigned to free him from serious dangers. In the second, the Church speaks. Before the Lord's coming she endured countless calamities, and subsequently He took pity on her. He granted her the healing of the holy incarnation, and by the gift of baptism He gathered the Christian people from the whole world. In the third part, the voice of the Saviour glides in like the dew of mercy. Here His strength and power are described with most beautiful allusions. In the fourth, the words of the Catholic Church again emerge, and the gifts of the Godhead are praised with great joy.[14]

As we can see, Cassiodorus does not hesitate to spread the speaking parts around. While he will identify most psalms as having only one speaker (140 psalms are allotted to one speaker), there are three speakers in this one. These three—the prophet David, the church, and Christ—are the three most common speakers that he hears within the Psalms. David and Christ are, of course, men in the biological sense; the church is always personified as a woman. A central theological idea for the church fathers was the notion of the church as the bride of Christ; hence, the church is always portrayed as female.

The designated sections are sometimes broken up by a "diapsalm," a feature of the text of the psalms that indicates a pause. This psalm doesn't have any diapsalms, though, but that does not daunt Cassiodorus. Numbered verses would not appear in Bibles until the printing press so he could not use them to designate his sections; we can, though. The first section that he indicates (the prophet speaking)

---

[14] Cassiodorus, *ExplPs* 18.div, p. 1.176.

includes Psalm 18:1-3. The second section (in the voice of the church) stretches from verse 4 through verse 31. The third section (spoken by Christ) begins with verse 32 and runs through verse 45. The fourth and final section (reintroducing the church) begins at verse 46 and goes until the end in verse 50.

As indicated in the interpretation of the title, Cassiodorus fully intends to find the developed doctrine and practices of the faith within this psalm. Note that in the second section he identifies key topics as incarnation and baptism. This is backed up by the mention of "beautiful allusions" in the third section. Cassiodorus is signaling that careful readers will have the right skills and techniques to properly identify what aspects of the psalm are allusions and to know what events or concepts the psalm might be alluding to.

By this point, we have covered all of the material on f. 101r; it's time to turn the page.

Proceeding Line by Line

The uppercase line that begins with a red initial signals that we are moving into the third part of Cassiodorus's four-part structure. This is a lengthy section where he goes through the psalm line by line. As he explains it:

> Thirdly, I shall try to show the hidden meaning of the Psalm [*arcanum psalmi*], which varies with the spiritual sense [*partim secundum spiritualem intelligentiam*], the historical [reading] [*partim secundum historicam lectionem*], and the mystical meaning [*partim secundum mysticum sensum*]. I shall discuss the fine points and the proper meanings of the words as opportunity presents itself.[15]

Again, there is the sense of deeper meanings, multiple meanings, puzzles to be found, solved, and resolved. But there may also be more clearly applicable material. Hence:

> Fourthly, I shall try briefly to expound the power of a passage as it demands, so that the purpose of a poem's division may by God's gift be clear to inner eyes. By the power of a psalm I mean

---

[15] Cassiodorus, *ExplPs* Pref.14, pp. 1.35-6. Adapted.

An Initial Glance at the Explanation of the Psalms 101

the divine inspiration by which God's purpose is revealed to us, keeps us clear of faults through David's words, and persuades us to lead an upright life.[16]

Thus if there is a broad theme or moral instruction to the psalm, Cassiodorus will discuss it in this run-through also.

The psalm opens with the words *Diligam te, Domine, virtus mea* ("I love you, O Lord, my strength"). This is explained by reference to another passage: "He loves the Lord [*Diligit dominum*],

Opening words of Psalm 18

for he obeys His commands devoutly. As Christ says in the gospel: 'He that heareth my commandments and keepeth them, he it is that loveth me [*diligit me*] [John 14:21].'"[17] Different forms of the verb *diligere* (to love) are being used here to make the connection between the psalm text and the gospel passage. This technique of chaining, where verses that share a significant word are connected with one another, is a very common technique in Cassiodorus's commentary and throughout patristic and early medieval texts.

Cassiodorus then explains the word itself: "*Diligo* (I love) derives from *de omnibus eligo* (I select from all)."[18] This passage in the text corresponds with the first marginal note that we saw in our initial scan of the page. Out to the left of this text in the margin is a connected ETH

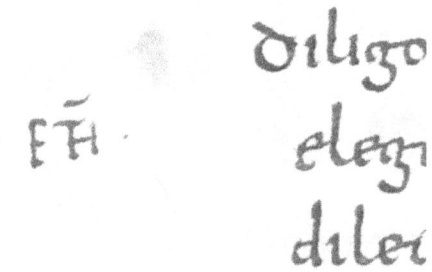

Marginal sign for an etymology

---

[16] Cassiodorus, *ExplPs* Pref.14, p. 1.36.
[17] Cassiodorus, *ExplPs* 18.1, pp. 1.176–77.
[18] Cassiodorus, *ExplPs* 18.1, p. 1.177.

with a line over it. If we were to consult the key to the marginal signs listed at the very beginning of the volume, we would see that this sign indicates an etymology. In the *Institutions*, Cassiodorus includes etymology at the very end of his grammar section and defines it as "a true or likely interpretation that explains the source of words."[19] Put simply—Cassiodorus loves etymologies. He cannot pass up the opportunity to trot one out. For him, this is not simply a tool for the interpretation for Scripture; rather, this is an all-purpose tool. Etymologies are scattered throughout the *Variae* as well, Cassiodorus using them to both craft a learned image for his Gothic overlords and impress the recipients with the depths of their knowledge. Of course, just as biology was in its infancy in those days, so too was linguistics. Most of the derivations that he gives would make a linguist groan, but that's not the point for him; he is delving into the very bones of the words themselves and using them to make connections between one thought and another.

He makes one more comment on *Diligam*, the first word of the psalm before moving on: "Note that the love promised for the future is such as is seen never to have failed."[20] He is noticing a grammatical point here—that the psalm opens with a word in the future tense. It doesn't say *diligo* ("I love") in the present tense but rather *diligam* ("I will love"); attention to the verb tense is what prompts this comment. The fact that he makes this observation tells readers something about the speed at which he is reading. He is taking the time to give a close and careful grammatical analysis of the text and to consider what even the choice of a verb tense might mean for what is being said.

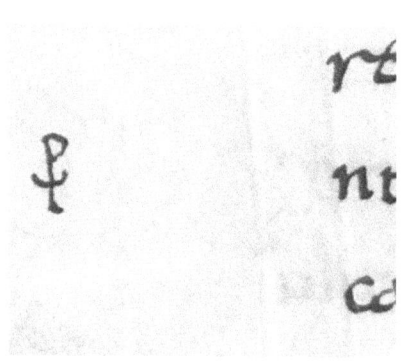

Marginal sign for a definition

Moving on to the next phrase, "my strength," we'll notice that

---

[19] Cassiodorus, *Institutions* 2.1.2, p. 1.177.
[20] Cassiodorus, *ExplPs* 18.1, p. 1.177.

the next marginal sign, a P with a partial circle through it, is next to this block of text. Cassiodorus writes:

> The prophet is freed from his foes, and rightly proclaims the Lord as His *strength*, for by His gift he was made to appear stronger to his enemies. This is the twelfth type of definition, which Greek calls *kat'epainon* and Latin *per laudem* [through praise]. His proclamation announces God's nature in individual and varying words: now *strength*, now [in the next line] *firmament*, now *refuge*, now *deliverer*, now *helper*, now *protector*, now *horn of salvation*. All these terms beautifully denote what the Lord is.[21]

This marginal sign is used to indicate a definition—one of the fifteen identified ways of defining a thing according to the canons of classical dialectic. That is, rather than choosing to define a thing by its essential nature, or by what it does, or by its characteristics (the first three kinds of definition), Cassiodorus sees the psalmist selecting this way of identifying God as calling specific attention to his best qualities for the sake of praise. All of the other terms that we will be encountering in the next few lines are also examples of this twelfth kind of definition.

The next large red initial, a "D" at the top of the left-hand column, silently signals that Cassiodorus is about to move on to the next line of the psalm: "The Lord is my firmament [*firmamentum*], my refuge, and my deliverer [*liberator*]: my God is my helper" (Ps 18:2a). What follows from the initial to the next punctuation mark, a comma at the end of the following line, is a quotation from the biblical text. Beyond the punctuation mark, the black initial "I" that pokes into the left margin also indicates that the quotation is over and that Cassiodorus's words are about to begin again.

Cassiodorus interprets these words with reference to David the prophet, the historical situation that he found himself in that prompted the psalm: "He justly calls the Lord his firmament [*firmamentum*], for He enabled him to stand firm [*firmus*] in the line against his enemies, and to fight with lively spirit."[22] David's word choice is connected to his experience of God within his historical context.

---

[21] Ibid.
[22] Ibid.

104   *The Honey of Souls*

A red initial "E" sticking into the margin indicates that we're going to move along to the next phrase: "*And my refuge*. Precisely so, for when he needed advice he took refuge in the Scriptures, and found what could help him through the prompting of the Godhead."[23] A modern reader might expect Cassiodorus to stick with the battlefield interpretation, but he is ready to move on to another sphere of David's life and experience. Just as David provides a good example of what to do in the battle line with the help of the Lord, so too he demonstrates the best place to look for advice.

Red initial indicates the start of next verse

As he moves on to the next epithet, Cassiodorus once again applies it to a different topic, picking up one of the hints from the psalm's title: "He rightly proclaims the Lord as his Liberator, for He freed him from the anger of Saul the most savage king as if from the mouth of hell."[24] David's historical experience of being delivered from Saul receives a spiritual interpretation. By denoting Saul as "the most savage king" and making reference to "the mouth of hell," Cassiodorus infers that Saul is functioning as a typological pointer to the devil; God is thus rescuing David from Saul in the same way that he rescues him from hell. We will see this kind of interpretation again in the commentary since Cassiodorus identifies a particular group of psalms as those "pointing through the deeds of David to the future mysteries of Christ the Lord."[25]

As we come to the bottom of the left-hand column of f.101v, Cassiodorus completes his interpretation of this line by addressing the final phrase:

---

[23] Ibid.
[24] Ibid.
[25] Cassiodorus, *ExplPs* 26.div, p. 1.263.

An Initial Glance at the Explanation of the Psalms   105

> *My God is my helper*: charmed by the sweetness of what has been granted him, he repeats in summary the earlier things he has said, for God was everywhere at hand, and guarded him with the protection of His strength. But note that he runs through all the epithets in such a way as not to presume that gifts have been bestowed on his own deserving merit.[26]

The prophet's use of the term "helper," then, is a summarizing epithet in which the others can be found. The last line takes a theological turn. Cassiodorus makes an Augustinian observation here; he emphasizes that God's grace and deliverance is not part of a transactional scheme that must be earned or merited in order to be received. Rather, God gives good gifts because God is good.

A few pages on, there is a marginal sign for a "schema," a figure of speech or thought. This one identifies an "idea" in verse 7, a figure where a future event is discussed in order to evoke an emotional reaction. There's another schema identified in verse 10: he takes the repetition (in the Latin) of the word "flew" as a hypothesis, when an author draws attention to something unusual by marveling at it. A schema marked a little later looks like a mistake. Based on the content, the scribe should have made the mark for a doctrine as Cassiodorus reads this same verse as referring to Christ being seated at the right hand of God.

Two conjoined "p"s at the top of f.104v signals an idiomatic expression in verse 11, and Cassiodorus reminds the reader that references in Scripture to "darkness" do not always refer to evil but sometimes to the deep and hidden secrets of God, dark to unenlightened minds. A marginal chi-rho identifies verse 16 as having particularly important doctrinal material. This verse refers to the marriage between Christ and his church, and the "mighty" waters can be interpreted in two ways: either as the many nations from which

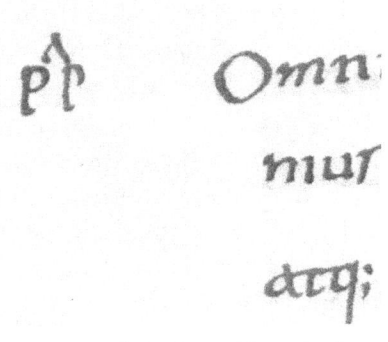

Marginal sign for an idiomatic phrase

---

[26] Cassiodorus, *ExplPs* 18.1, p. 1.177.

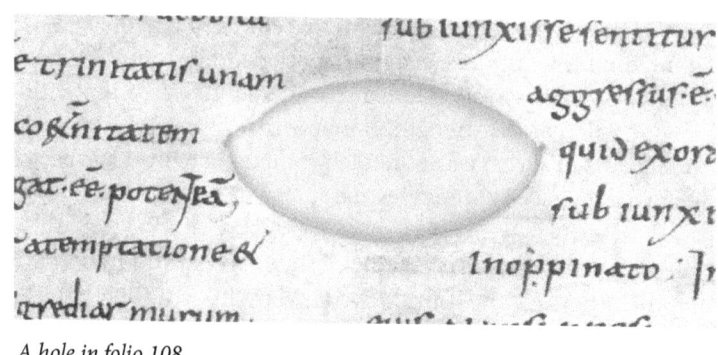

A hole in folio 108

the Gentiles were called to form the church or as baptism, the waters through which people are brought into the church.

A "TOP" at the side of verse 26 marks a "topic" or a method of making an argument, also part of the art of dialectic. Cassiodorus sees an argument from externals here when a bad man is subverted by his companions.

Folio 108 displays an interruption in the orderly march of columns down the pages; there's a sizeable football-shaped hole toward the bottom of the page. Who knows what made it—perhaps an imperfection in the skin, a slip of the knife in the butchering process, or a weakness in the hide exposed when it was stretched and rubbed smooth in the process of preparation? Clearly it occurred in the preparation phase and did not happen after the text had been written, as four lines in the right-hand column have been adjusted in order to account for it.

A few pages and a few more schemes and points of doctrine pass until we reach a new figure, a line-crossed circle on f.111v; if we consult the key on the first two and a half folios of the manuscript, we won't find this one. It's in the margin next to verse 46. One possibility is that this may be marking the start of the fourth section of the psalm as Cassiodorus renders it. No such symbols mark the other section beginnings, though. Another possibility might be related to the collapse of word spaces. As the pages have gone on, some of the words have gotten tighter together. If we quickly skim the line across from this mark, it looks like there is a reference to mathematics there. Unfortunately, math is not mentioned in the text here, but it popped out of

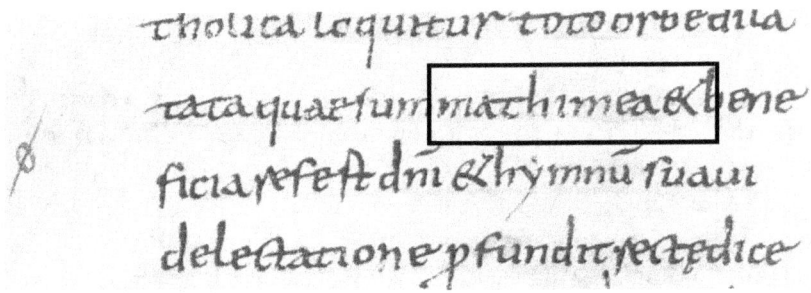

A new symbol for a scribal error?

the scribe's hand nonetheless. The words ought to be *quae summatim et beneficia refert Domini* ("briefly both recounting the Lord's benefits"), but somehow the scribe, likely working off a manuscript with few word breaks, rendered the line "quaesum*mathimea&*bene," turning the end of "summatim" and the "et" into a new word entirely—and then helpfully marking a nonexistent point on mathematics!

Jumping to the Conclusion

Turning the page once more finally brings us to folio 112, the end of this long psalm, and a red line of writing in the middle of the left-hand column announcing *Conclusio Psalmi* ("The Conclusion of the Psalm") to mark the fourth section of Cassiodorus's four-part interpretive scheme. This is a short summary that ends midway down the right column of folio 112's *verso* with a red block of uppercase letters announcing the ending of this psalm and the start of the next.

In the concluding section, Cassiodorus hopes to accomplish a couple of goals. First:

> When necessary I shall mention the numbers attached to the psalms, for this has been consecrated with a distinction afforded to the most venerable topics. I confess that it has been difficult for me to do this in the case of each and every psalm, because even the authority of the Fathers has left this matter undecided and in the air. The remaining numerations the researcher must carefully work out for himself, for many things in divine Scripture which at present seem hidden become clear with the passage of time.[27]

[27] Cassiodorus, *ExplPs* Pref.14, p. 1.36.

The fathers didn't leave numerology undecided for lack of trying; lots of numerological schemes were floated in lots of writings by Hilary, Augustine, Jerome, and many others. Cassiodorus, never one to be shy when obscure classical learning is called for, is eager to put forth his own interpretations.

In addition, the concluding section must also serve as a conclusion, a point that Cassiodorus does not miss: "In the final section I draw together briefly a summary of the whole psalm, or say something in opposition to heresies which are to be extirpated, for true love of the Lord lies precisely in regarding His foes with perfect hatred."[28] Fighting heresies—especially trinitarian and christological heresies—is an important part of faith formation for Cassiodorus. His citation of Psalm 139:22 ("I hate them with perfect hatred"), though, does come across a bit strong to modern ears.

His conclusion to Psalm 18 offers a summary and numerology but no heresy fighting. Here is the conclusion in full:

> With what remarkable interweaving of words is the action of this psalm enacted, retaining its impact by variation of speakers, as alternating speeches replace and succeed each other! Let us realise how mighty is this glorious alliance of the chorus. Even the Lord Himself has deigned to add His words of salvation on behalf of those for whom He did not refuse to assume the lowliness of the incarnation. Even the number of the psalm encloses the Law's great mysteries: the ten refers to the decalogue of the Old Testament, the seven to the seven-formed Spirit. Brought into a single partnership, they form seventeen, so outstanding mysteries of the holy Law are embraced by the number of this psalm.[29]

The major theme that Cassiodorus focuses on in the summary is the number of speakers and their harmonious interrelation among one another. Although heresies are not mentioned, Cassiodorus does take the opportunity to reinforce the incarnation of Christ. The numerology presented here is rather tame as far as these things go.

---

[28] Ibid.
[29] Cassiodorus, *ExplPs* 18.concl, p. 1.195.

A Few Observations

The Visual Texture and Its Uses

The first thing to note from our run-through of this manuscript is the visual nature of the experience. We talked quite a bit in chapter 2 about orality—how the liturgy and the memorization of the psalms serve to bring the Scriptures out of a strictly textual paradigm and into an oral one. A culture bereft of literacy could hear the Word being proclaimed to them. Cassiodorus's psalm commentary goes in the other direction. This cannot be an oral experience. There are a number of purely visual cues that help make this commentary what it is. That is to say, imagine trying to read this aloud in the monastic refectory while the other monks were eating and trying to convey what's here. You'd have to stop and say something like "And then this part is in red" or "He's got a squiggle out here in the margin to let us know that he thinks this point is important." This can't be oral: rather, this text takes reading to the next level. It requires literacy in order to engage it fully, and in engaging it, the reader's literary abilities are boosted and improved.

It ought to be said too that this particular manuscript is not even the most visual kind of experience possible. This copy indicates a verse of the psalm by only coloring in the initial that starts a psalm quotation—this is the laziest way to make this indication. In some manuscripts of the commentary, each quotation from the psalm is written in uppercase letters to differentiate it from the text around it. A manuscript from St. Gall, written in the last half of the 700s, is an example of this approach.[30] Red letters are used sparingly—just to signal the start of each of Cassiodorus's four interpretive sections—and the initials in the line-by-line section are drawn larger in black and the uppercase text sets off the psalm text. Another St. Gall manuscript, written at the end of the 800s, quotes the psalms in lowercase letters but these are all in red.[31] The psalm fragments leap off the page and announce their presence visually much more than in the St. Emmerman's manuscript.

---

[30] Schaffhausen, Stadtbibliothek, Ministerialbibliothek, Min. 78. See this manuscript here: http://www.e-codices.unifr.ch/en/sbs/min0078/79v/0/Sequence-1039.

[31] St. Gallen, Stiftsbibliothek, Cod. Sang. 200. This manuscript is located here: http://www.e-codices.unifr.ch/en/csg/0200/101/0/Sequence-386.

The second thing to note flows from the first. Cassiodorus has created a visual apparatus for engaging his text for multiple purposes. At the most basic level, this manuscript can be read straight through. The red titles for each interpretive section will help orient us and give us a sense of what we are reading; the initials that poke into the margins will give us a sense of when a psalm phrase and its interpretation are stopping and starting. We don't have to engage the marginal symbols if we don't want to.

But another way to use the manuscript is explicitly for the symbols. If a schoolmaster ordered a young monk to look at the etymologies in the first twenty psalms, he could do that. By paging through the manuscript and scanning the margins for the symbols, he could find the kind of information that he was looking for. We modern people have the luxury of using an index (often), but an index requires a stable page—we have to know that a particular word or topic will remain in the same place—which is simply not possible in a hand-copied manuscript. Cassiodorus's marginal symbols are the next best thing, but one that will function in the context of hand-copied manuscripts where an index would not.

Here's the other function of this system of marginal notes, though. Cassiodorus and Pope Agapetus wanted to create a publicly funded school where the interpretation of the Scriptures could be taught. The Gothic Wars, the depopulation of Rome, and the presumed sack of the initial library they had gathered together revealed the futility of relying on institutions in an age where institutional systems were crumbling around them. With a detailed system of marginal notes, combined with the overview of the liberal arts in the *Institutions*, Cassiodorus is trying to create a system of self-study where enterprising students could learn without needing a physical teacher. Even without a schoolmaster, monks or nuns possessing a well-copied manuscript of the *Explanation of the Psalms* could read the text and use the marginal notations to educate themselves whether they had the benefit of a good teacher or not.

Some Favored Reading Strategies

Even without going through the entirety of Psalm 18, we can start to pick out how Cassiodorus goes about his interpretive work. First, Cassiodorus is very much a structured and disciplined teacher. He is organized and orderly and he offers a uniform framework for approaching each psalm:

- the interpretation of the title
- the division of the psalm into parts by speaker and/or topic
- the line-by-line interpretation of every verse
- the summary

Cassiodorus will even hold to this pattern in the case of Psalm 1—a psalm without a title. Rather than skipping the first section, he has a section explaining why this psalm does not have a title!

Second, Cassiodorus is a christological reader. That is, his approach to the Psalms is thoroughly invested in reading them through the New Testament experience and finding Christ within them. The interpretation of the title of Psalm 18 alone demonstrates this tendency, and it will be reinforced throughout his interpretative work.

Third, in order to perform his christological reading of the text of the Psalms, Cassiodorus understands the spiritual meaning of the text to be the primary meaning. Sometimes this level of meaning corresponds to the literal level of the text—sometimes it doesn't. For instance, in his reading of "God is my helper" in Psalm 18:2, the literal meaning of the text (the psalmist is calling God his helper to describe his experience of the divine) is also the spiritual meaning. Just prior to that, however, when he is interpreting the epithet "refuge," the literal meaning would suggest a place of safety in battle or war. And that would make sense, especially because that topic (warfare) had been introduced by the title and makes sense in relation to the other titles. Cassiodorus goes with a spiritual reading, however, seeing this epithet referring to David's reliance on the Scriptures.

Fourth, because the emphasis on the spiritual level of the text frees the meaning from directly literal applications, Cassiodorus is able to imagine a wider range of speakers. That is, if Cassiodorus were reading the psalms strictly as historical documents from the time of David, the available speakers would be limited to David, some other Israelite of the time, or a worshiping congregation in the temple or some other place of assembly. By focusing on the spiritual level of the text and emphasizing the prophetic origin and character of the Psalms, Cassiodorus is able to place the passages from the text into the mouth of David the prophet, or Christ, or the church, or other speakers as deemed appropriate.

Fifth, in addition to being a bureaucratically minded organizer, Cassiodorus is an enthusiast for the glories of classical learning. At every opportunity, he points out aspects of the Psalms that embody the principles codified in the arts of grammar, rhetoric, and dialectic. We didn't see any of the others in this brief dip into the commentary, but he will also bring in the higher mathematical arts as well when he can: arithmetic, music, geometry, and astronomy. The fact that the scribe attempted to create a mathematical entry and marginal note indicates that this was precisely the kind of thing that he expected to see from Cassiodorus!

Sixth, Cassiodorus is very attentive to the words on the page. Several times in just this short run-through, I needed to include the Latin term present in the text in order to clarify what he was saying. That is, he will see a word, and then engage with that word on a couple of different levels in order to make his point. A perfect example is the way that he worked with the very first word of the psalm, *diligam* ("I will love"). He noted the presence of the word. Then, he connected this verse to another verse halfway across the canon because they share that same verb. After that, he uses the word for its etymology, breaking it into parts and using a connection drawn from that (dubious) verbal analysis to make another point. Finally, he draws attention to a grammatical matter, the use of the future tense, to make a theological point. Thus, the verbal texture itself is important.

Seventh, linking Scripture passages together, as he did with *diligam*, is a core reading strategy. He links Psalm 18:1 with John 14:21—which is a theologically fruitful connection—on the strength of memory. Think about this for a minute, and the kind of rigorous reading that this both implies and requires. Because I have an electronic concordance at my fingertips, I can tell that—taking the various forms of the word into account—there are more than five hundred instances of the verb *diligere* ("to love") in the Vulgate. Only four of them are in the first-person future state: Psalm 18:1; Hosea 9:15; 14:5; and John 14:21. I had to look that up; Cassiodorus simply knew it because of his reading, memorization, and meditation on the text. It is easy for modern readers to look at some of these verbal connections and jumps made by patristic readers and be skeptical of the connection or the conclusions they come to; what we so often forget, however, is the amount of reading and familiarity with the biblical text necessary in order to perform these interpretive feats. The amount of Scripture that they held in memory and were able to deploy at a moment's notice is staggering.

Finally, Cassiodorus is not just a teacher of reading practices; he is conscious of his role as a theologian. He uses the Psalm commentary to teach doctrine, to reinforce theology (particularly the Augustinian form current in the Italy of his day), and to fight the many heresies that he sees assailing the church. We only saw a little bit of that here, in his explanatory note on "helper" in verse 2, but we will see far more of it as we plunge deeper into his text.

Summary

When discussing an early medieval work, there's nothing like digging into a manuscript. Modern printed editions are much more legible. Modern translations are much easier to read (especially if we don't know Latin!). But whether we can puzzle the letters out or not, whether we can read the language or not, there's nothing like getting the feeling of the manuscripts themselves through which these works were transmitted to us. It's easy to forget the ways and forms in which these texts have been transmitted to us through the centuries. Hand copying is the way it happened: copies of copies of copies filtered down through the ages until presses began printing them. The experience of encountering such a text is incomplete without the physical component of the books themselves—if only from a digital image.

In this brief glance at a ninth-century manuscript of Cassiodorus's *Explanation of the Psalms*, we got an initial sense of the ways that Cassiodorus conducts his interpretive task. He is a structured reader who follows a christological paradigm for spiritual readings. He sees the psalms as speeches or even dramas where the speakers must be identified, and the meanings fit to the words from this proclamatory context. He uses the classical arts of reading not only to interpret the text but also to initiate his readers into these practices. In doing so, in concert with a set of marginal notations, he seeks to construct a self-interpreting text that communicates biblical interpretation, classical reading strategies, and solid Augustinian theology in place of a flesh-and-blood teacher.

CHAPTER FIVE

Cassiodorus and the Interpretive Framework

Searching for a Big Picture

Cassiodorus's commentary seems like a self-contained, stand-alone work. On the one hand, it is. We can pick it up (or at least, one volume at a time) and read through it. It will teach us what we want to know from the perspective that he is working from. Cassiodorus has chosen an inductive approach to teaching; indeed, that's one of its great strengths and the reason that the commentary enjoyed the popularity that it did.

Speaking broadly, there are two main avenues for teaching something. The first and probably more common is the deductive method. That's where a topic is approached as a whole and then broken down into logical sections. Then, each of those sections is broken down into logical sections, and the information is passed on to the students by showing them the whole and then walking them through the parts. It starts with a big picture and zeroes in from there.

The other main approach is the inductive method. An inductive approach starts with a close-up. It takes a single thing, then plays with it for a while, and looks to see what it's connected to. As the investigation moves up from smaller structures to larger structures the mental image slowly zooms out. If we at arrive at a comprehensive big picture, it's only at the end of a process of pulling back from an original tight focus.

While he does start with some prefatory chapters, the commentary is fundamentally an inductive experience as Cassiodorus guides the reader through the text, pointing out definitions, explaining etymologies, finding Christ in the most unusual places, and calling out figures of speech and thought. He never quite zooms out to give us a sense of the bigger picture. This is where the *Institutions* comes in. In essence, the *Institutions* supplies a bigger-picture view, in that book 1 attempts to communicate methods and resources for reading the Scriptures, and book 2 gives a quick yet broad tour of the three liberal arts (grammar, rhetoric, and dialectic) and the four mathematical arts (arithmetic, music, geometry, and astronomy).

On the other hand, looking over Cassiodorus's idea of a big-picture view is precisely what tells us that we can't treat his work on the Psalms on its own. The problem for modern readers is that Cassiodorus's big picture isn't quite big enough. The reason is because Cassiodorus is immersed in a particular spiritual and theological culture that we are not. He is writing for an audience with whom he shares fundamental assumptions learned from Greco-Roman late antiquity and the early medieval world that are foreign to us—thoughts about the nature of the universe, the basics of biology, the relationship between the natural and supernatural, and so on.

Furthermore, he is presuming a shared microculture with the people to whom he is writing. Not only do they live within early medieval Italy, but also he is writing to and for monks whose environment and experience is structured by liturgical prayer. Prayer, especially as lived in the early medieval world, bears within it interpretive strategies and suggestions. The practice of using hymns, antiphons, responsories, and other kinds of prayer texts that piece biblical materials together teach interpretive methods and assumptions that may never be clearly articulated. Sermons and homilies from the fathers are read on a regular basis; hearing these texts read aloud within the liturgies forms communities in interpretive practices even if these techniques are not being taught explicitly.

Cassiodorus's *Institutions* served as a fine big-picture view of reading and interpretation for people immersed in that culture. For us, it's just not sufficient. We lack the yearslong processes of formation, the process of habituation, that would allow us to natively enter into the Psalms commentary. As a result, we have to do some deductive catch-up work in order to understand exactly where Cassiodorus and his monks are coming from and why it matters.

Constructing a Conversation

My middle-school-aged daughter plays a literary game with her friends. One person will write a paragraph and then pass the paper along to the next person, who will then write the next paragraph of the story before passing it to another. As young, undisciplined writers, each person often brings only his/her preoccupations and ideas about what makes a story good or fun or funny. As we can imagine, it doesn't take long at all before the evolving story becomes quite silly! Characters appear and disappear at a whim and act with no consistent motives or plans. The attempted tale is usually a disjointed band of paragraphs whose unity is largely based on the fact that they occupy the same sheet of paper, not because of any true storyline or coherent idea.

On the other hand, I used to play that same game with some of my English-major friends in college. One would start with a paragraph and hand it off to the next—just as in the middle-school version. But what happened next would be quite different. A new paragraph would appear, yes, but its construction would arise from the paragraph before it and would interweave themes or structures or details from the previous paragraphs, grounded in a knowledge of the previous allusions and intentions and based in a familiarity with the person passing around the page. Sophisticated narratives would arise within minutes as each person brought depth, insight, and an awareness of where the other people were coming from. Not simply a game, these could be experiences of surprising intimacy as we shared our own thoughts and sought to blend our own ideas and feelings with what had gone on the page before us.

The difference between the middle-school version and the college version is intentionality, sensitivity, and skill. In both cases each subsequent author is building on the work that has come before. The middle-school version usually disregards what has come before or engages it in a cursory fashion—the authors are usually more interested in shaping the story according to their own ideas and desires. The college version allows the plot to unfold as it will, and skillful authors will temper their desires to put their own mark on the story by discerning where the communal plot seems to be taking it and permitting it to flower in that direction.

Early medieval Scripture interpretation is often accused of being "derivative." That is, it is simply copying that which came before, usually the works of the church fathers, which are conventionally defined as the writers of the church's first five hundred years. Sometimes the last of the Western church fathers is identified as Gregory the Great, the reforming pope who died in 604. Others reckon the final Western father as the Venerable Bede who died around 735.

Is this a fair charge? Well—there's derivative and then there's *derivative*. Some early medieval authors were little more than copyists. And before we dismiss copyists, we'll remember again that the work of preserving the wisdom of former times was an essential activity in a time where the only books that would survive were those that got copied in the first place! But compositionally, some truly were little better than copyists.

Others were editors. Yes, they might only have copied down the words of others, but they made intelligent decisions about what material to copy and for what purpose. A skillful digest or extract can preserve the genius of an earlier author's work in far less space, particularly if that writer had a tendency to ramble. Cassiodorus recognized his contemporaries Eugippius and Dionysius Exiguus in his own day as doing this kind of work. (We'll say more about them later.) Other early medieval interpreters had the skill and sensitivity, however, to enter into the work of their earlier partners in reading. They communicated what they found there but also allowed the flowering of the plot line of Holy Scripture that their predecessor had noticed.

Relegating early medieval interpretive work to the derivative bin is a modern judgment based on the modern condition. Merely repeating things that other people said is not necessary in our time and place. We can almost always go back to the original text or look it up on the internet. There was no such luxury in the early medieval world. Identifying and communicating wise things that other people said will always have value. Identifying something profound and bringing it to the attention of others is an important work of communication. In the early medieval world, such work prevented wisdom from being lost when the destruction of written documents was a real danger. In the modern world, careful curation prevents wisdom from being drowned out in an environment of constant communication where the noise-to-signal ratio conspires to fill our ears with the static of frivolity or venality.

If the modern world accuses the early medieval of being derivative, the early medieval world would charge the modern with the error of novelty: that we are constantly coming up with something new simply for the sake of doing something new. In our lust for the new and different, we frequently fail to take deep stock of what has come before us and to consider why some paths were taken and others avoided, which avenues will lead to human flourishing and the flourishing of our actual embodied communities rather than games that serve only for intellectual diversion. It's the difference in attentiveness between the paragraphs of middle schoolers who can't wait to put their own mark on a narrative rather than a more mature and substantial reflection to see where the plot is unfolding of its own accord.

When we look at early medieval writing, we have to see it against its own environment and understand the pressures that conspired against the handing on of wisdom. We must judge the works we have received with an awareness of the challenges of the time. But—more than that—studying these writings will attune us to that sensitivity of spirit that enters into the forebearers' works and continues them rather than simply introducing novelty into the discussion for novelty's sake.

In order to approach the commentary of Cassiodorus properly, we have to see it within the perspective of "traditioning." Scholar Thomas O'Loughlin emphasizes that for authors in the time of Cassiodorus, the concept of tradition was a central one. While we generally think of tradition as a thing, a body of ideas, they understood it as an activity, a means of comprehending the wisdom of the past and passing it along to the next generations.[1] And, indeed, that's what the Latin verb *traditio* means: to hand over. The Latin fourth century was an age of genius. Three of the four greatest Doctors of the Latin Church—Ambrose, Augustine, and Jerome—were not just alive and writing during that time; they were writing to one another and bouncing ideas off one another, disagreeing, and learning from one another. Having to follow

---

[1] Thomas O'Loughlin, "Individual Anonymity and Collective Identity: The Enigma of Early Medieval Latin Theologians," *Recherches de Theologie et Philosophie medievales* 64, no. 2 (1997), 291–314, at 294.

such authors, the thinkers of the fifth and sixth centuries saw their task in relation to their predecessors. O'Loughlin suggests that these authors understood their role as follows:

> To mop-up in the aftermath of genius, rather than to try to compete with them, or do something new: what more could be said, who could consider themselves equal to such authorities? Their task was not to add new materials, but to master, organise into a manageable form, retain, and teach what they had inherited. There seemed to be so much work involved in this process that it appears they felt that until this had been done it would be premature to add new material, and possibly that when the sifting task was complete, there might be little need, or possibility, of further developing the ideas.[2]

Ambrose, Augustine, and Jerome had done terrific work—but they left it in a bit of a mess! Augustine didn't finish any commentaries on the letters of Paul but left all sorts of wise thoughts and sharp observations on Paul scattered across ninety-three published works. Furthermore, if you wanted the best pithy statements on grace and free will you'd have to go searching across at least fifteen of these works—assuming your library even had them all. Something had to be done.

The answer was to rework and repackage; the goal was utility. In one sense, these three great Doctors stood on the far side of the dividing line in the world of late antiquity, a world where Roman learning and authority were still respected and understood. The compilers lived on the side of the early medieval, in times and places that lacked the trade, resources, leisure, and frequently safety to maintain large libraries with comprehensive sets of the works of the fathers. O'Loughlin suggests that they embraced a corporate identity and a collective sense of excellence: they all worked to hand the wisdom of the fathers to the next generation in the most useful form possible.[3]

The irony, though, is that the reformulation of the fathers was itself an innovative process. Biblical scholars like to say that every act of translation is an act of interpretation; there's no such thing as a neutral translation. The same is true of the editing process as well.

---

[2] Ibid., 297.
[3] Ibid., 303–6.

Whether they were aware of it or not, trimming, altering, excerpting, and editing the texts of the fathers transformed these works into something different. Some editors altered by accident more than anything else, but some were much more intentional and not only altered but created something new through a synthesis of the tradition they had inherited. This is where Cassiodorus falls.

If we listen to Cassiodorus as he explains himself in his introduction to the *Explanation of the Psalms*, we'll hear him insist that there is nothing—or very little—new or original about this work. That's a lie. But it's an important lie for him to tell. It is a lie that allows him to remain within the mainstream of those largely anonymous workers who were doing the hard work of traditioning—of handing on knowledge and spiritual wisdom from one generation to another. In truth, Cassiodorus was a synthesist. While he relied chiefly on the work of Augustine for his inspiration, he produced a commentary that neither looks nor functions like Augustine's, that pulls in material from other authors, and that communicates a paradigm built on Augustinian ideals for reading that is vastly different from Augustine's commentary. In order to properly begin our investigation of the *Explanation of the Psalms* by Cassiodorus Senator, we must begin by understanding the streams of tradition that fed into his work.

When we look at how Cassiodorus handles the biblical text—fundamental assumptions, basic tools, interpretive reflexes—I see him operating in the midst of three major traditions. The first major tradition is the Alexandrian School of biblical interpretation. The big name here is Origen of Alexandria: he was the one who established a thoughtful, philosophically grounded, interpretive school known for its use of allegory and spiritual readings of the text. Origen, in turn, influenced the nascent monastic tradition and therefore John Cassian, who, in turn, pulls together monastic methods of praying, reading, and living, synthesizes them, and transmits them to the West in his *Conferences*. Hilary of Poitiers, a bishop from Gaul exiled into Asia Minor after losing a political fight with Arians, discovered Origen and his books and taught them in his own writings. Jerome, Doctor of the Church, ascetic, translator, and bad-tempered polemicist, made a career for himself translating Origen's Greek works into Latin for the circles of ascetic women to whom he ministered.

The second major tradition that influenced Cassiodorus was Augustine of Hippo. Augustine wrote broadly enough that he deserves to merit being a school all by himself. While he largely follows Alexandrian strategies and assumptions, he puts his own spin on them and has left us a general text on biblical interpretation—*Christian Instruction*—as well as his own commentary on the Psalms. Cassiodorus explicitly saw himself as an Augustinian thinker and communicates himself as one in his writings. Because of the special regard for Augustine that Cassidorus himself had, Augustine must loom large in our understanding of how Cassiodorus read and interpreted.

The third major tradition is the Antiochene School. It is usually associated with the figure of Theodore of Mopsuestia and is often placed into deliberate opposition with the Alexandrian school. Antiochene approaches are known for rejecting an overreliance on spiritual or allegorical interpretation and giving more weight to the literal or historical sense. Care must be taken with these interpreters, though, lest they—incorrectly—be cast as early forms of modern biblical scholars. They were not and had different aims, methods, and understandings.

These three groups, then, the Origenists, Augustine, and the Antiochenes, form the big-picture milieu that Cassiodorus communicates in his writings. We have to get a sense of them and how he used them in order to see how they influenced his work. Then, there are three specific works on the Psalms that were important resources in putting the commentary itself together: Augustine's *Enarrations on the Psalms*, Hilary of Poitiers's *Tractates on the Psalms*, and *The Letter of Athanasius to Marcellinus*. Once we have constructed a big-picture view, we can pick up some details from these to flesh out the specific approach that Cassiodorus will use to address the Psalms.

The Alexandrian School: Origen and Friends

On Origen

Origen of Alexandria is rightly reckoned among the top ten most influential Christian thinkers ever. That may sound like a grand claim for someone that many Christians have never even heard of, but that doesn't make it any less true! The modern academy and seminaries within it create logical divisions between disciplines so they can be studied more thoroughly. As a result, the study of Origen tends to be spread across at least three departments: biblical studies, the history of theology, and spirituality. But there were no such divisions when Origen was writing. Influenced by Neoplatonism, Origen put forward a remarkable body of work that melds biblical interpretation with disciplined reflection on the art of prayer to create a vision of Christian practice and experience that would set an agenda for the church for centuries to come.

This brilliance did not come without a heavy price, however. Jealousy from his bishop caused him to be defrocked, excommunicated, and exiled. After that bishop died, Origen tried to return but was once again excommunicated and exiled by the new bishop—who was one of his own former students! The bishop of Caesarea in Palestine, ignoring the Alexandrian decrees, invited him to come and teach there, and Origen set up a catechetical school at Caesarea along the same lines that he had in Alexandria. It was, however, no safer in Caesarea than it was in Alexandria; Origen was repeatedly captured by the Roman authorities and tortured for his faith. His death in 215 was due to the aftereffects of his mistreatment at government hands.

The church historian Eusebius of Caesarea tells us in his *Ecclesiastical History* a bit about the early life of Origen. It was a difficult time for the church: Septimus Severus was on the throne, and in the year 203 Christians were being persecuted in Egypt. Origen's father was arrested and sentenced to die. Remember, as the early church saw it, martyrdom was something to be avoided, yes, but at the same time, it also remained the most perfect form of the imitation of Christ. Just as Christ was killed by the hostile empire for his message of love and grace, so too his followers walked in his footsteps if they met the same end. Caught up in the spirit of the moment, Origen wanted to imitate both Christ and his father and achieve a martyr's death; the only way his mother was able to keep him from going out to be arrested was by hiding his clothing. Origen had to settle for sending his father a letter, praising him and urging him to stay the course of martyrdom without fear for his family. His father did die, his property was seized, and the family was left destitute.

By the time he was seventeen, Origen was a renowned teacher of the faith in Alexandria. Despite the persecutions, crowds of both men and women went to him for instruction. The problem for him, apparently, was the women, as he was still a young man with a young man's desires. Eusebius says it like this:

> About the same time, while responsible for the instruction at Alexandria, Origen did a thing that provided the fullest proof of a mind youthful and immature, but at the same time of faith and self-mastery. The saying "there are eunuchs who made themselves eunuchs for the kingdom of heaven's sake" (Matthew 19:12) he took in an absurdly literal sense, and he was eager both to fulfill the Saviour's words and at the same time to rule out any suspicion of vile imputations on the part of unbelievers.[4]

In a very delicate and roundabout way, Eusebius is telling us that Origen castrated himself due to his reading of the gospel text. A few modern scholars believe that, whether intentionally or not, Eusebius is repeating false slander about Origen and that this story isn't actually true. Most believe, though, that Eusebius is giving us the straight story. If nothing else, the fact that this story has been believed for so long and is entirely believable indicates that there were real practical ramifications based on how a person read. For people whose connection to the biblical text was so intense that they were willing to die or mutilate themselves based on how they heard God speaking in the Scriptures, that made how they listened to it all the more important.

Origen's most significant contribution to thinking about interpretation is his metaphor comparing Scripture with a human person. Just as a human being has a body, a spirit, and a soul, so too does Scripture. It has a bodily sense (the literal and historical meaning), a spiritual sense (that which pertains to Christ and the faith), and a moral sense (that which pertains to how Christians ought to behave). The literal is the most basic sense, the spiritual drives toward the truest meaning of the text, then—once that has been grasped—the moral meaning lets readers know how they should act and behave in light of the text. This communicates that multiple meanings can be found in a single passage. Identifying one meaning does not mean that the interpretive work is finished; a text can have a host of simultaneous complementary

---

[4] Eusebius, *Ecclesiastical History* 6.8 (Williamson, 186).

meanings operating at different levels of signification, all doing different things and communicating a variety of things to the reader.

The part that makes modern literalist readers the most suspicious of Origen is this statement that he makes while explaining the metaphor: "There are certain passages of Scripture where this 'body,' as we termed it, i.e., this inferential historical sense, is not always found . . . but where that which we termed 'soul' or 'spirit' can only be understood."[5] Origen is saying that Scripture always has a spiritual or moral sense but does not always have a literal sense. He is denying that the literal, plain-sense meaning of Scripture is true and dependable in all places. This is a bold statement; it's perfectly understandable why it makes people a bit nervous. The most important thing to realize is that Origen is not saying this because he is only a casual reader of Scripture. Rather, this observation is born out of a thorough, exhaustive, comprehensive knowledge of the Scriptures. That is, he knows the texts of Scripture too well to make the claim that they are always correct and never contradictory. He is too good of a reader to make that kind of a claim. Where other readers may harmonize, elide, or simply overlook troublesome passages, Origen demands an integrity from both the text and its interpretation.

When pressed on this claim, Origen begins with the very beginning. He asks how Genesis 1 can have a literal sense if it insists that there are "evenings" and "mornings" before the sun and moon are created on day 4. Evening and morning are defined by the disappearance and appearance of the sun; we can't have either without it. Continuing on to Genesis 2 he asks if we should take literally the idea of God walking around a garden and not being able to find Adam and Eve. Could God—who has no physical form and sees all things—be either crushing grass with his feet or be at a loss as to where his creatures had gotten to? He contends that impossibilities or contradictions or factual errors in the Scripture are signals that there is a deeper spiritual meaning that the text is trying to communicate. Rather than obsessing about a mistake in the text or trying to rationalize it, he counsels that readers should be looking for the spiritual truth concealed within the letter of the narrative.

---

[5] Origen, *First Principles* 4.1.12 (ANF 4.360).

Origen defines an interpretation as spiritual:

> when one is able to show of what heavenly things the Jews "according to the flesh" served as an example and a shadow, and of what future blessings the law contains a shadow. And, generally, we must investigate, according to the apostolic promise, "the wisdom in a mystery, the hidden wisdom which God ordained before the world for the glory" of the just, which "none of the princes of this world knew."[6]

The image of "shadow" is an interesting one. The notion that we get here is of some major event in the life of Christ or in the history of salvation that, illuminated from the far side, casts an image of itself back into the past so that its general shape can be discerned, but not the details. Origen sees the Old Testament littered with such images that signify something then but that point forward to a more complete reality in the future.

Origen concludes this definition with a reference to Paul writing in 1 Corinthians 2:6-8, which establishes for Origen the idea that Scripture is deliberately structured to be a mysterious document containing concealed truths that must be read out of it. The reference to Paul is not a tangent, though—indeed, Origen continues with a list of passages that demonstrate that this spiritual interpretation was essential to Paul's own method of reading Scripture. Against his critics, Origen is deploying a most compelling argument: if we take issue with the way that he is reading, we are simultaneously taking issue with the way that Paul himself argues in inspired Scripture. Thus, Origen cites Paul's words in 1 Corinthians 10:11 ("These things happened to them to serve as an example, and they were written down to instruct us, on whom the ends of the ages have come") as a programmatic statement on a means of reading, then offers specific examples like 1 Corinthians 10:4 ("For they drank from the spiritual rock that followed them, and the rock was Christ"), Hebrews 8:5 ("They offer worship in a sanctuary that is a sketch and shadow of the heavenly one"), and the lengthy allegory (Paul uses the word specifically) in Galatians 4:21-31 where Hagar is compared to the present Jerusalem and Sarah is compared to the New Jerusalem.

---

[6] Origen, *First Principles* 4.1.13 (ANF 4.362).

From these starting points, Origen wrote a host of commentaries and homilies on Scripture that deeply influenced writers in both East and West. Modern Roman Catholic theologian Henri de Lubac rightly notes that Origen

> was destined to be, almost directly, one of the foremost educators of the Latin Middle Ages. His "vision" of the Bible and of the Christian life was destined to govern the underpinnings of its customs and methods. Together with Saint Augustine, he was destined to be "the doctor of the spiritual sense of history." More than any other figure in the fields of hermeneutics, exegesis, and spirituality, he would be the grand master.[7]

Despite this influence, Origen himself would be anathemized not only in his own lifetime but long afterward as well. Origen had the misfortune of writing before language about the Trinity had been formally and finally decided by the ecumenical councils. As a result, some later readers questioned his orthodoxy because of his terminology around the Trinity. Others were concerned about the ramifications of his teaching about souls. Conflict over Origen and his orthodoxy drove a wedge between the two greatest Latin translators of Origen, Jerome and Rufinus. Once friends, the argument caused them to write bitter polemical treatises against one another. Ultimately, during the lifetime of Cassiodorus, the ecumenical council gathered to anathematize the Antiochene Three Chapters placed Origen under anathema as well.[8] Thus, Origen—one of the greatest teachers of the church—is reckoned among the church fathers but despite his work and witness never received recognition as a saint, had many of his works destroyed, and persists under a theological cloud.

A Spin from John Cassian

Cassiodorus is influenced by a stream of interpretation that comes from Origen and was mediated to the Latin West through several

---

[7] Henri de Lubac, *Medieval Exegesis*, vol. 1, trans. Mark Sebanc (Grand Rapids, MI: Eerdmans, 1998), 159.

[8] This was the event we touched on in chapter 3 that caused Justinian to kidnap Pope Vigilius and imprison him in Constantinople until he changed his mind.

channels. Jerome and Rufinus clearly were the main hands at work directly translating Origen's works. His influence, though, is found far beyond their works. The interpretive handbook of Eucherius of Lyon is strongly Origenist, and the initial section sets up an Origenist method of interpreting as read through Cassian. While Jerome did more direct translation of Origen than anyone else, Cassian's presentation of the methods of Origen proved very influential in the West and particularly in the monastic traditions.

Cassiodorus praised Cassian highly, both the *Conferences* and the *Institutes*. While warning his monks about Cassian's problematic passages on the freedom of the will, he nevertheless recommends him to be read and studied as a guide to monastic life.[9] In his opening chapter on study and the Scriptures, Cassiodorus refers to Cassian explicitly noting an interpretive event in the *Conferences* and implicitly when he recommends the kind of meditative repetition that Cassian insists on.[10]

Cassian's *Conferences* are a strange and wonderful collection of conversations. The story goes that Cassian and his friend Germanus, after spending some time in a monastery in Bethlehem, took the theological equivalent of a Gap Year and set off to see the sites—in the Egyptian deserts. They hiked around the wastelands of northern Egypt, meeting and interviewing the famous hermits of the desert and gaining wisdom from them about the spiritual life. Many years later—probably in the opening decades of the fifth century—after founding two monasteries around modern-day Marseilles, Cassian wrote down the conversations as the *Conferences* and, in so doing, created the first great work on the nuts and bolts of Christian spirituality in the West.

Translating and transmitting a spirituality born of experience in the desert, rooted in the teachings of Origen, Cassian's writings were invaluable to the emerging monastic movement in the West. Benedict praises him and advises his monks to read Cassian (RB 73.5). As monastic reformations periodically swept through the church in the course of the Middle Ages, Cassian's books in general and the *Conferences* in particular are cited again and again with approval.

Cassian's fourteenth conference portrays a conversation between Cassian, Germanus, and an old man known as Abba Nesteros that is

---

[9] Cassiodorus, *Institutions* 1.29.2, pp. 162–63.
[10] Cassiodorus, *Institutions* 1.pref.7, p. 108.

focused on the topic of spiritual knowledge. As they delve into the topic, Abba Nesteros begins talking about the ways to interpret and understand the Scriptures. First, he separates spirituality in general into two parts. The words that he uses are the "practical" and the "theoretical," but it's better to say that one part is the active, external part while the other is the internal, meditative part. That is, the central task of the active/practical part is the control of the body and mind—built on a foundation of fasting and self-mortification—whereby one focuses on sinning less. Once that task has been fully engaged and some progress has been made the turn to the interior life will bear fruit. This is where he gets to the Scriptures.

Abba Nesteros explains that the study of Scripture is divided into two main parts: "historical interpretation [*historicam interpretationem*] and spiritual understanding [*intelligentiam spiritalem*]."[11] In making this division, he lays down the two major modes of interpreting that writers of the early medieval period will prefer. He splits the spiritual interpretations into three subcategories: allegory, anagogy, and tropology. After identifying these four (the historical and the three subdivisions of the spiritual), he explains them a bit. The historical sense is not just about the past but includes what we would consider the literal meaning of the text. In particular, the Abba says that history pertains both to things that happened in the past and to visible things. Hence, an interpretation relating to natural science would be a historical reading in the sense of the phrase "natural history." Allegory is the mystery that is prefigured by the historical/literal events. Said another way, allegory is the means "by which the things that the historical interpretation conceals are laid bare by a spiritual understanding and explanation."[12] Anagogy "mounts from spiritual mysteries to certain more sublime and sacred heavenly secrets."[13] This is restated a little better to clarify that it is the means "by which words are directed to the invisible and what lies in the future." Tropology, at least, is more clear: "moral explanation pertaining to correction of life and to practi-

---

[11] John Cassian, *Conferences* II.14.8.1, p. 509.
[12] John Cassian, *Conferences* II.14.8.5, p. 510.
[13] John Cassian, *Conferences* II.14.8.2, p. 510.

cal instruction."[14] More helpful than his definitions, though, is his example in which he demonstrates what these four look like in practice:

> The four figures that have been mentioned converge in such a way that, if we want, one and the same Jerusalem can be understood in a fourfold manner. According to history it is the city of the Jews. According to allegory it is the church of Christ. According to anagogy it is that heavenly city of God "which is the mother of us all." According to tropology it is the soul of the human being, which under this name is frequently reproached or praised by the Lord.[15]

While a theoretical distinction is made between these four senses, as far as early medieval writers are concerned, there are two broad senses: the historical and the spiritual. Only rarely will an early medieval author specify what kind of spiritual interpretation they are using and, in practice, the categories are very fluid. Indeed, the fact that only three kinds of spiritual understanding are described seems to have more to do with scriptural proof texts than actual practice. Abba Nesteros cites two different biblical texts, one that refers to three things, Proverbs 22:20[16] ("Have I not written for you [three] sayings of admonition and knowledge"), and one that refers to four, 1 Corinthians 14:6 ("If I come to you speaking in tongues, how will I benefit you unless I speak to you in some revelation or knowledge or prophecy or teaching"). In each case, we get the sense that the numbers recorded in Scripture are driving the enumeration of elements rather than the methods themselves. In practice, there are many more modes of spiritual interpretation than three, and not all of them are clearly defined or delineated. We will come back to this point later as we discuss how we actually see spiritual interpretation happening in Cassiodorus and other authors.

Modern readers—and especially biblical scholars looking for the history of the discipline—tend to focus in on this section of this conference. However, this is just one part of a larger argument, and it deserves to be put into the proper context. Again, this whole conference

---

[14] Ibid.

[15] John Cassian, *Conferences* II.14.8.4, p. 510.

[16] Looking this up in the Bible might cause a bit of confusion. The "three" here comes from the textual tradition of the Septuagint, the Greek translation of the Hebrew Bible; the Hebrew and modern translations that follow it read differently.

begins with the idea that the first step of proper interpretation is the purification of the body, mind, and spirit. Those undisciplined who persist in their sin simply cannot read the Scriptures rightly—they don't yet have the right frame of mind to read what is found there. As a result, after talking about interpretive method, Abba Nesteros returns to hammer this point again:

> Maintaining the diligence in reading that I think you have, then, make every effort to get a complete grasp of practical—that is, ethical—discipline as soon as possible. For without this the theoretical purity that we have spoken of cannot be acquired. The only people who attain to it, possessing it as a reward after the expenditure of much toil and labor, are those who have found perfection not in the words of other teachers but in the virtuousness of their own acts.[17]

This is a key point and leads to an emphasis on doing rather than teaching. Scripture must be put into practice; those who wish to teach it must first demonstrate with their actions their deep grasp of its teachings. Knowing with the mind is not enough; no one should presume to teach Scripture until its truths have been—literally—embodied in habits and actions. Abba Nesteros explains that this is essential for two reasons. First, because we cannot presume to teach what we do not know and knowledge comes only by putting it into action. Second, because putting the teaching of Scripture into action is itself a sign of the converting presence of the Holy Spirit—the true guide to right reading and interpretation: "For it is one thing to speak with ease and beauty and another to enter deeply into heavenly sayings and to contemplate profound and hidden mysteries with the most pure eye of the heart, because certainly neither human teaching nor worldly learning but only purity of mind will possess this, through the enlightenment of the Holy Spirit."[18]

Humility and the other virtues, then, are the central prerequisites to reading Scripture well. From that point, Abba Nesteros describes the proper practice of engaging Scripture. While he had talked about

---

[17] John Cassian, *Conferences* II.14.9.2, p. 512.
[18] John Cassian, *Conferences* II.14.9.7, p. 513.

technical matters of interpretation in the earlier part of the dialogue, he now turns to what this looks like in day-to-day experience:

> Then, once all worldly cares and preoccupations have been cast out, you must strive in every respect to give yourself assiduously and even constantly to sacred reading. Do this until continual meditation fills your mind and as it were forms it in its likeness, making it a kind of ark of the covenant. . . . All of these are guarded by two cherubim—that is, by the fullness of historical and spiritual knowledge, for the cherubim are interpreted as the breadth of knowledge. . . . Hence the successive books of Holy Scripture must be diligently committed to memory and ceaselessly reviewed. This continual meditation will bestow on us double fruit. First, inasmuch as the mind's attention is occupied with reading and with preparing to read, it cannot be taken captive in the entrapments of harmful thoughts. Then, the things that we have not been able to understand because our mind was busy at the time, things that we have gone through repeatedly and are laboring to memorize, we shall see more clearly afterward when we are free from every seductive deed and sight, and especially when we are silently meditating at night. Thus, while we are at rest and as it were immersed in the stupor of sleep, there will be revealed an understanding of hidden meanings that we did not grasp even slightly when we were awake. But as our mind is increasingly renewed by this study, the face of Scripture will also begin to be renewed, and the beauty of a more sacred understanding will somehow grow with the person who is making progress.[19]

In this set of statements, Abba Nesteros, speaking to us through Cassian, reveals the incredible profundity that we encounter again and again in the wisdom of the desert fathers and mothers: they have a remarkable grasp of the habits of the mind, displayed here in the discussion of the processing power of the subconscious mind, that seems amazingly modern yet is centuries old. In the spiritual laboratory of the desert, these hermits and anchorites observed and taught about the power of habit and the functions of the conscious and subconscious mind in ways that would not be replicated again until the rise of psychology in the twentieth century.

---

[19] John Cassian, *Conferences* II.14.10.2, 10.3, 10.4–11.1; pp. 514–15.

The pattern, then, is clear: memorize and rehearse. Soak the soul in Scripture, and Scripture itself will transform the soul to be more like Scripture. In so doing, the soul's perception of Scripture will be transformed and freed to perceive more and deeper meanings within Scripture.

Reading with Augustine

Augustine of Hippo: Theologian of the West

Saint Augustine of Hippo looms large over Western theology. Standing in a succession of important Latin-speaking African theologians stretching back through Cyprian (d. 258) and Tertullian (d. 240), Augustine dominates the Latin patristic age because of his intellect, his personality, and his prolific energy. Like Tertullian, Augustine was born of Berber stock in the North African Roman province of Numidia. Augustine started life in the year 354 in the town Thagaste in modern-day Algeria, the son of a local official and a devoutly Christian mother. He studied grammar and rhetoric as young men of substance did and began a career teaching rhetoric, eventually moving to Carthage, to Rome, and finally to Milan. Dismissing the Christianity of his upbringing as childish and unsophisticated, he wandered through a variety of belief systems, including Manichaeism, before rediscovering Christianity in Milan through the preaching of Ambrose, the city's persuasive bishop. Augustine was baptized there by Ambrose in 387. Returning to Africa with the intention of settling down and living a simple monastic life in Hippo, a coastal city about sixty miles from his birthplace, his plans were interrupted by the recognition of his many gifts. Against his wishes, he was ordained priest in 391 and then elected and consecrated bishop in 396. He spent his episcopate preaching, writing, and attending councils until his death in 430, three months into the Vandal siege of Hippo.

Augustine-bashing has become fashionable in some sectors of the church and academy. Whether fairly or not, criticism over Christian attitudes toward sexuality and procreation, the doctrine of original sin, denigration of the originally good created state of humanity, church collusion with the coercive power of the state, and other matters have all been laid at Augustine's feet. And yet these issues are tangential to what Augustine's voluminous writings actually accomplished. Augustine was the architect of a remarkable and long-standing synthesis that gave a philosophical and scientific underpinning to Christian doctrine that would remain unchallenged until the rediscovery of Aristotle in the High Middle Ages. Despite challenges to his authority, his thought was a primary driver of the Protestant Reformation in Europe, and he remains a potent presence in theology today as well. Ironically, modern attacks against Augustine pay homage to his importance and continuing influence.

The weakness of his synthesis is part of what gave it its tremendous strength: Augustine insisted on connecting his theology to the very best philosophy and science of his day. After fifteen centuries, though, the biology, physics, and medicine of his day are no longer persuasive. We know far more about the human body and the wonders of the cosmos on both the universal and atomic levels than he ever dreamed of. This is not his fault. His attempts to describe a biological mechanism for original sin made perfect sense within the context of fourth-century science but seem ridiculous to modern readers. To put this in perspective, cutting-edge theology these days attempts a rapprochement with quantum physics and string theory; consider how well these efforts will be regarded a century from now—let alone from a vantage point fifteen centuries hence!

Augustine was a tireless author, a man with nary an unpublished thought. As he looked back over his literary life in his *Retractions*, he identified some 232 books spread over ninety-three works, not even bothering to account for his letters and treatises. His friend and chronicler Possidius added an index onto his biography of the bishop; the list identifies 1,030 separate texts and apologizes for not including those additional items not catalogued within his system. These works range from books on theology to controversies within the church to letters to other bishops or authors (like Jerome) to homilies. His most famous works include the *Confessions*, an intimate spiritual autobiography that examines his youth and conversion from the vantage point of middle age. His *On the Trinity* in fifteen books became the central lens through which the Western church understood both Christology and trinitarian theology—the interrelations between the three persons in the Godhead and the theological and pastoral implications thereof. The *City of God* in twenty-two books was a grand defense of the church from the charge that the Gothic sack of Rome in 410 was but a culmination of punishments from the gods for the empire abandoning the old faith and embracing Christianity.

For Augustine—as for most authors in this period—there was no dividing line between doing theology and doing biblical interpretation: they were one and the same. To do theology was to think through the Scriptures. Despite his massive amount of writing, Augustine left little behind in the way of direct commentaries on the Scriptures. When biblical scholars survey his work, there appear to be only three complete substantive commentaries that appear among the piles of books that he produced: the *Tractates on John*, *Tractates on the First Epistle of John*, and the *Enarration of the Psalms*. (There are a number of false starts on Genesis and Romans that are important works in their own right, but even Augustine was not able to make much headway through these two books, given the level of detail and theological attention he devoted to each phrase!)

Even these three works are not properly commentaries in the formal sense, however; they are sets of sequential sermons. Augustine was first and foremost an orator. He was a preacher. And, sure enough, the commentary on the Psalms that we have from him is a collection of sermons on individual psalms delivered and collected over the course of decades. While reading Augustine's commentary, it's easy to form a mental picture of his compositional style: Augustine has walked into the pulpit holding nothing but a Psalter and is expounding on it line by line before an eager crowd while a scribe in the first row is feverishly scribbling down his words into a tablet for review and transcription onto parchment later in the day. Augustine doesn't cite authorities; he doesn't rely on a great deal of prior research. The effect is listening to a man who has been reading and pondering the Scriptures for years, standing before a crowd and speaking off the cuff, indulging in digressions, and making connections across the canon that occur to him on this particular day. This impression is only reinforced on the occasions where Augustine's commentary contains two or three different sermons on the same psalm. A different day brings a different message on the same text.

O'Donnell, in his biography of Augustine, contrasts the African preacher with Jerome:

> [Augustine] did [interpretation] as a performer, not a scholar. The pulpit and its extemporaneity offered the focus for his biblical

interpretation. While his contemporary Jerome was dictating volume after volume of careful biblical commentary in his study, sometimes following Greek authorities and sometimes simply translating them, Augustine the exegete shied away from that practice as time went by. He only turned his hand to writing formal Scriptural commentary a half-dozen times, and only once as a bishop, and never used an authoritative source or sources.[20]

The contrast with Jerome holds true for Cassiodorus as well—perhaps even more so. Cassiodorus was no preacher. Rather, he was a man who reveled in the written word. Fitted to his bureaucratic life by his temperament, the writing of Cassiodorus is structured, organized, and analytical.

The Augustinian Framework

Out of all of Augustine's writings, the most important for our purposes is the one that modern scholars refer to as *Christian Instruction*. I have to hedge that a bit because the actual Latin name is *De Doctrina Christiana*. Many have been tempted to translate this title as "On Christian Doctrine" because the Latin words look like the English words. This is the option taken by the translation that I normally use, that of D. W. Robsertson Jr. The problem is that the Latin *doctrina* and the English "doctrine" are false friends—they look very similar and are even related to one another linguistically, but they have important differences in meaning. Another translation option is "On Christian Teaching," which better conveys what the term *doctrina* is trying to accomplish; the recent translation by R. P. H. Green uses this as an English title. Despite these options, the official style guide of the Society of Biblical Literature insists on *Christian Instruction* as the preferred title. Therefore, be aware that all four of these titles do, in fact, refer to the same book.

Augustine wrote this work in two parts. The bulk of books 1 through 3 were written in 397, just after his consecration as bishop; the last part of book 3 and book 4 were written some thirty years later

---

[20] James J. O'Donnell, *Augustine: A New Biography* (New York: HarperCollins, 2006), 133.

in 427. The first three books lay out Augustine's theory of signs and figures and how reading ought to be done. Book 4 draws on rhetoric to talk about how to preach.

Augustine's *Christian Instruction* forms the baseline for Cassiodorus's reading practices. Indeed, much of the advice given in the *Institutions* is a simplified form of the methodology described in *Christian Instruction*. After a brief overview of signs, book 2 of *Christian Instruction* gives a succinct summary for approaching Scripture:

> In all of these books [of Scripture] those fearing God and made meek in piety seek the will of God. And the first rule of this understanding and labor is, as we have said, to know these books even if they are not understood, at least to read them or to memorize them, or to make them not altogether unfamiliar to us. Then those things which are put openly in them either as precepts for living or as rules for believing are to be studied more diligently and more intelligently, for the more one learns about these things the more capable of understanding he becomes. Among those things which are said openly in Scripture are to be found all those teachings which involve faith, the mores of living, and that hope and charity that we have discussed in the previous book. Then having become familiar with the language of the Divine Scriptures, we should turn to those obscure things which must be opened up and explained so that we may take examples from those things that are manifest to illuminate those things which are obscure, bringing principles which are certain to bear on our doubts concerning those things which are uncertain. In this undertaking memory is of great value, for if it fails rules will not be of any use.[21]

We are in familiar territory here: read over all of the Scriptures continually, whether you think you are getting everything or not; read seeking the will of God (not just information); put the open, clear, and basic rules of faith and belief into practice; only then worry about the obscure stuff.

But what to do with the obscure stuff? Augustine has a very simple rule to determine if any given passage in Scripture is meant to be taken literally or if it is intended to be taken figuratively:

---

[21] Augustine, *Christian Instruction* 2.9.14 (ChrDoc, pp. 42–43).

> A method of determining whether a locution is literal or figurative [*propriam quasi figuratam*] must be established. And generally this method consists in this: whatever appears in the divine Word that does not literally pertain to virtuous behavior or the truth of faith you must take to be figurative. Virtuous behavior pertains to the love of God and of one's neighbor; the truth of faith pertains to a knowledge of God and of one's neighbor. For the hope of everyone lies in his own conscience in so far as he knows himself to be becoming more proficient in the love of God and his neighbor.[22]

Although this seems pretty clear, Augustine doesn't hesitate to repeat his point just to make sure that it has been properly understood:

> But Scripture teaches nothing but charity, nor condemns anything except cupidity, and in this way shapes the minds of men. . . . I call "charity" the motion of the soul toward the enjoyment of God for His own sake, and the enjoyment of one's self and of one's neighbor for the sake of God; but "cupidity" is a motion of the soul toward the enjoyment of one's self, one's neighbor, or any corporal thing for the sake of something other than God. That which uncontrolled cupidity does to corrupt the soul and its body is called a "vice"; what it does in such a way that someone else is harmed is called a "crime." And these are the two classes of all sins. . . . On the other hand, what charity does to the charitable person is called "utility"; what it does to benefit one's neighbor is called "beneficence." . . . The more the reign of cupidity is destroyed, the more charity is increased.[23]

The interpretation of Scripture is about forming Christians who demonstrate their Christianity through love. Vice is rooted out of the soul in order that charity might prevail.

Furthermore, if a reader encounters a passage that does not appear to either promote charity or condemn vice, Augustine has a clear directive: "What is read should be subjected to diligent scrutiny until an interpretation contributing to the reign of charity is produced."[24]

---

[22] Augustine, *Christian Instruction* 3.10.14 (ChrDoc, pp. 87–88).
[23] Augustine, *Christian Instruction* 3.10.15-6 (ChrDoc, pp. 88–89).
[24] Augustine, *Christian Instruction* 3.15.23 (ChrDoc, p. 43).

In a sense, this opens the door wide for the unlimited allegorizing of texts. Augustine has laid out the answer key and informed his readers what every text in the Bible is about. Now they are told to go and figure out how that can possibly be the case—how to make any passage conform to this meaning. This could open things up for a complete free-for-all, but Augustine maintains that there are certain controls within the interpretive system.

A fundamental principle for Augustine and those who follow his strategy—like Cassiodorus—is that "hardly anything may be found in these obscure places which is not found plainly said elsewhere."[25] As a result, this kind of interpretation is not simply a matter of making things up—or formulating something new on the spot. Rather, Augustine suggests that one reason why the scriptural teachings are veiled is because they exercise the minds of those who study it, and that those who take delight at discovering a veiled doctrine, although it is taught openly elsewhere, will be the more likely to follow it because of the work exerted.

Another principle is that there will always be some kind of connection, however remote, that will signal the connection between the plain matter and the obscurity: "When a figurative locution appears, the words of which it is composed will be seen to be derived from similar things or related to such things by some association."[26] This principle is behind several different kinds of connection making that Augustine, Cassiodorus, and other interpreters commonly used, including word-chaining, etymology, typology, and allegory.

Sometimes the way that a particular image or topic is used in one place in Scripture carries over to many others: "In those places where things are used openly we may learn how to interpret them when they appear in obscure places."[27] This is the idea behind the large collection of identifications in Eucherius of Lyon's *Formulas of Spiritual Understanding*, a work that Cassiodorus also favors. Drawing primarily from the Psalms, Eucherius provides lists of how certain images like "javelin" or "chariot" or "rod" can be interpreted. Drawing chiefly from the Psalms but also the Prophets and various New Testament

---

[25] Augustine, *Christian Instruction* 2.78 (ChrDoc, p. 38).
[26] Augustine, *Christian Instruction* 3.25.34 (ChrDoc, p. 99).
[27] Augustine, *Christian Instruction* 3.26.37 (ChrDoc, p. 101).

texts, this kind of a reference can be helpful when confronted with an unfamiliar image or a familiar term used in an unusual way.

Augustine does point out, however, that this doesn't always work, reminding his readers that one similarity alone does not make an open-and-shut case: "But since things are similar to other things in a great many ways, we must not think it to be prescribed that what a thing signifies by similitude in one place must always be signified by that thing."[28] Cassiodorus will also affirm the same thing; in his discussion of Psalm 11:1, for instance, he points out that neither the terms "mountain" nor "sparrow" can be understood the same way in every context.

At the end of the day, Augustine's guidance on the interpretation of the Scriptures comes down to the transformation of the reader. The kind of reading that Augustine is most interested in discussing in *Christian Instruction* is reading for edification—for the building up of the soul—and for transformation. While he certainly will, and does, read the Scriptures doctrinally and fight against heresies from the Scriptures, his chief concern here is guiding regular readers to see that the purest encounter with Scripture is one of transformation toward the virtues of Christ. As a result, the accuracy of a reading is less important to him than whether the act of reading has the proper effect and result:

> Whoever, therefore, thinks that he understands the divine Scriptures or any part of them so that it does not build the double love of God and neighbor does not understand it at all. Whoever finds a lesson there useful to the building of charity, even though he has not said what the author may be shown to have intended in that place, has not been deceived, nor is he lying in any way. . . . But anyone who understands in the Scriptures something other than that intended by them is deceived, although they do not lie. However, as I began to explain, if he is deceived in an interpretation which builds up charity, which is the end of the commandments, he is deceived in the same way as a man who leaves a road by mistake but passes through a field to the same place toward which the road itself leads. But he is to be corrected and shown that it is

---

[28] Augustine, *Christian Instruction* 3.25.35 (ChrDoc, pp. 99–100).

more useful not to leave the road, lest the habit of deviating force him to take a crossroad or perverse way.[29]

Augustine is not trying to say that there are not wrong interpretations; he specifically says that there are. Furthermore, those who interpret wrongly ought to be corrected. There are rules here; there are things we can and cannot do while reading; there are interpretations that are better than others. Nevertheless, the end—the purpose—of reading is the building up of love in the Body of Christ.

An Antiochene Structure?

There has been speculation as to the amount of influence the so-called Antiochene school of interpretation had on Cassiodorus's commentary. This school gets its name from the city of Antioch in Syria where it was based. It is a profoundly Eastern method; its proponents were from the farthest eastern reaches of the empire, and sometimes beyond it, into Persian territory. We know Cassiodorus was in touch with this tradition as he recommends the handbook of Junillus Africanus, which transmits an Aristotelian logic for approaching the Scriptures and the kind of interpretive speech the Antiochene works have in them. O'Donnell notes that Cassiodorus is largely responsible for the circulation of Junillus's text in the West.[30] Since Junillus was in Constantinople in the 540s, it is quite likely the two men knew each other. Cassiodorus also mentions the work of Adrian, an author whose work survives primarily in Greek.

Scholars of biblical interpretation tend to argue over a theory that pits a fundamentally Origenist Alexandrian school that embraces allegory against an Antiochene school, represented chiefly by Theodore of Mopsuestia, that eschews allegory for a historical/literal method of reading. One particular version of this theory celebrates the Antiochenes over the Alexandrians because it sees in them a foreshadowing of modern biblical scholarship with a preference for the literal and historical meanings over allegorical ones. This view over-argues the evidence and ignores the kind of moral, doctrinal, and spiritual

---

[29] Augustine, *Christian Instruction* 1.36.40-41 (ChrDoc, pp. 30–31).
[30] O'Donnell, *Cassiodorus*, 247–49.

readings that the Antiochenes do perform on a regular basis. A more nuanced—and evidence-based—approach championed by Frances Young does find value in the distinction between the two schools even if it is not quite as hard and fast as some try to make it.[31] With regard to the Psalms, Theodore of Mopsuestia in his commentary rejected the notion that Christ was speaking any of the psalms. Rather, he emphasized that David was the speaker of them and that the psalms should be read with reference both to their historical situation and understanding David as a true prophet who could speak of future events—including events involving Christ.

In Cassiodorus's commentary, we do see David—sometimes just referred to as "the Prophet"—as the speaker in most of the psalms; David as psalmist and prophet is identified as the sole speaker in sixty-four psalms. Jesus himself is, however, appointed as the sole speaker in twenty-one. Among these is Psalm 22, a psalm that Theodore identified as improper in the mouth of Christ because the speaker mentions committing transgressions. There's no evidence that Cassiodorus used Theodore's Psalm commentary nor did he recommend it. It is beyond a doubt that he was aware of it, though; the controversy that had brought Pope Vigilius to Constantinople was about the condemnation of Theodore and two other Antiochene authors suspected of Nestorian beliefs.

While not embracing specifically Antiochene ideas on the Psalms, there is a clear connection between the two Antiochene handbooks—that of Junillus and Adrian—and Cassiodorus's commentary. Both of these works are deeply invested in building on the Greco-Roman tradition of literary and rhetorical interpretation far more than any of the Western handbooks. Augustine says that learning the figures of speech and thought are useful but will not teach them; both Junillus and Adrian do teach them and describe how they apply to Scripture. Furthermore, the rhetorical emphasis of the Antiochene writers leads them to consider the flow and scope of an argument. Western interpreters frequently get stuck in the sentence-level reading of a text and forget to zoom back out to get a sense of how each piece fits together into a coherent whole. Young notes that it is not uncommon to have

---

[31] See in particular Frances Young, *Biblical Exegesis and the Formation of Christian Culture* (Peabody, MA: Hendrickson, 1997).

summaries of sections of arguments in Antiochene works. Keeping a sense of the motion of the argument is important, and this particularly comes into play when such things have to be tracked over chapters as we see in Paul's letters.

Two of the unusual aspects that set Cassiodorus's Psalms commentary apart from all other Psalms commentaries in the early medieval West are his attention to the structure and flow of the argument within each psalm and his rigorous application of the technical vocabulary of Greco-Roman grammar, dialectic, and rhetoric. Furthermore, each psalm receives—in effect—three different summaries. It is summarized as Cassiodorus identifies the major sections from which it is composed. He offers a summary of each section at the start of each section in his verse-by-verse run-through. Finally, he draws the themes together again when he offers a conclusion to each psalm before making final comments. There is an attention to the interpretive big picture lacking in the Western sources but that is a feature of the Antiochene approach. Just as Boethius promised a synthesis between the philosophies of Plato and Aristotle, Cassiodorus appears to have created a synthesis between the dominant Alexandrian method of spiritualized interpretation and the Antiochene school with its emphasis on the rhetorical and grammatical integrity of the text.

Cassiodorus's Interpretive Big Picture

Cassiodorus lays out his own sense of the interpretive big picture in book 1 of the *Institutions*. In the preface to the *Institutions*, Cassiodorus gives clear instructions on how monks should learn to interpret the Scriptures. He invokes Jacob's ladder as a key image for a set of steps by which a monk learns the arts of contemplation: "For commentary on Scripture is, as it were, Jacob's ladder, by which the angels ascend and descend."[32] The very first step is, naturally, memorizing the Psalms. Once the Psalms have been learned, Cassiodorus directs that they proceed to the rest of Scripture. They "should study the divine text in corrected books until, by continuous practice, with God's help, it is known to them."[33] He mentions the phrase "depths of memory [*memo-*

---

[32] Cassiodorus, *Institutions* 1.Pref.2, p. 106.
[33] Ibid.

riae sinibus]" twice in this section, and by the end the implication is not that the monks have simply read Scripture once but that a great part of it has also been memorized already. This introductory stage must therefore take a considerable amount of time. If the learning of the Psalter by heart takes between six months and two years, then reading of the Scriptures in this deep and intensive way will take at least another two years—if not longer—and only then will the student be at the proper point for benefiting from the *Institutions*: "Therefore, dearest brothers, after the soldiers of Christ have filled themselves with divine study [*divina lectione*] and, grown strong by regular reading [*frequenti meditatione*], have begun to recognize passages cited as circumstances indicate, then they may profit from going through this guide."[34]

The next nine chapters of book 1 of the *Institutions* move through the ninefold division of the Scriptures and identify for each the most important authors and their works. For instance, in his chapter on the Psalms he states that "Blessed Hilary, blessed Ambrose, and blessed Jerome have treated some of the Psalms, but blessed Augustine in a scholarly manner more fully treated all."[35] After mentioning his own commentary, following Augustine, he also includes a notice of "the short book of Athanasius, bishop of Alexandria, that he sent to Marcellinus as a sweet refreshment after his illness."[36] As we read through these sections, we get the sense that Cassiodorus is doing two things. On one hand, he is giving a general set of directions as to what authors should be read and sought after. Much like Jerome's listing of reputable Christian authors in *On the Illustrious Men*, he is telling us whom we ought to be reading and, by omission, whom we shouldn't. On the other hand, he is giving us a guided tour of the library; he will often mention where a text is located or will indicate that he has had some of the smaller treatises bound together into one volume. There is a sense of place and location that comes out of this section of the *Institutions* that frequently reminds readers that this is an instruction book prepared for small groups of men who are settling into the religious life in one particular converted villa in Southern Italy. There are tiny intimacies that ground the reader in a particular place and time.

---

[34] Cassiodorus, *Institutions* 1.Pref.3, p. 106.
[35] Cassiodorus, *Institutions* 1.4.1, p. 120.
[36] Cassiodorus, *Institutions* 1.4.3, p. 120.

After this run through the approved commentaries, Cassiodorus lists a six-step method for tackling a text if a reader happens to get stuck on a particular point of interpretation. The first step is to read through the *Institutions* themselves to see if they help solve the problem. The second is to check the introductory manuals. Cassiodorus has bound five works into a single volume for ease of reference: "Tyconius the Donatist, St. Augustine [*Christian Instruction*], Adrian, Eucherius, and Junillus."[37] These works represent a range of approaches containing everything from general directions on how to interpret to very specific explanations of what individual figures of speech could mean. The third step searches through the approved commentaries to see what their authors suggest. The fourth step is to carefully read the orthodox teachers to see if they have clarified the point in question. The fifth step is to examine the annotated listing of illustrations that the fathers scatter throughout their writings in hopes that this issue will have been treated by one of them. The sixth step is to engage in conversation with learned elders and to seek the wisdom of those the reader trusts.

Finally, after discussing various reputable authors and church fathers, Cassiodorus provides a concluding summarization of what he has been doing up to this point in book 1:

> But to summarize the essential points: everything that the ancient commentators have spoken of in a laudable way ought to be grasped eagerly. But those subjects that they did not deal with should be scanned first to avoid being worn out by fruitless toil, to discover their strongest points and to what knowledge they may lead us and finally what they intend us to draw out of them in our reading. For although the text may seem to be perfectly clear and splendid in a literal meaning [*historica relatione*], even so it also urges justice or reproves impiety, either preaches tolerance or attacks the vices of inconstancy, either condemns pride or exalts the virtues of humility, either checks those who are not at peace or consoles those who are most full of love, or tells something that urges us to good conduct and turns us away from evil thoughts by its respect for goodness. For if God promised rewards to the good only, his forgiveness would be ignored and fade; and if he always

---

[37] Cassiodorus, *Institutions* 1.10.1, p. 133.

> threatened destruction to those who are evil, despair of their salvation would drive them on to vice. Thus the Holy Redeemer for our salvation has ruled in such a way that he both frightens the sinners with the punishment he announces and promises worthy rewards to the good.
>
> Therefore let our minds be ever intent on the general meanings of the books, and let us set our minds on that contemplation that does not merely sound in our ears but lights the interior eye. Although the narrative may seem to be simple, Divine Scripture contains nothing empty, nothing idle. It always speaks to some purpose that the righteous may profitably extract. When good actions are reported, let us be aroused immediately to imitation; when it tells of punishable deeds, let us fear to do them. Thus it happens that we always obtain something useful if we observe why these points are mentioned.[38]

This passage reminds us of some major points that are worth underscoring. First, Cassiodorus and his monks are not interested in reading Scripture for the sake of figuring it out; it is not simply an intellectual puzzle to be solved. Rather, Scripture is a set of directives on how the holy life is cultivated and lived. We don't have to understand everything in it as long as we embody what is most important about it and keep chewing away at the parts that puzzle us—if they are worth it. When Cassiodorus recommends letting some questions go as not worth pursuing, he is redirecting his monks back to this point: monks aren't called to solve all the problems of Scripture—they are called to live it as thoroughly as they can.

Second, however edifying the literal or historical sense of Scripture is, there is always a moral sense that urges monks to live correctly, either by embracing virtues or by avoiding vices. Cassiodorus sets up a variety of dichotomies here that pit virtues against their vices. The central one—love or charity—is missing, however; it seems to be assumed rather than stated and is seen in its parts in the virtues that build up to it.

It is quite easy to look at the *Institutions*, its comprehensive list of commentaries, and to assume that Cassiodorus is only interested in directing his monks to a blind reliance on prior authorities. This is not

---

[38] Cassiodorus, *Institutions* 1.24.2-3, pp. 156–57.

true and mistakes his intention. Remember, the material contained in the *Institutions* is not the starting place. Scripture itself is the starting place. The Psalms must be memorized first, then the rest of Scripture has to be read through until the reader has a solid familiarity with all of it. The process of reading and interpreting has already begun. Readers have been brought to the text, and their own thoughts and imaginations have been engaged here at this initial level. Only then is the material in the *Institutions* to be learned. Furthermore, readers are encouraged to apply the material here, apply the directions on reading from the various handbooks even before commentaries are sought out. But even then, the purpose of interpretation is not to think new thoughts—the point is to live like a Christian, to be formed into the contemplation of God and the behaviors of loving God and neighbor most thoroughly.

Based on what he recommends and the practices that he actually enacts in both the *Institutions* and the *Explanation of the Psalms*, Cassiodorus is working from an interpretive synthesis that is built on a framework of Augustinian exegesis, read through Cassian and structured by means of Antiochene principles.

Conclusion

We have to get a sense of the big picture in order to understand what the *Explanation of the Psalms* is trying to do and to get a sense of the interpretive world from which it comes. Cassiodorus is not a modern reader, does not hold modern reading sensibilities, and is not struggling with the same questions, concerns, and issues as modern readers. Rather, the interpretive world that he inhabits is shaped by three major strands: the allegorical methods of Origen, the figural strategies of Augustine, and the Antiochene model of rhetorical interpretation. Taking these three as complementary rather than opposed, he will create a means for exploring the Psalms that will educate monastic readers in their literal, spiritual, and moral meanings. Having tried to get a sense of the big picture, we will now return to the commentary and start getting a sense of how Cassiodorus introduced his work to his readers.

CHAPTER SIX

The Preface to the Commentary

Having thought about the big picture, it's time to get back into the *Explanation of the Psalms* itself. If the *Institutions* and the background material provide us with a big-picture understanding of what Cassiodorus is up to, the next best thing to do is to read the preface to the Psalms commentary.

The Marginal Notes

Before the Preface

The preface consists of a few basic parts. The very first section is the notes section that explains the system of marginal signs that Cassiodorus invented and deployed to mark major items throughout the text. In the manuscripts that have it—not all of them do—this appears even before the preface proper. The marginal note is given, an explanatory line in red capitals describes it, then text in

Start of the Notes, f. 1r

the regular black lowercase letters explains what it means. He provides signs for thirteen different items:

- idiomatic expressions
- Christian doctrines
- definitions
- schemes (figures of speech or thought)
- etymologies
- interpretation of names (like etymologies but with names)
- rhetoric
- topics (a term from dialectic: a categorization of arguments based on kinds of evidence or strategy)
- syllogisms (a term from dialectic: different kinds of logical steps in constructing an argument)
- arithmetic
- geometry
- music
- astronomy

Not all occurrences of these items receive a marginal note; it's not always clear why that is. Was Cassiodorus's intention to mark only the ones he thought the most important, or did the marks fall away in the course of transmission?

Unfortunately, neither the initial guides to the notes nor the locations of the notes themselves are included within Walsh's English translation of the *Explanation of the Psalms*. This is a shame, because they do constitute an important part of Cassiodorus's overall plan of formation enacted within this work.

The Arts of Reading in Antiquity

When we started this investigation, we observed three broad themes that kept popping up in the lives of the early ascetics: an emphasis on the centrality of the Psalms, the importance of literacy, and the connection between the gospels and the Psalms. The marginal notes demonstrate how Cassiodorus goes all-in on the importance of literacy: he sees the Psalms as the ideal starting place for literacy, uniquely suited as a text from which to learn to read and to acquire the deeper arts of reading and learning.

Men like Ambrose, Augustine, Prosper of Aquitaine, and Cassiodorus were highly trained in the classical arts of reading: grammar, dialectic, and rhetoric. Indeed, these were the essential arts for a young man of good birth looking to make his way in the world. Education was rarely education for its own sake; rather, it was education for the purpose of becoming a skilled and effective public speaker within the courts of law. Since these courts occurred within the marketplaces and were attended almost as a form of spectator sport, they were a central means by which an ambitious young man could earn a spot in the public eye, attract attention from those in positions of power, and gain a position in the government.

The first study undertaken was grammar. Latin is a highly inflected language, meaning that prefixes and suffixes on the beginnings and ends of words give a great deal of information about how the word is functioning in a sentence. In English, word order and the use of prepositions are key means for determining the meaning of a sentence. Latin is quite different. Word order gives a general sense of emphasis while the beginnings and endings of words determine how they interact with one another. As a result, learning how to read, write, and speak correctly started with learning the parts of speech and wrapping one's head around the proper ways that nouns and verbs of various sorts were correctly ended or transmuted in order to get one's point across.

Advanced grammar branched out into the various kinds of ornamented language, conventionally divided into two major groups: figures of speech and figures of thought. Some kinds of ornamentation were about sound. For instance, students were introduced to rhyme, assonance, and alliteration, that is, sonic connections between one or more words because of shared sounds at the ends, middles, or beginnings of words. Some kinds of ornamentation are about the arrangement of words. For instance, it was one kind of figure if succeeding sentences all started with the same word, but another if one sentence ended and the next sentence began with the same word. In some, conjunctions were avoided and nouns were piled together; in others an almost excessive use of conjunctions separated every word in a list. Tropes were another kind of ornament, where a word is used but its meaning is shifted in some way. There were several kinds of comparisons like metaphors and similes, or forms where reference to part of something is intended to refer to the whole or vice versa, or where naming a container refers to the contents or vice versa. Allegory and parable and enigma and analogy are all forms of using words that ostensibly refer to something else entirely to shed light on the topic of discussion.

Dialectic is the art that defines the logically valid ways of arguing. It includes the fifteen different ways to define a person or thing and the various kinds of syllogisms used to make logical arguments. It also explores the different valid ways of categorizing things. While many of the topics in grammar and advanced grammar are still taught as aspects of English classes today, dialectic tends not to be covered as much. It seems like the kind of material that debate teams might get into but that most modern readers have never heard of.

Rhetoric deals with rules for creating a literary composition; since its practical application in the ancient world was oratory in the law courts, rhetoric also includes the arts of speaking effectively in public. One part of rhetoric deals with the various steps of composition: in invention we decide what it is we want to say; in arrangement we figure out which pieces of our argument should go where; in style we decide which figures of speech and thought to use and how many of them to strike the right tone; in memorization, we learn strategies that help us memorize what we've written; and in delivery we learn the skills of speaking, including how to speak loudly, clearly, and with the proper use of pauses. Another part of rhetoric focuses on the kinds of compositions and how they should be structured for maximum effect. Since classical rhetoric focuses on arguing legal cases, there is a whole field of stasis or status theory to determine what kind of arguments are possible or preferable based on a client's guilt or innocence, how much evidence does or does not exist, and to what degree the law does or does not address the kind of event that transpired.

At a certain level too, these three arts were bound up with the study of philosophy. The general theories of knowledge had practical implications in terms of how definitions were split and how arguments structured, what topics were or were not effective ways to approach ideas or events. Most of the people we think of as major philosophical figures of antiquity—Plato, Aristotle, Epictetus, and others—wrote books used as introductory works in these arts. In the later Latin tradition, philosophy became thoroughly tangled with the arts of reading and writing through towering figures who were both orators and philosophers like Cicero and Boethius.

The Problem with a Classical Education

There was one major problem here. These major fields of classical learning were deeply invested in and were communicated through classical culture. The two appeared to be inseparable. To learn grammar and dialectic and rhetoric was to learn it through immersing oneself in the epics, plays, hymns, and poetries of classical Greece and Rome. It meant memorizing the stories of Zeus lusting after nymphs, the trysts of Mars and Venus, the seductions of Apollo, and the deeds of heroes aided or hindered by the gods. There was no option between a Christian education or a secular education; there was no such thing as a secular education: it was a thoroughly and deeply pagan education.

There was a range of Christian responses. One was to flee learning entirely. Gregory the Great records that this was St. Benedict's decision; faced with the moral quandaries of education, he turned his back on the schools of Rome and headed into the mountains, founding—as his Rule puts it—a "school [*schola*] for the Lord's service" (RB Prol.45). Others were more ambiguous: scholars continue to argue over just how faithful a Christian Boethius was. His indebtedness to Neoplatonism, his ready personifications of Wisdom and Fortune, his lack of reference to biblical texts or theological wisdom, make him a suspicious character in the eyes of some. While there are theological treatises ascribed to him, some scholars doubt whether his was the hand that wrote them.

The greatest depiction of the struggle between classical education and Christian truth is undoubtedly a nightmare that once afflicted St. Jerome. In one of his letters to Eustochium, he recounts a terrifying experience brought on by a fever in the midst of Lent. He had, at that time, been alternating his reading between Scripture and the plays of Plautus and the philosophical writings of the orator Cicero. Sick—probably from excessive fasting—Jerome dreamt that he had been called before the great judgment seat of Christ in the midst of a host of saints and heavenly beings. He writes:

> I cast myself on the ground and did not dare to look up. Asked who and what I was I replied: "I am a Christian." But He who presided said: "Thou liest, thou art a follower of Cicero and not of Christ. For 'where thy treasure is, there will thy heart be also.'" Instantly I became dumb, and amid the strokes of the lash—for

he had ordered me to be scourged—I was tortured most severely still by the fire of conscience, considering with myself that verse, "In the grave who shall give thee thanks?"[1]

The bystanders cry out for mercy and Christ relents after Jerome makes a solemn vow never to take up pagan books again. On waking in the morning, he found his shoulders black and blue with bruises; they ached for several days afterward from the phantom whipping he had received. He tells Eustochium that after that point he redoubled his efforts in reading the sacred books, but he doesn't actually mention if he kept the vow made in a dream, extracted under torture. Whether he did or not, this episode dramatically illustrates the conflict between Christian wisdom and pagan education.

A Middle Way

The strongest strand of the tradition found a suitable middle way. In a line of thought pioneered by the great interpreter Origen of Alexandria, Augustine's *Christian Instruction* addresses the problem of pagan learning by reference to the plundering of the Egyptians. In an often overlooked detail of the escape from Egypt, Scripture records the Israelites taking gold, silver, and garments from their Egyptian neighbors in Exodus 12:35-36. Augustine, following like-minded church fathers, insists that all truth is God's truth; if there are truths to be found in pagan writings and wisdom, they originally come from God and may be safely and profitably applied to God's work if cleansed of their overtly pagan elements:

> If those who are called philosophers, especially the Platonists, have said things which are indeed true and are well accommodated to our faith, they should not be feared; rather, what they have said should be taken from them as from unjust possessors and converted to our use. . . . [A]ll of the pagan teachings contain not only simulated and superstitious imaginings and grave burdens of unnecessary labor, which each one of us leaving the society of pagans under the leadership of Christ ought to abominate and avoid, but also liberal disciplines more suited to the uses of truth, and some useful precepts concerning morals. Even some

---

[1] Jerome, Letter 22.30 (NPNF[2] 6:35).

truths concerning the worship of one God are discovered among them. These are, as it were, their gold and silver, which they did not institute themselves but dug up from certain mines of divine Providence, which is everywhere infused, and perversely and injuriously abused in the worship of demons. When the Christian separates himself in spirit from their miserable society, he should take this treasure with him for the just use of teaching the gospel.[2]

Once these arts are cleansed of their pagan past, then they are not only acceptable but also profitable for Christian use and teaching.

There is within this description, though, another possibility hinted at by the phrase "dug up from certain mines of divine Providence," which is also offered at a different point in Augustine's book. He also refers to what Ambrose taught him regarding such matters. Apparently some pagan skeptics had approached Ambrose of Milan and pointed out to him the similarities between the teachings of Christ and the teachings of Plato. Because Christ obviously came after Plato, they reasoned, is this not a clear sign that Christ learned all of his lessons from Plato? Augustine demonstrates the utility of studying history by telling what Ambrose did next:

> Did not the famous bishop, when he had considered the history of the pagans and found that Plato had traveled in Egypt during the time of Jeremias, show that Plato had probably been introduced to our literature by Jeremias so that he was able to teach or write doctrines that are justly commended? Pythagoras himself did not live before the literature of the Hebrew nation, in which the cult of God took its origin and from which Our Lord came "according to the flesh," was written. And from the disciples of Pythagoras these men claim that Plato learned theology. Thus from a consideration of times it becomes more credible that the Platonists took from our literature whatever they said that is good and truthful than what Our Lord Jesus Christ learned from them. To believe the latter view is the utmost madness.[3]

In laying this out, Ambrose is actually drawing on an argument originally established by the Jewish Alexandrian philosopher Aristoboulos

---

[2] Augustine, *Christian Instruction* 3.40.50 (ChrDoc, p. 75).
[3] Augustine, *Christian Instruction* 2.28.43 (ChrDoc, p.64).

and subsequently picked up by the better-known Jewish interpreter Philo Judaeus who made just this point: the wisdom of the Platonists and Pythagoreans comes from contact with Moses and Jeremiah in Egypt rather than the other way around.

Although Augustine recommends the classical disciplines and goes deeply into the interpretation of figured language—the bulk of book 3 is dedicated to this task—he tells his readers to learn these arts from some other source:

> Lettered men should know, moreover, that all those modes of expression which the grammarians designate with the Greek word *tropes* were used by our authors, and more abundantly and copiously than those who do not know them and have learned about such expressions elsewhere are able to suppose or believe. Those who know these tropes, however, will recognize them in the sacred letters, and this knowledge will be of considerable assistance in understanding them. But it is not proper to teach them to the ignorant here, lest we seem to be teaching the art of grammar. I advise that they be learned elsewhere, although I have already advised the same thing before in the second book where I discussed the necessary knowledge of languages.[4]

This, then, is part of the broader Augustinian vision of instruction in the art of sacred reading: the need for basic instruction in the schemes and tropes—those figures of speech and thought that belong to advanced grammar—and in the arts of dialectic and rhetoric that enable the kind of reading strategies that Augustine expounds in *Christian Instruction*.

Cassiodorus and the Implementation of the Augustinian Vision

Augustine points the way but does not go there; Cassiodorus embraces this as his task. The Psalms are poetry. A fundamental characteristic of poetry across every human language is, among other things, a particularly rich use of ornamented language. If we want to teach ornamented language in Scripture, there is no book better suited to it than the Psalms. The marginal notes literally point the way to an

---

[4] Augustine, *Christian Instruction* 3.29.40 (ChrDoc, pp. 102–3).

education in advanced literacy through the Psalter. What is implicit in them is made explicit a bit later in the preface: chapter 15 of Cassiodorus's preface is the longest of the chapters and sets forth his theory of language and its use in the Psalms. He begins by establishing that the figures of speech and thought are found in the Scriptures and that anything identified by the classical teachers appeared in Scripture first:

> [The divine law] exploits its varieties of language in sundry ways, being clothed in definitions adorned by figures, marked by its special vocabulary, equipped with the conclusions of syllogisms, gleaming with forms of instruction. But it does not appropriate from these a beauty adopted from elsewhere, but rather bestows on them its own high status. . . . Those experienced in the secular arts, clearly living long after the time when the first words of the divine books were penned, transferred these techniques to the collections of arguments which the Greeks call topics, and to the arts of dialectic and rhetoric. So it is crystal clear to all that the minds of the just were endowed to express the truth with the techniques which pagans subsequently decided should be exploited for human wisdom. In the sacred readings they shine like the brightest of stars, aptly clarifying the meanings of passages most usefully and profitably. I shall draw attention to them briefly at the most suitable places, for it will be most convenient to cite the passages in which the expression of the meaning will shine out more clearly.[5]

He defends his decision with an appeal not just to the words of Augustine cited above but also by pointing to the works of Jerome, Ambrose, Hilary, and others, establishing most clearly that he is not the originator of this idea but is only making explicit what other Christian authors have indicated. Against the objections of those who argue that the Scriptures never identify these grammatical and rhetorical devices, he insists that their presence is sufficient to demonstrate the usefulness of their explanation:

> Someone, however, may say: The premises of syllogisms, the names of figures, the terms for the disciplines, and other items

[5] Cassiodorus, *ExplPs* Pref.15, pp. 1.37, 38.

of this kind are not found at all in the psalms. But they are clearly found in force of meaning, not in the utterance of words; in this sense we see wine in vines, a harvest in the seed, foliage in roots, fruits in branches, and trees conceptually in nuts. Moreover, succulent fish though invisible to the human eye before being hooked are caught from the deepest pools. So we rightly proclaim the existence of the techniques which we feel are equally present because of their force. Paul bids us not to be seduced by the empty wisdom of the world, but he does not deny the presence of these techniques in the divine letters. At any rate, let us turn to the psalms, and investigate the reliability of the facts, which is superior to any contention.[6]

At this juncture, Cassiodorus and Benedict reveal themselves to be kindred spirits, but ones who choose to exercise their intellectual gifts in complementary directions. On being confronted with the wholesale paganism of classical education, Benedict turns his back on it in order to create a school for the Lord's service that will form Christians in the deeper arts of embodying the Scriptures in a psalm-soaked life of obedience and humility. Cassiodorus uses his intellectual gifts and training to prepare a purified Christian curriculum for just such an endeavor likewise grounded in the Psalms.

The commentary that Cassiodorus prepares will frequently depart from the text of Augustine for the sake of exploring and explaining the arts of reading that Augustine acknowledges to be essential but does not teach.

Cassiodorus, though, doesn't leave it at that. The Scriptures generally and the Psalms in particular are streams of divine wisdom. Why should they restrict themselves to contain only the essential of some of the learned arts? Surely a divinely inspired source of wisdom would bear within itself subtle clues to the other human arts and sciences as well! Sure enough, Cassiodorus makes clear that the Psalter not only teaches the three fundamental arts of reading—grammar, dialectic, and rhetoric—but also teaches the four arts of mathematics: arithmetic, music, geometry, and astronomy. He concludes his verse-by-verse interpretation of Psalm 150 with a grand statement to this effect:

---

[6] Cassiodorus, *ExplPs* Pref.15, p. 1.38.

Indeed, we have shown that the series of psalms is crammed with points of grammar, etymologies, figures, rhetoric, topics, dialectic, definitions, music, geometry, astronomy, expressions peculiar to divine Scripture, in so far as the Lord has deigned to grant this. Thus those who have already read these features may gladly acknowledge them, and those who are as yet novices may observe them most clearly delineated without coming to grief.[7]

At a handful of points he makes reference to an arithmetic computation or refers to geometry when he is talking about the shape of the earth. He does discuss music quite a bit at the mention of instruments, and the catalogue laid out in the final psalm gives him an opportunity to discuss both the kinds of instruments and the nature of harmony but—truthfully—the mathematical arts receive only the most token glances. Cassiodorus is not trying to, and does not need to, teach them in the same way that he is teaching the arts of reading. His goal is to demonstrate that the seeds of all human arts can be found in the divine wisdom of the Psalter; he accomplishes this to his satisfaction even if he does not go on at length about the mathematical arts.

Notice that the list Cassiodorus rattles off in relation to Psalm 150 is almost exactly the listing of the marginal notes:

Marginal Notes	Psalm 150
Idiomatic expressions	Expressions peculiar to Divine Scripture[8]
Christian doctrines	
Definitions	Definitions
Schemes (figures of speech or thought)	Figures (*schematibus*)
Etymologies	Etymologies

---

[7] Cassiodorus, *ExplPs* 150.6, p. 3.465.

[8] This is the alternate heading in the marginal notes, which reads in full "Here are idioms, that is, expressions peculiar to the divine Laws [*Hoc in idiomatic id est propriis locutionibus legis divine*]." The last four words in Latin are the precise phrase used in Psalm 150 and translated by Walsh above.

Marginal Notes	Psalm 150
Interpretation of names	
Rhetoric	Rhetoric
Topics	Topics
Syllogisms (a term from dialectic)	Dialectic
Arithmetic	
Geometry	Geometry
Music	Music
Astronomy	Astronomy

One of the ironies of intellectual history is that Cassiodorus does not get credit for so much of the effort expended here. Modern scholars of grammar and rhetoric pass off the contribution of Cassiodorus to these arts as negligible—chiefly because they are looking in the wrong place: the *Institutions*. George Kennedy's otherwise insightful history of classical rhetoric is a great example. After summarizing Cassiodorus's drive-by of the arts of grammar, dialectic, and rhetoric in the *Institutions*, he concludes with this comment:

> Although Cassiodorus had earlier mentioned figures of speech as a subject common to grammar and rhetoric, his discussion of rhetoric is chiefly devoted to summaries of stasis theory and rhetorical argumentation. Thus its logical side is emphasized, but nothing is done to illustrate how this knowledge can be applied to the study of the Scriptures or the teaching of Christianity.[9]

This notion is thoroughly contradicted by "Appendix D: Figures of Speech and Thought" in the first volume of Walsh's translation of Cassiodorus's Psalms commentary, where scores of occurrences of 108 different figures are listed across four pages. In each of these cases,

---

[9] George A. Kennedy, *Classical Rhetoric and Its Christian and Secular Tradition from Ancient to Modern Times*, 2nd rev. ed. (Chapel Hill: University of North Carolina Press, 1999), 201.

Cassiodorus identifies a figure in the text of the psalm, provides the name of the figure, and explains how it functions.

Conclusion

Thus, Cassiodorus leverages the Psalms as the perfect basis from which to teach the seven liberal arts of the classical curriculum. In doing so, he makes a clear departure from the Psalm commentary of Augustine, who never could have explored this territory in sermons preached from the pulpit. Cassiodorus, however, is enacting a necessary but unfulfilled portion of the Augustinian interpretive vision by presenting a thoroughly Christian program of instruction through the Psalms. The marginal notes are, further, an ingenious method for creating a program of self-study: a book that can visually instruct a student if there is no competent teacher on hand.

Introducing the Commentary

After the section introducing the marginal notes the preface proper begins. Cassiodorus gives a basic introduction to why he wrote the commentary and what we should expect to see within it. He tells us of his initial puzzlement over the Psalms in Ravenna, his relief at finding answers in Augustine's work, and his desire to create something a bit more manageable. He celebrates the Psalms with elaborate language, including the epigram that inspired the title of this book, "Honey of Souls." Quoting Athanasius, he describes the Psalter as the enclosed garden that bears all the different fruits of Scripture.

The most important focus in the central part of the introduction, though, is on the Psalms as the sung praises of God. This is very significant. Here, at the beginning of his work, he explicitly describes the psalms as the central experience of monastic liturgical prayer:

> Finally, the psalms make our vigils [Vigils/The Night Office] pleasant when in the silence of the night the choirs hymn their praise. The human voice bursts into melody, and with words skilfully set to music it leads us back to Him from whom divine eloquence has come for the salvation of the human race. The united voices of the singers become a song which delights ears and instructs souls. In company with the divine angels whom we cannot hear,

we mingle words of praise through Him who came from the seed of David, the Lord Christ. As He Himself says in the Apocalypse: *I am the root and source of David*. From Him we have both obtained our saving religion and have come to know the revealed mysteries of the holy Trinity. So the psalms rightly unite the undivided glory of Father, Son, and Holy Spirit, so that their praise is proved to be perfect. They beguile the approaching day with early-morning joy [Matins],[10] they dedicate for us the first hour of the day [Prime], they consecrate for us the third hour [Terce], they make joyful the sixth hour [Sext] with the breaking of bread, they end fasting at the ninth [Nones], they bring to a close the last hours of the day [Vespers], they ensure that at the onset of night [Compline] our minds are not darkened. In their own words, *The night is a light in my pleasures, since the darkness will not be your doing, O Lord*. So if a person does not enjoy the sweetness of this gift, he is right to believe that he is a stranger to true life.[11]

Cassiodorus clearly identifies the eight prayer offices that defined monastic life by name, making his intentions quite obvious. This is a commentary on the praises sung every day, week in, week out, year after circling year by a community of monks. The psalms are the heart of the Daily Office, the liturgical round, and Cassiodorus intends his work for this purpose and setting. As we will see when we dig into specific psalms, the liturgical environment of the Mass and Office is never far from his mind—but he (and those to whom he writes) is so saturated within this environment that he rarely bothers to call it to mind. He expects his readers to pick up these references easily and naturally, making it that much harder for those of us who do not live within these cycles of prayer.

Given the massive number of times that terms like "sing," "praise," "exult," and the like appear in the psalms, liturgical praise of the divine is never far from mind. Cassiodorus will frequently use these triggering words as occasions to refer to the church or people within the church

---

[10] In common with the other sixth-century Italian monastic materials, the Rule of the Master and the Rule of Benedict, Cassiodorus uses the term Vigils (*vigilias*) for the long Night Office and then Matins (*matutina*) rather than the alternative Lauds for the same early morning Office.

[11] Cassiodorus, *ExplPs* Pref.Intro, pp. 1.24–25.

singing the Lord's praises, also holding before his readers the psalms as liturgical prayers past, present, and future.

It's worth noting in connection with this point that Cassiodorus sometimes includes short citations from the church fathers to explicate some point or other; among these, Cassiodorus quotes five times from the Office hymns attributed to Saint Ambrose, usually mentioning its liturgical use by season or office when citing it.

The Prefatory Chapters

Cassiodorus closes out the introduction by dedicating it to an unnamed "apostolic father," who is Pope Vigilius, and providing a list of seventeen chapters that will provide the bulk of the preface:

- Chapter 1: Prophecy
- Chapter 2: Why do we find various names of apparent authors in the Psalm-headings
- Chapter 3: The meaning of "unto the end" which often appears in headings
- Chapter 4: What a psalterium is, or why psalms are so-called
- Chapter 5: What a psalm is
- Chapter 6: What a canticle is
- Chapter 7: What a psalm-canticle is
- Chapter 8: What a canticle-psalm is
- Chapter 9: The fivefold division [of these title terms]
- Chapter 10: A general consideration on the inscribed psalm headings
- Chapter 11: What a diapsalm is
- Chapter 12: Should the text of the psalms be divided into five books or one book
- Chapter 13: How we are to regard the Lord Christ in the Psalms
- Chapter 14: How this commentary on the Psalms is divided
- Chapter 15: The eloquence of the entire divine law
- Chapter 16: The particular eloquence of the Psalter
- Chapter 17: Praise of the Church

The ordering of these chapters is a bit odd. Generally speaking, he is literally starting from the top (of a psalm) and spends the first ten chapters on things that appear in psalm headings or how the psalm headings are to be understood. Then he moves into general material, seemingly taking up more big-picture items in the block from chapters 14 to 16. Another organizational factor at play is the way that he distributes chapters around the three chief speakers of the Psalms: the first two chapters cover David and his prophetic role, then Christ appears toward the middle in chapter 13, and the chapters conclude with a rousing praise of the church in chapter 17.

Although it will not completely solve the riddle or answer all of the questions about structure, the chapters that Cassiodorus chooses to include and how they relate to one another will become more clear once we consider their inspiration, the *Tractates on the Psalms* of Hilary of Poitiers.

A Brief Introduction to Hilary

We don't know much about Hilary of Poitiers; probably born in Gaul around 310 or so, he was a pagan who received a good education and converted to Christianity as an adult along with his wife and daughter. Around 350, he was unanimously elected bishop of Poitiers, a city in western France, and consecrated. Most of his career was embroiled in controversy with the Arians. In 356, he was exiled to Phrygia in modern Turkey; it's not entirely sure what prompted this, but his stay in the East was worthwhile. He continued to administer his diocese and to write, penning polemical works against the Arians, but he also discovered the biblical interpretation of Origen. Jerome writes that, in addition to some histories and letters to emperors, he:

> composed twelve books *Against the Arians* and another book *On Councils* written to the Gallican bishops, and *Commentaries on the Psalms* that is on the first and second, from the fifty-first to the sixty-second, and from the one hundred and eighteenth to the end of the book. In this work he imitated Origen, but added also some original matter. . . . Also a book of *Hymns* [and *On the Mysteries*], a commentary *On Matthew* and treatises *On Job*, which he translated freely from the Greek of Origen, and another elegant little work *Against Auxentius* and *Epistles* to different persons. They say he has written *On the Song of Songs* but this work is not known to us.[12]

---

[12] Jerome, *On Illustrious Men* 100 (NPNF[2] 3:380). Amended. The NPNF translation elides the *Book of Hymns* and the separate work, *On the Mysteries*.

Sometimes Jerome's record refers to books that no longer survive; we know we have gaps because of works he has described but that no longer exist. In an odd reversal of the usual pattern, we have more of Hilary's Psalms commentary than Jerome records. In addition to the ones listed here, we also have commentary from Hilary on Psalms 9, 13, 14, 63–69, and 91, and there are signs that there were more that didn't survive—or maybe are waiting to be found.[13]

On the Mysteries is not about the Psalms per se but has bearing on them as what survives of it deals with the Christian interpretation of the Old Testament. What Hilary writes here is strongly reflected in his Psalms commentary:

> [A]ll of Scripture declares the Incarnation of Christ whether in deeds or in words. . . . Christ is prefigured in the sleep of Adam, the flood of Noah, the blessing of Melchizedek, the justification of Abraham, the birth of Isaac, and the servitude of Jacob. The events recounted are real ones, but God works through man so that the human actions are imitations of the divine plan, in the sense that those events were especially willed by God to prefigure and symbolize the future reality of the Incarnation.[14]

Writing around the time Augustine was born, Hilary manifests one of the fundamental principles of the patristic reading of the Old Testament: Jesus is the key that unlocks the meaning of the Scriptures. This is also something he addresses in his work on the Psalms.

Hilary's Introduction to His Tractates on the Psalms

Hilary's *Tractates on the Psalms* opens with an introduction made up of twenty-four chapters on a variety of topics. It's worth taking a look at these for a couple of reasons. First, this is—to the best of our knowledge—the first time a Latin-speaking author has laid out a comprehensive approach to the interpretation of the Psalms. In comparing what Hilary writes here with what history has ascribed to Origen, it seems quite likely that Hilary's work is more or less an adaptation of Origen's work on the Psalms and some of his more general interpretive

---

[13] Johannes Quasten, *Patrology*, 4 vols., trans. Placid Solari (Notre Dame, IN: Christian Classics, 1986), 4:50.

[14] Quasten, *Patrology*, 4:52.

ideas compiled from the *Philocalia*, a guide to Origen's teaching extracted from his writings by two of his best students, Basil of Caesarea and Gregory Nazianzen. Thus, even though most of this material does not consist of new ideas or information, Hilary is the first to collect it or translate it from Origen's Greek.[15] Second, as the first guide to reading the Psalms and the material at the heading of a substantial set of tractates, it was widely read and accepted by authors like Augustine and Jerome and therefore influential. Third, Cassiodorus starts his commentary with a set of seventeen chapters that address introductory topics on the Psalms. Some of these are taken over directly from Hilary; others address the same topics but come to very different conclusions. Thus, because this introduction literally introduces a comprehensive theory of reading the Psalms to the Latin West and was an important conversation partner for our author, we'll run through them.

The first chapter in Hilary's introduction tackles the question of whether the Psalms should be referred to as one book or five books; he notes that Jewish sources divide it into five sections at the points where psalms end with *fiat, fiat* ("Amen, Amen").[16] Next, three chapters take up the topic of authorship, which Hilary resolves by a direct appeal to the text: the psalms were written by whoever is indicated in the title. Following Origen, but in contrast to most other early interpreters, Hilary rejects Davidic authorship of the whole Psalter and has no qualms about multiple authors. The next three chapters establish a christological reading of the Psalms, clarifying that the Psalms are fundamentally about Christ but are intentionally veiled. How and why he handles this is important, and we'll come back to these.

The next six chapters of Hilary's introduction begin with the editing of the psalms but move into numerological mysteries connected with the editing and arrangement of the psalms. Thus, Hilary starts with the idea that Ezra, the scribe who reconstituted the Law after the Babylonian exile and who has a book of the Bible named after him, is the editor

---

[15] There is a Latin commentary in PL 21 tentatively attributed to Rufinus that covers the first seventy-five psalms; the introduction looks very similar to Hilary's. It may be a Latin translation of Origen or an amalgam of materials that is already borrowing from Hilary. If the work is by Rufinus, Hilary's work would have predated it by about two decades. If it is not by him, there is no telling when it may have been done.

[16] Most English study Bibles indicate these divisions.

who collected the scattered psalms and formed them into a single book. The ordering does not, however, reflect a temporal sequence, but the psalms are grouped by topics and mystical meanings. This leads into the numerological significance of the number fifty and why it is significant that there are three sets of fifty psalms. This road continues for a while with discussions of the subtle meanings of the numbers seven and eight.

Numerology leads down an odd path for the next three chapters. Our Psalm 119 was reckoned in their count as Psalm 118; Hilary uses the presence of the number eight—about which he had been speaking—to delve into his Psalm 118 which is divided into twenty-two sections of eight verses each; that's because this psalm is a giant acrostic: the first letter of each section of eight starts with the same letter of the Hebrew alphabet. Thus, the first eight verses start with the first letter *aleph*, then the next eight verses all start with the second letter *beth*, and so on. Hilary explains what an acrostic is and that there are twenty-two Hebrew letters, and then he states that there are twenty-two books in the Hebrew Scriptures that correspond numerically to the alphabet. Then, following that massive psalm are the Songs of Ascent, a grouping of fifteen psalms that Hilary uses the previous numerology to identify as inclusive of the mysteries of the numbers seven and eight. Not only that, fifteen was the number of the steps into the holy of holies in the temple, indicating that these Songs of Ascent taken as a group had a mystical shape and purpose regarding the soul's ascent into the holy of holies and the presence of God.

The next six chapters drop the topic of numerology and move to the superscriptions or titles that stand at the head of the psalms. He gives particular attention to five items that appear regularly: the phrase *In finem* ("to the end") and what he identifies as the four kinds of music (psalm, canticle, canticle-psalm, and psalm-canticle). All of these are clues to the mystical meanings contained in the psalm that follows. After that, a single chapter explains the "diapsalm," which appears in most English translations as the Hebrew word "Selah." These indicate a change of some sort—either in the person speaking, the topic, or the music of the psalm. A single final chapter leaves us with an image directly from Origen—it's such a memorable one that Jerome will also borrow it to begin his sermon on Psalm 1.[17] The Psalms are like a great

---

[17] See Jerome, *The Homilies of Saint Jerome*, vol. 1, trans. Marie Ligouri Ewald, FOTC 48 (Washington, DC: The Catholic University of America Press, 1964), 3.

166   *The Honey of Souls*

and beautiful city filled with many different buildings. Not only does the city need a key to unlock it, but each building requires its own key also which must be sought through careful research and consideration.

Let's pause for a moment and pull out three essential aspects of Hilary's introduction: that Christ is the true meaning of the Psalms, that the true meaning of the text is deliberately veiled and hidden, that the study of the Psalms is the investigation of a deep and wonderful mystery that will be challenging and frustrating but ultimately beautiful. The first and second are interconnected and lead to the third.

First, that Christ stands at the center of the psalm is a fundamental conviction that Hilary receives from Origen. The three christological chapters of the introduction (chaps. 5–7) insist that all of the events surrounding the begetting, life, death, and resurrection of Christ are foretold in the psalms. A chapter titled "The Psalms Sing the History of the Gospel; Prophecies of Christ Are Shut Up and Sealed from the Ignorant" begins with a direct statement to this effect:

> There is no doubt that what is said in the Psalms ought to be understood according to the Gospel proclamation. From whatever person the Spirit has spoken prophecies, still all of it refers to the knowledge of the coming of our Lord Jesus Christ, and his Incarnation, and his passion, and his reign, and to the glory and power of our resurrection.[18]

Likewise, the next chapter appeals to the book of Revelation and the vision of the book sealed with seven seals. Hilary understands these seven to signify "his Incarnation, and passion, and death, and resurrection, and glorification, and reign, and judgement."[19]

The third and last chapter of this section does something a bit different; instead of insisting on Christ as the content of the Psalms, it considers the relationship between Christ, his Body (the church), and the production of sound and therefore the spiritual content of the Psalter. Hilary draws a visual comparison between a psaltery—the instrument from which the psalms derive their name—and the Body of Christ. Hilary informs us that a psaltery, when played, produces sound from the top part. This shape is analogous to the Body of Christ. Christ

---

[18] Hilary, *Tractates* Prol.5, PL 9 col 235a.
[19] Hilary, *Tractates* Prol.6, PL 9 col 236b.

as the head, the top part, the section nearest the heavens, sounds out his truth to the earth. Thus, the whole body of Christ is involved in the process of producing the sound, but it properly proceeds from Christ at the top.

The second essential theme of the introduction lies in how and why prophecies regarding Christ have been hidden with the Psalms. In the first chapter, immediately after the assertion I quoted above about everything referring to Christ, Hilary goes on to say, "However, all prophecies are shut up and sealed from worldly perceptions and the wisdom of the age."[20]

This is a reading that comes straight out of Origen. That is, the truth of Christ is taught throughout the Old Testament and especially within the Psalms. However, these truths have been hidden from those who do not know that secret.

Likewise, in the next chapter, Hilary appeals to the vision of the sealed book in Revelation, saying that it contains all of the prophetic truths about the past and the future but is sealed and cannot be opened except by a single figure. Explicitly quoting Revelation 3:7, he identifies it as Christ who says to the church at Philadelphia: "These are the words of the holy one, the true one, who has the key of David, who opens and no one will shut, who shuts and no one opens." Christ alone opens the seals (which are the mysteries about himself), revealing the truths of all past, present, and future prophetic mysteries.

For Hilary and Origen, from whom he learns this method of reading, difficulty and obscurity on the part of the text is not a bug. It's a feature; it was designed to be that way. Origen's religious world was one marked by two aspects: first, initiations into secrets and mysteries were expected when dealing with cosmic and divine truth; second, it also comes out of an experience of persecution. Remember, Eusebius informs us that Origen's father died under the headsman's axe for his faith, and the only reason Origen did not die alongside him is because his mother hid his clothes to prevent him from going out of the house![21]

In Origen's Alexandria, catechumens—those who came seeking baptism—had to receive instruction in order to understand the faith

---

[20] Hilary, *Tractates* Prol.5, PL 9 col 235a.
[21] Eusebius, *Ecclesiastical History* 6.1 (Williamson, 180).

they would be baptized into. Likewise, the unbaptized were only allowed at the church services for certain parts. Only the initiated—the baptized—could be present for the recitation of the creeds and the celebration of the Eucharist. The modern Christian idea of drawing new followers is that the Good News of the Gospel is told abroad, hoping to attract those who are interested by the message. Origen explicitly rejects this as being proven not to work. Instead, he recommends, following standard practice for many of the religions of his day, that the secrets ought to be hidden so the mystery itself will draw adherents who are looking for holy truth. If it is broadcast widely, they won't really learn it, or learn it deeply, because they assume they already know it from the parts that they have heard publicly.

Obscurities in the text were useful because, on the one hand, it concealed the divine secrets until readers had been properly initiated and, on the other hand, persecuting authorities would not understand the full meaning of the text. Hilary, as a former initiate in the mysteries of Neoplatonism—which was as much a religion as a philosophy in those days—would have (and clearly did) find this a compelling position. He speaks of all of these mysteries of Christ being hidden under "allegories and types [*allegoricis et typicis*]."[22]

All of this talk of mysteries, of hidden meanings, of numerological secrets, of a great and beautiful city evoking images of the city built of flashing jewels described in Isaiah 54 and Revelation 21 invites the reader into adventure of the spirit. Promising that each psalm may be unlocked only through patient research, but that doing so will yield the secrets of salvation, creates a sense of anticipation and excitement. The psalms are not just obscure poems that talk about things that don't seem to have much relevance; they are a playground of hidden meanings and secrets waiting to be uncovered. Like some visually luscious seek-and-find game on an iPhone to be taken out and played at will, the psalms invite exploration and just need us to notice a line or angle that seems out of place or a shape that doesn't quite blend with its environment or an image that doesn't quite fit to open into a mystical signification of something greater and deeper.

---

[22] Hilary, *Tractates* Prol.5, PL 9 col 235b.

How Cassiodorus Uses Hilary

Cassiodorus takes up Hilary's introductory chapters. Some he borrows whole cloth, others he discards, and in others he borrows the topic or concept but replaces it with different material more congenial to his Augustinian reading. Cassiodorus's first two chapters take up authorship, the first describing the phenomenon of prophecy and the second focusing on David and the many names in the psalm titles. He comes down on the opposite side of the question from Origen and Hilary: for Cassiodorus, all of the psalms were written by David; the other names indicate what people or groups were expected to sing them in the temple.

Next, he appears to jump to the end of Hilary's chapters. Having introduced the superscriptions through the discussion of authorship, he runs with that topic with eight chapters on the titles of the Psalms. Here, Cassiodorus shows clear influence from Hilary but not textual dependence. That is, he's borrowing the order of topics and thoughts from Hilary (Cassiodorus also starts with *in fine* and then discusses the four musical titles), but he doesn't normally borrow his vocabulary or expressions, even when he is saying the same thing. He too takes the same description of the Psaltery and its spiritual meaning from Hilary's chapter on christological reading and inserts it in this section on the titles, but he doesn't attribute it to Hilary. Rather, he beefs it up with additional description from Jerome (who himself seems to be working from Hilary here) and attributes the later father instead. After discussing the titles, Cassiodorus takes up the diapsalm and comes to the same conclusion as Hilary—although he bases his decision on appeals to Jerome and Augustine.

Then, Cassiodorus jumps back to the beginning of Hilary's introduction. He had been distracted by the topic of psalm titles but now returns to the question of how many books the Psalms contains: one or five? He agrees with Hilary and, after noting Jerome's evidence of five books from the Hebrew, goes with the answer of one. Then, following Hilary's order, he discusses how Christ should be considered within the Psalms. The way he answers the question, though, is very different from the way Hilary does. While he is going to read the Psalms in the way Hilary will, he gives a three-point answer: the Psalms speak with reference to the humanity of Jesus and recount what happened to him during the incarnation, they reveal him to be coequal and coeternal with the Father, and they describe him in connection to the limbs of the church. (That is, if there ever seems to be a place where Christ refers to his own sins, rest assured that he is speaking of the sins of the church as he has no sins to recall.) Whereas Hilary's section on Christ was primarily about interpretation, Cassiodorus's is primarily about Christology.

While Hilary then goes on to talk about the editing of the Psalms and the numerology of their overall composition, Cassiodorus heads on a different tack. He talks about how his own commentary will work and the approach he has chosen to use. This leads into two chapters on eloquence, the first on the eloquence of the Scriptures in general, then a follow-up on the Psalms themselves. Finally, Cassiodorus ends with a chapter praising the church, which has no analogue in Hilary's introduction.

Clearly, then, Hilary's introduction to his commentary is a major influence on Cassiodorus, both in terms of its content and its structure. The interpretive techniques that Hilary lays out are adopted and adapted by both Augustine and Cassiodorus; the structure becomes a conversation partner that Cassiodorus uses to construct his own but with whom he can argue and disagree. It is odd, though, that Hilary's name is never mentioned in Cassiodorus's introduction. Both Augustine and Jerome appear, sometimes in places where the thoughts being primarily borrowed belong to Hilary. This seems particularly unusual since it is evident that Cassiodorus had nothing against Hilary and, indeed, admired him; one of the churches connected to the Vivarium was consecrated in the name of Saint Hilary.

The Question of Overall Structure

There is one more takeaway that Cassiodorus gleaned from Hilary's introductory chapters. When it came to dividing his work into multiple volumes, it's my belief that Cassiodorus borrowed a rationale for the division from Hilary's introduction, not once, but twice.

In the form that we have received it, Cassiodorus's *Explanation of the Psalms* is a three-volume collection. He directs future scribes as such in the introduction: "I have divided this book into three sections, each containing fifty psalms preceded by introductions. By this means the clarity of the script will appear clearer to older eyes, and the division of the book's content can meet the needs of the brothers at their reading."[23] Most of the surviving manuscript sets follow this directive.[24] Based on the length of the book, three volumes is the logical division. Furthermore, this division mirrors Hilary's comments in the eleventh chapter of his introduction where he discusses the 150 psalms as composed of three sets of fifty: The first set of fifty represents the instruction that leads to salvation; the second set, the new life of grace after penitence (remember that in their numbering system the first set ends with our Psalm 51, the preeminent penitential psalm); the third set of fifty, the consummation of glory in the new Jerusalem.

However, there are a few suggestions that this division was not Cassiodorus's original intention. On one hand, he promises introductions to each volume, but there are none. Psalm 51 ends and Psalm 52 begins; Psalm 101 ends and Psalm 102 begins.[25] On the other hand, there are several references throughout the work that refer to a scheme that splits the Psalter in two, one section containing seventy psalms and the other eighty. In the discussion of the Songs of Ascent, the fifteen Gradual Psalms that span from Psalm 120 to 135, Hilary describes the number fifteen as being made up from seven and eight: since seven represents the Sabbath, the first seven psalms represent the Old Testament; since eight represents Sunday, the day of resurrection, the following set of eight psalms represent the New Testament.

Cassiodorus's interpretation of Psalm 71 (his Psalm 70) ends with the usual summary of the psalm, but then the conclusion switches topics:

> Our fathers believed that the aggregate of the psalms was to be apportioned between the mysteries of the Old and New Testaments. They allotted seven decades to the sabbath, which undoubtedly belongs to the prior mode of worship, and eight decades to our period, for we revere the Lord's Resurrection every week on the eighth day. Thus by this double reckoning the sacred total of the psalms is seen to contain both Old and New Testaments; for what

---

[23] Cassiodorus, *ExplPs* Intro.Pref, p. 1.24.
[24] The exception is a manuscript tradition that puts it all into a single volume!
[25] Remember, due to the difference in numbering between the Vulgate and the modern Hebrew-based numbering system, the numbers the medieval were working from is usually off by one from ours.

can count as one hundred and fifty individually can indicate fifteen decades if considered in groups of ten. So this total of psalms is appropriately adapted to the New and Old Testaments.[26]

This is the logic that we saw Hilary apply to the Songs of Ascent. It's not one, though, that he applied to the whole Psalter. It's unclear who these other fathers that Cassiodorus is referring to might be.

After discussing this point and the contents of the two sets of psalms, Cassiodorus writes: "So let us draw this present volume [*praesenti operi*] to a close [*terminum*], that this brief respite may rekindle the reader's enthusiasm, and the ensuing separate section of psalms on the significance of the New Testament may be fittingly commenced. Amen."[27] This looks very much like the ending of a volume, and before the next psalm gets underway there is another statement to the effect that the reader has finished the seven decades of psalms pertaining to the Old Testament and is now entering the eight decades that pertain to the New Testament. It is an introduction to a second volume.

In addition to the presence of this conclusion and reintroduction between Psalms 70 and 71, Cassiodorus makes reference to this means of dividing the psalms in two other places, once in the midst of the Songs of Ascent, the other at the end of his work.

His summary of Psalm 126 ties together several threads. First, this psalm is the seventh of the Songs of Ascent; as Hilary indicated in his preface, numerologically this psalm closes out a Sabbath count of psalms that prefigure the Old Testament. Cassiodorus will mention this but will also draw attention to the name that appears in the superscription of the next psalm, Solomon. The only other time that Solomon appears in a title in the Latin Psalter is in its Psalm 71 (our Psalm 72), where it opens the group of eight decades:

> How splendidly has this seventh consecutive step prophesied to us the Lord's first coming as a prefiguration in the Old Testament! It has foretold the joy of salvation to be bestowed on the people, so that the group of eight would be left which we have earlier said relates to the Lord's resurrection. The next heading reveals this dichotomy, for its formulation is "Canticle of the steps of Solomon."

---

[26] Cassiodorus, *ExplPs* 71.conc, p. 2.179.
[27] Ibid.

> Solomon means "man of peace," a term especially relevant to the Lord Christ, who reconciled the world to God, and who said: My peace I give to you, my peace I leave to you. In short, the psalm is shown to reveal not a future prophecy but the very fruit of the womb; so it may be clear beyond doubt to all that indications of the New and Old Testaments, designated by the decades of the whole work, are contained in Psalm 71, and that here the same indications are revealed by the individual psalm-numbers.[28]

Just as the reader has arrived at this pivot point between the Old and New Testaments as interpreted by Hilary, so Cassiodorus reminds his readers that their Psalm 71 serves the same function for the Psalter as a whole.

In the final wrap-up of the final psalm, Psalm 150, we also find another reference to this twofold scheme:

> However, so far as human intelligence could trace it, the entire series of psalms has been surveyed in its twofold mystery. First, as has been said on the authority of the Fathers, it embraces the mysteries of the Old and New Testaments, for seven decades are relevant to the sabbath, which undoubtedly is connected with the earlier form of religious worship; and then eight decades are ascribed to our own time, for with sacred devotion we revere the Lord's resurrection on the eighth day.[29]

The text does not say that the scheme of seven and eight decades is used to structure the work as a whole, but—again—the significance is implied and such references may have been edited out in Cassiodorus's successive revisions of the work.

Thus, the evidence suggests that Cassiodorus had originally envisioned a two-volume work on the Psalms, divided according to Hilary's reckoning. When he discovered that his text went beyond what was manageable in two volumes, he adopted a threefold scheme, also inspired by Hilary's preface.

---

[28] Cassiodorus, *ExplPs* 126.concl, pp. 3.295–96.
[29] Cassiodorus, *ExplPs* 150.concl, p. 3.466.

Listening for Voices

Aside from the introduction, Hilary's tractates provided one more essential part of the interpretive tradition that would shape the reading of the Psalms in the Latin West and that we see represented in Cassiodorus's prefatory chapters. Hilary's tractate on Psalm 1 opens with a methodological statement (borrowed from Origen);[30] the voices of the speakers must be properly distinguished in order to hear the psalms properly:

> The primary condition of knowledge for reading the Psalms is the ability to see as whose mouthpiece we are to regard the Psalmist as speaking, and who it is that he addresses. For they are not all of the same uniform character, but of different authorship and different types.[31]

Hilary asserts that "we constantly find that the Person of God the Father is being set before us"[32] but also acknowledges "in what we might call the majority of Psalms the Person of the Son is introduced."[33] In the case of Psalm 1, though, Hilary (and likely Origen before him) contends that the pronouns and the use of "Lord" do not make it likely for either God the Father or God the Son to be the speaker and concludes that it should be understood as coming from the psalmist himself: "Here, then, we are to recognise the person of the Prophet by whose lips the Holy Spirit speaks, raising us by the instrumentality of his lips to the knowledge of a spiritual mystery."[34] This gives us the foundations of a reading strategy. The Psalms ought to be read as a classical reader would read an oration or a drama and decide from careful attention to verb endings and pronouns who is speaking to whom.

Both Augustine and Cassiodorus adopt this strategy, and it becomes an important part of situating the interpretation of each psalm: Who

---

[30] Origen also discusses this principle in relation to Psalm 1. See Origen, *Philocalia* 7.1-2.
[31] Hilary, *Tractates* 1, NPNF² 9a.236.
[32] Ibid.
[33] Ibid.
[34] Ibid.

speaks? Are there any changes of speakers? As Hilary noted in his introduction, the diapsalm frequently marks a shift of some sort within the body of a psalm and may, in fact, alert the careful reader to a shift between different speakers. Cassiodorus picks up this same interpretation of the diapsalm in his own prefatory remarks and employs it throughout his commentary.

Conclusion

The prefatory chapters represent Cassiodorus's clearest indications of how he intends to treat the Psalms. He sends several important signals here that will be put into practice throughout the commentary. He clarifies his position that the classical liberal arts are implanted within Scripture and that proper interpretation can not only uncover them but also turn them to their properly divine purposes. He establishes how he will read and break down each psalm, using the fourfold scheme that we observed with Psalm 18: interpreting the heading; dividing the psalm into speakers and topics, more often than not using the diapsalm; providing line-by-line analysis; and offering a final conclusion. In support of this process, several chapters preemptively discuss the most commonly encountered terms in the psalm titles, while another four introduce the three central speakers: David the prophet, Jesus Christ the God-Man, and his bride the church.

Gathering Psalms

The final piece of the preface that appears after chapter 17 has concluded is a section titled the Prolegomena in some manuscripts. This add-on section discusses an ordering of the psalms by means of grouping them. This is an idea that Cassiodorus has borrowed from Athanasius. In the *Letter to Marcellinus*, which I introduced back in chapter 1, Athanasius identifies thematic patterns within the Psalter. That is, he will identify groups of psalms that have related themes or content. Sometimes he will identify psalms as belonging to a group on the strength of a single verse; these aren't collected together in any way but are mentioned throughout the rather loose structure of the letter. Here's a chart that shows the psalms that he groups together:

Psalms about Creation	19, 24
Exodus from Egypt	87, 105, 106, 114
Return from Exile in Babylon	122, 126
The Coming of Christ	33(:6), 45, 50(:3), 87, 107, 110, 118(:26-27)
The Sufferings of Christ	2, 22, 69, 72, 88(:7), 138(:8)
The Ascension of Christ	24, 47
The Judgment of Christ	9(:7), 50(:7), 72, 82, 110
Expressions of Faith and Prayer	11, 12
Praise in the Midst of Persecution	54, 56, 57, 142
Narrative on the Spiritual Life	73, 78, 114, 115
Exhortations to the Spiritual Life	32, 97, 103
Prayers to God	6, 16, 54, 102
Thanksgiving and Praise	8, 98, 117, 125
Declare Blessing	1, 32, 41, 112, 119, 128
Thanks at Affliction's End	4, 75, 116
Against Enemies	17, 86, 88, 140
For Vindication	26, 35, 43
Self-Dedication	30, 127
Goodness of God/ Ungratefulness of Humanity	44, 78, 89, 105, 106, 107, 114, 115
For Testifying about God	9, 71, 75, 92, 105–8, 111, 118, 126, 136, 138
How to Praise God Rightly	105, 107, 113, 117, 135, 146–50
Prayer and Supplication	5, 141–43, 146

Just as different levels of interpretation could be applied to verses of the biblical text, so too several of these groupings operate at different levels of meaning. Hence, a psalm like 105 can appear on this list several times—as a historical psalm, as a psalm testifying to the goodness of God and the ungratefulness of humanity, and as a psalm of praise to God. Its presence in multiple groups is in no way contradictory, because none of these groups require exclusive groupings.

No other Latin patristic commentary groups psalms in this fashion. Cassiodorus is the first to imitate this practice, but he does not use the same categories that Athanasius does; Cassiodorus borrows the idea but uses his own themes. He performs this grouping in two ways. First, they are laid out explicitly in the Prolegomena. In this section he provides a list of twelve groups of psalms. He appears to be moving in canonical order—just as Athanasius had—but his references to the various groups are unclear; he doesn't refer to the psalms by number but in loose generalizations. Some can be clearly identified; others cannot:

> Before tasting the honey of the heavenly psalter and before setting foot with God's help on those fields so famed of the most glorious passion, there are certain preliminaries or introductory headings which seem to me to fall into separate sections, and to inform us about the framework of the actual poems. So I can instruct the reader more clearly and hasten through the poems without coming to grief.
>
> In the first category the bodily life of the Lord is described.
>
> In the second, the nature of the Godhead Himself is subtly indicated.
>
> The third enumerates the manifold people who strove to destroy him.
>
> The fourth continues with the same warning, prophetically urging the Jews to cease to plan and commit evil, since they know that they must be destroyed by the power of God.
>
> In the fifth, the Lord Christ cries to the Father that His prayers be heard, and that through His resurrection the Father may grant future benefit to the world.
>
> Sixth come the words of the penitent throughout a whole Psalm, to which are appended another six of the same type, these being described at the end of Psalm 51. [These are the seven Penitential Psalms: 6, 32, 37, 51, 102, 130, 143.]
>
> In the seventh, Christ humbly asks to be helped by the Father. He is confident enough to hold a direct conversation more appropriate to His divinity, but after the fashion of the humanity which

He has assumed He asks for help that the devil may not plunder His soul through his wicked presumption, and that His glory may not be dragged in the dust and annihilated.

In the eighth, parables and figurative allusions are gathered, and the ensuing action is completed with everything referring to the Lord Christ by allegorical comparison. I mention those figures at the most suitable places, and draw the clearest attention to them so that all ambiguity is removed for the studious reader.

The ninth has diverse praises beginning with His divinity or His humanity, and then there is a change of speakers and headings with the word *Alleluia*, which means "Praise the Lord." [In the Vulgate, Pss 104–6 and Pss 110–19 begin with "Alleluia."]

Tenth come the psalms of the steps, which lead our minds through chaste and humble satisfaction to the Lord Saviour. [These are the Gradual Psalms, Pss 120–34.]

In the eleventh, they once again with verbal variation hymn together the Lord's praises with joyful song. This section proclaims the majesty now of the Father, now of the Son, now of the holy Spirit, so that no-one is in doubt that the holy Trinity is uniquely omnipotent in all that It wishes to perform in heaven and on earth. [Based on the groups before and after, would these be Pss 135–43?]

The seven remaining psalms form the twelfth group. They celebrate with devotion of heart the entire glory of the holy Trinity in general, with joy in song. [These appear to be Pss 144–50.] So the text of the whole psalter is divided into twelve parts, the number of the apostles, and it comes to a close with wondrous praise in achieving what we know God's followers achieved.[35]

The more the groupings move toward the conclusion of the list, the more they seem to identify sequential sections rather than disparate psalms pulled together based on common themes.

Cassiodorus will also create groups that he mentions within the commentary itself, tucking references to these groupings into his conclusions to the various psalms. These are the groups that he identifies:

---

[35] Cassiodorus, *ExplPs* Pref.Prol, pp. 1.43-44.

Psalms that briefly touch on the Passion and Resurrection	3, 16, 28
Pointing through the deeds of David to the future mysteries of Christ	7, 27, 34, 144
Psalms of the Passion	22, 35, 55, 69, 109
Psalms on the 2 natures of Christ	2, 8, 21, 72, 82, 108, 110, 139
Incomplete Acrostics	25, 34, 37, 145
Complete Acrostics	111, 112, 119
Psalms that prophesy concerning the first and second comings of Christ	50, 96, 98
Psalms on the coming of the Antichrist	9, 52
Psalms announcing the chastening and conversion of the Jews[36]	14, 53, 58
Psalms that instruct the faithful	1, 15
Psalm of lamentation for the temple	74, 79, 137
Psalms designated as prayers	17, 86, 90, 102
Penitential Psalms	6, 32, 38, 51, 102, 130, 143
Psalms relating miracles that announce sacraments	78, 105

While there is a similarity between some of the categories that Cassiodorus lists and those used by Athanasius, there does not seem to be much direct borrowing going on. The two groups that will be the most important for the piety of the later church are the Penitential Psalms and the Psalms of the Passion. Cassiodorus is the first source to identify a discrete body of psalms for each.

These groups are important for Cassiodorus because of the way that they provide interpretive contexts for one another. That is, Cassiodorus

---

[36] Cassiodorus's attitude toward the Jewish community will be addressed more fully in chapter 8 with reference to Psalm 22.

will use a common strategy to interpret all of the Penitential Psalms; when he interprets the psalms lamenting the destruction of the temple he is able to assign each of the three psalms to one of the three great acts of violence against the temple. Not only does creating groups help his readers get a big-picture view of the sorts of groups that exist within the Psalter, but they also assist in the work of interpretation.

Summary

Cassiodorus uses the preface to the *Explanation of the Psalms* to lay out a comprehensive approach to interpreting the psalms. Moving in order, he establishes a set of marginal notations for indicating the presence of thirteen different important kinds of information found within the Psalms. He presents a four-part scheme for analyzing every psalm in the Psalter, providing preemptive materials on commonly found terms in the headings and introducing the three main speakers. He then provides a complete—if vague—set of interpretive contexts by grouping the psalms into twelve roughly sequential groups. These groupings will be reinforced by more clearly identified interpretive collections that he will call out in the commentary itself.

Of the many issues that Cassiodorus raises in the preface and its chapters, two in particular deserve a more complete treatment before returning to the psalms themselves. First is the relationship between his *Explanation of the Psalms* and the *Enarrations on the Psalms* by Augustine of Hippo. How and to what degree did Cassiodorus use Augustine's work? Second, at several points in the preface and its chapters, Cassiodorus refers to "allegory" and to "the hidden meaning of the Psalm which varies with the spiritual sense, the historical perusal, and the mystical meaning"[37] and to the Psalms as a whole as "the key to the heavenly mysteries and a herald of sacred language."[38] What is Cassiodorus's method for conducting spiritual reading of the psalms? We shall take up these two questions next.

---

[37] Cassiodorus, *ExplPs* Pref.14, p. 1.35.
[38] Cassiodorus, *ExplPs* Pref.17, p. 1.42.

CHAPTER SEVEN

Editing Augustine and Reading the Scriptures

Managing Augustine

Admirers of Augustine

Writing in the decades after Cassiodorus, some two hundred years after Augustine himself, Isidore of Seville comments that anyone who claims to have read the complete works of Augustine is a liar. There are two ways that we need to take this comment. First, as we've already discussed, Augustine wrote an enormous amount. Working through a corpus of that size is literally the work of a lifetime. Second, there is the issue of access. Thanks to the lists in the *Retractions* and in Possidius, early medieval readers knew how much Augustine there was to read—but laying their hands on it was another story entirely. Remember, in a world of hand-copied works, neither the production nor the circulation of texts was a controlled process. Possidius appears to have been working off the list at Augustine's home library, a great repository in Hippo of everything that he ever kept copies of. But knowing titles and having books are two different things. The Vandal siege that cost Augustine his life and the subsequent sack of the city likely destroyed the library or, at the least, scattered its contents, dealing a huge setback to the circulation of his works.

Remember that monastic library from the ninth century we looked at when we were considering biblical manuscripts? Right after the initial entry with the biblical manuscripts it lists its holdings of the works of St. Augustine. Of the ninety-three books that Augustine recorded in his *Retractions*, the library at Reichenau had only twenty-four—and not all of those were complete. For instance, it had the beginning of the *City of God*, but only the first ten chapters; the last twelve are missing. Of the *Enarrations on the Psalms*, it had Psalms 30–40 and also Psalms 101–50. If we are relying on Augustine for our treatment of the psalms, fewer than half are actually present. Nevertheless, several other works are scattered through the library if an informed reader knows what to look for. They had Prosper of Aquitaine's *Epigrams* in one volume; they had Cassiodorus's *Explanation of the Psalms* in three volumes; they had the *Books of Excerpts from the Works of Saint Augustine* by Eugippius in one volume.

Since Augustine didn't edit his own works, the church stepped in and took care of it for him. A cottage industry sprang up to work with Augustine's texts, whittling them down and culling material so that the good stuff could be more easily found, circulated, read, and used. Michael Gorman writes:

> Students of Augustine in the early Middle Ages were as aware as we are that an editor was needed to trim his rhetoric down to manageable proportions for post-classical tastes, budgets and life-styles. Epitomes made it possible to acquire an excellent, detailed knowledge of the content of Augustine's long and difficult works without ever having to actually read them. This was one of the advantages offered by the genre. Another was the economic factor: an epitome was much cheaper to produce than a manuscript of the complete work. By the year 800, if not perhaps well before, it was possible to read and study most of the major works of Augustine in epitomes or abbreviated versions, including *On Genesis Literally Interpreted*, *Tractates on the Gospel of John*, *The Trinity*, *Confessions*, *Christian Instruction*, and *The City of God*.[1]

Let's define some terms here: a florilegium is a series of quotations pulled directly out of an author's work with no context provided

---

[1] Michael Gorman, "The Oldest Epitome of Augustine's *Tractatus in Euangelium Ioannis* and Commentaries on the Gospel of John in the Early Middle Ages," *Revue des Études Augustiniennes* 43 (1997): 63–103, at 66. I have changed his citation of the Latin titles into their English counterparts.

(maybe it would tell us what work it came from, maybe not). An epitome is a work where only the author's words are used; no one else's words appear, but the text is excerpted and stitched together to create an abridgement of the author's thought. A summary is where the author's words may or may not be used; the author's ideas are being transmitted, usually in fewer words, sometimes in smaller or less technical words as well.

Florilegia, epitomes, and summaries of Augustine's works began to be produced right around the time he died. Prosper of Aquitaine was a major supporter of Augustine's ideas on grace and free will against the supporters of Cassian in a theological dustup in southern France that occurred around 426. Prosper even wrote to Augustine for assistance and the African bishop sent two books back from Hippo to help the cause. After Augustine's death, Prosper created the *Book of Sentences Plucked from the Works of St. Augustine*, the earliest known Augustinian florilegium that contains 392 sayings. These were sayings particularly useful in theological debate and, because of their lack of context, tend to exaggerate Augustine's positions a bit. Later in life Prosper also wrote a poetical text, *Epigrams from the Sentences of St. Augustine*, that puts 106 statements from Augustine into verse form. This proved a definite hit and became a standard part of the education of early medieval monks. Particularly for those who lived in small monasteries or who would become priests serving rural parishes, Prosper's *Epigrams* might be the principal explicitly theological text they would study.

In addition to these, Prosper also wrote a summary of Augustine's *Enarrations on the Psalms*. It was incomplete, only tackling Psalms 100–150. It did not see the same kind of circulation that the *Epigrams* did; Reichenau owned Prosper's *Epigrams* but not his summaries on the psalms.

In the *Institutions*, Cassiodorus mentions another great scholar of Augustine, Eugippius. Originally from the region of Austria and pushed into Italy by barbarian attacks, Eugippius founded a monastery in Naples and specialized in the works of St. Augustine. In the *Institutions*, Cassiodorus indicates that the two men had met; the entry, however, seems a bit curt and perhaps a little cold.[2] Eugippius was patronized by the great Anicii clan, one of the two great Roman senatorial

---

[2] Cassiodorus, *Institutions* 1.23.1, p. 154.

families who looked down on the Cassiodori as provincial newcomers. Eugippius even dedicated his greatest work, a massive florilegium of 338 chapters titled *Excerpts from the Works of Saint Augustine* to Proba, a member of the Anicii clan and a church mother in her own right. She had written a life of Christ pieced together entirely out of quotations from the first-century pagan poet Virgil. Cassiodorus also claimed kinship with Proba, but how they were related is not entirely clear. Cassiodorus's final comment on Eugippius is a telling one regarding the state of Augustinian survivals in the sixth century: "This book is recommended reading, since this diligent scholar set down in one collection what can scarcely be found in a great library."[3] As a man who had access to all of the greatest libraries of the age in Rome, Ravenna, and Constantinople, Cassiodorus surely knew of what he spoke.

For what it's worth, the monastery that Eugippius founded in Naples seems to have been quite similar to that of Cassiodorus in that it became a major center of Augustinian manuscript production. Medieval tables of contents would frequently offer brief summaries of what was contained in the various books and chapters that made up a work to help readers find what they were looking for; for Augustine's works, most if not all of these summaries appear to be the work of Eugippius or his monks.[4] Despite that, there seems to have been very few if any copies of the *Enarrations on the Psalms*; had they been available, Cassiodorus would certainly have collected more than twenty of Augustine's psalm treatments. Furthermore, there are few if any citations from the *Enarrations on the Psalms* included in the florilegium of Eugippius.

In addition to Eugippius, Cassiodorus also mentions another author, Peter of Tripoli. The comments of Cassiodorus on Peter's work are instructive because of the perspective they provide on the question of originality at the start of the early medieval age:

> Peter, the abbot of the province of Tripoli, is said to have annotated the epistles of St. Paul with examples from the shorter works of the blessed Augustine. He declares the secret of his own heart with

---

[3] Ibid.
[4] James O'Donnell, "Eugippius," in *Augustine through the Ages: An Encyclopedia*, ed. Allan D. Fitzgerald (Grand Rapids, MI: Eerdmans, 1999), 337–38, at 338.

the tongue of another and he has fitted these examples so suitably to individual passages that you might think that the whole had been accomplished rather by the effort of blessed Augustine. For it is remarkable that one author has elucidated the text from another commentator in such a way that he seems to have expressed the desires of his own heart without adding a word of his own.[5]

The wonder is that Peter has so deeply internalized both the words and the messages of Augustine that he is able to produce a text constructed entirely out of Augustine's own words that express what Peter also thinks and feels. A modern perspective would simply see this as an unusual form of plagiarism; Cassiodorus sees it as not only a sign of respect for but also a mastery of Augustine's wisdom. Whereas the original quotations would have been scattered throughout Augustine's works, now someone reading Peter's text would have access to Augustinian thought on the Pauline Epistles through a single manuscript.

It's likely that Peter's work never actually made it to Vivarium or, if it did, it did not circulate widely, because the Venerable Bede ended up doing the same work around the end of the seventh century. When Bede lists the texts that he has written at the end of his great history, *A History of the English Church and People*, he describes his life's work by saying, "I have worked, both for my own benefit and that of my brethren, to compile short extracts from the works of the venerable Fathers on Holy Scripture and to comment on their meaning and interpretation."[6] Among the works is this one, "*On the Apostle [Paul]*: in which I have carefully transcribed in order whatever I have found on the subject in the works of Saint Augustine."[7]

Of all of Augustine's works that received abbreviation, the foremost among them was the Psalm commentary. Gorman describes it thus:

> To judge from the number of items in *Codices Latini Antiquiores*, Augustine's *Enarrations on the Psalms* was far and away the most widely diffused of all his works in the early Middle Ages. I count twenty-five items which are manuscripts, fragments or excerpts

---

[5] Cassiodorus, *Institutions* 1.8.9, p. 129.
[6] Bede, *A History of the English Church and People* 5.24, trans. Leo Sherley-Price, rev. R. E. Latham (New York: Penguin Books, 1968), 336.
[7] Bede, *History of the English Church* 5.24, p. 337.

of the *Enarrations*. Just how significant this number is can be appreciated by comparing it with the relevant numbers for the other major works of Augustine: eleven entries for the *Tractates on the Gospel of John*, six for *The Trinity*, five for *The City of God*, four for *On Genesis Literally Interpreted*, three for *Christian Interpretation*, and three for the *Confessions*. It is thus not surprising that the *Enarrations* was an especially popular object for those who practised the epitomist's craft.[8]

Gorman then goes on to describe five different surviving epitomes created from the *Enarrations* between the sixth and the ninth centuries.

Cassiodorus and Augustine

This is the environment within which Cassiodorus is creating his Psalms commentary. Had he desired, he could have chosen any of the three options: florilegium, epitome, or summary. In his own preface he implies that he has created an epitome of sorts. After describing his initial difficulties in wrestling with obscurities in the Psalms, Cassiodorus tells us that he found the answers that he sought in Augustine and then says this:

> I had recourse to the highly esteemed commentary of our most eloquent father Augustine. There is such abundance of words gathered there that we can scarcely keep in mind the extensive exposition even after rereading. I imagine that he was eager to satisfy the people's great longing with an ecclesiastical feast, and inevitably his great preaching flowed out in a stream. So mindful of my own weakness, through the grace of God's mercy and in brief summary I turned into shallow streams that ocean of Augustine which wells from the springs of certain psalms; so I have embraced in one volume the wide range of topics which Augustine marvellously unfolded in his fifteen decades.[9]

We get the sense that he is giving us Augustine—and he says little to disabuse us of that notion. At the end of a paragraph filled with effusive praise of Augustine and his works, however, he does admit this: "There

---

[8] Gorman, "Oldest Epitome," 67. Gorman uses the Latin titles for all of Augustine's works, which I have changed to English for the sake of consistency.
[9] Cassiodorus, *ExplPs* Pref, p. 1.23.

are some new interpretations framed since the time of that wonderful master; I have inserted these solely through presumption in the Lord, who gives confidence to little ones, sight to the blind, speech to the dumb, and hearing to the deaf."[10] This makes it sound like maybe—just maybe—a few other quotations from someone else have been added. What he doesn't say is that he has completely reframed Augustine's work, in some places summarized Augustine's thought, and in others gone in entirely new directions on his own in addition to inserting several different classes of topics that Augustine never touched on.

Augustine was the preacher; Cassiodorus was the author. Augustine gives us a massive set of sermons that, when delivered properly, convey a strong sense of the orator's flair and personality.[11] Indeed, O'Donnell suggests that the best way to get in touch with Augustine is not through his works on the Trinity or even *The City of God*; rather, "If a modern reader would like to get the flavor of Augustine's religion as his followers did, seeing and hearing him preach in church week in and week out, those sermons on the Psalms are the best place to go to listen."[12] Cassiodorus, on the other hand, was a completely different kind of author. If Augustine was an orator, Cassiodorus was a composer. His writing shows organized composition both at the level of the individual psalm and across his work as a whole. His work on the psalms is not a collection of individually gathered elements, let alone homilies. Rather, it is planned, carefully charted out, logically structured, with consistently executed internal logic and cross-references. Cassiodorus was not standing in a pulpit by any stretch; he was sitting with several wax tablets of his own notes. Some of these bore notes on the specific psalm at hand; others related to the work as a whole, identifying groupings of psalms categorized by theme, topic, and theological import so that after the treatment of each psalm, its placement in the group could be identified and the other members in the group cross-referenced.

---

[10] Cassiodorus, *ExplPs* Pref, pp. 1.23–24.

[11] One of my greatest joys in a classroom was teaching an evening preaching class at Emory's Candler School of Theology in Atlanta. The majority of the students were from the Black Church tradition; exploring Augustine as, first and foremost, an African preacher was a thrilling and eye-opening experience for us all!

[12] O'Donnell, *Augustine*, 28–29.

Cassiodorus intended his work to be experienced in a very different way from Augustine's. Despite its written form, Augustine's commentary represents the spoken word, frozen in a moment and preserved for later ages. It was thoroughly oral and was designed to be heard rather than read. The work of Cassiodorus is designed and laid out to be looked at. Even the experience of reading Cassiodorus aloud is not the same experience as reading Cassiodorus and looking at his pages. It was designed to be seen. As a result, Cassiodorus treats Augustine by reframing his text into a new static, written format.

The best way to understand what Cassiodorus is doing with Augustine is to take seriously what he says in the *Institutions*. After recommending several authors in his section on the Psalms, Cassiodorus says this about Augustine:

> And as one draws light from light, so with the Lord's bounty, I have written drawing on him [sc. Augustine], so that the famous line of the Bard of Mantua should be truly fulfilled in my case, "and I cackle as a goose among the melodious swans" [Virgil, *Eclogues* 9.36]. In this work I have not disturbed the Psalm text under discussion by straying from the subject, but in place of glosses I have stated briefly on each passage as the nature of the text demands it.[13]

Augustine frequently wanders off topic. To be fair, given the nature of his orations and their liturgical context, he is sometimes pulled off topic by one of the other texts proclaimed within the liturgy. Nevertheless, Cassiodorus is promising not to do this. He will stick to the point, but he will also give the text the coverage it needs, not just be brief for the point of being brief.

Generally, speaking, Cassiodorus stays in contact with Augustine's text. That is, there are usually signs that Cassiodorus has read Augustine recently. He will borrow images that Augustine has used as well as Scripture quotations; sometimes logic jumps will make more sense if we glance back at Augustine. Nevertheless, he rarely, if at all, cites Augustine's *Enarrations* verbatim. He is far more likely to quote other works of Augustine verbatim, but he does not do so with the Psalms commentary.

---

[13] Cassiodorus, *Institutions* 1.4.2, p. 120.

Let me show what I mean. Let's consider for a moment a passage from Psalm 147. I'm deliberately selecting something from the end of the Psalter. If Cassiodorus were to start getting lazy, it would be toward the end; it would be easier to simply copy the source text directly than to write new words with similar thoughts. Psalm 147:15-16 reads: "[The Lord] sends out his command to the earth; his word runs swiftly. He gives snow like wool; he scatters frost like ashes." Both interpreters see the use of "word" in verse 15 as a reference to the Christ as the Logos described in John 1. With such a setup, they will not read what follows as a reference to standard weather events. This is how Augustine and Cassiodorus treat the references to "snow" and "wool":

Augustine, EnnPs 147.26, NPNF[1] 8:671.	Cassiodorus, ExplPs 147.17, pp. 3.446–47.
We then are burdened by the sluggishness of this cold body, and the bonds of this earthly and corruptible life; have we no hope of receiving "the Word," which "runneth even unto swiftness"? or hath abandoned us, though by the body we are depressed to the lowest depths? Did not He predestinate us, before we were born in this mortal and sluggish body? He then, who predestinated us, gave snow to the earth, even ourselves. For now let us come to those somewhat obscure verses of the Psalm, let those entanglements begin to be unrolled. Behold, we are sluggish on this earth, and are as it were frozen here. And just as happens to the flakes of snow, for they freeze above, then fall down; so as love groweth cold, human nature falleth down to this earth, and involved in a sluggish body becometh like snow. But in that predestined	After prophesying the Lord's coming, he next explains by metaphorical allusions what His blessings provide. This figure is called *parabole*, for things dissimilar to each other in kind are compared. All the things mentioned, *snow*, *mist*, *crystal*, *cold*, are ills of this world which grip tight mortal hearts with the frost of sins, and cause them to remain in a rock-like stupor unless they are melted by the Lord's warmth. But let us observe how apt healing is afforded in each case. He says: *Who giveth snow like wool*. *Giveth* means "makes," just as in common speech we say "He gave us an indication" when we state that we have been shown and taught something. So He makes *snow like wool*, so that what previously was frozen with bitter cold is transformed into woolly softness. This happens precisely when He has guided men's hearts when at their coldest through sins to the warmth of satisfaction.

sons of God. For, "He giveth snow like wool" (ver. 16). What is "like wool"? It meaneth, of the snow which He hath given, of these, who are as yet slow in spirit and cold, whom He hath predestinated, He is about to make somewhat. For wool is the material of a garment: when we see wool, we look on it as a sort of preparation for a garment. Therefore since He hath predestinated these, who at present are cold and creep on earth, and as yet glow not with the spirit of love (for as yet He speaketh of predestination), God hath given these as a sort of wool: He is about to make of them a garment.	*Snow* describes man when he removes himself from the Lord; *wool*, when he has deserved to attain His healing.

Both interpreters are reading this text in the same way: The references to cold weather in the psalm are actually references to humanity in a state of sin: they are—metaphorically—cold, frozen, and sluggish until they are warmed by the heat of God's love. (This reading is anticipating verse 18, "He sends out his word, and melts them," where the Word [Christ] will unfreeze sluggish humanity.) Both interpreters read "snow" as humanity frozen by sin; both see "wool" as reference to a healing or warming. At this point, Augustine will go on in some detail and describe the wool as raiment for the church in connection with the transfiguration of Christ. Cassiodorus doesn't go there at all but proceeds directly to the meaning of the term "frost." We can tell from the English what is confirmed by checking the Latin: Cassiodorus is in touch with Augustine's thought broadly, even uses some of the same spiritual interpretations, but does not borrow Augustine's words or phrases directly.

The best way that I've found to think of how Cassiodorus uses Augustine is to consider the practical logistics of how he might have encountered the commentary. If Cassiodorus is doing much of the composition of this work in Constantinople, he likely did not have the opportunity to take any volumes of it he might have owned or accessed in Ravenna with him when he traveled. Rather, he may well have been relying on the Imperial Library in Constantinople. I imagine Cassiodorus going to the Imperial Library and requesting Augustine's work. An ancient library is not necessarily like a modern one—we must not imagine him pulling out his library card to check out a stack of books at the circulation desk! A far better scenario to imagine is an attendant, likely a slave, coming to meet him with a single scroll under his arm—the requested portion of the text—who would then stand and read the scroll as the patron sat or reclined, taking notes on a wax tablet. The utility of this system is obvious: the library employee retains physical possession of the text (ensuring no unauthorized exits of rare or valuable texts), a patron can access a work regardless of their level of literacy, and—provided a sufficient supply of multilingual attendants—the text could be translated on the fly into the patron's mother tongue from Greek, Latin, Syriac, or Coptic at need.

Cassiodorus, therefore, is likely not copying from one manuscript to another. Instead, he is listening and jotting down notes—capturing the thoughts of Augustine in his own words. These he will then transcribe later, perhaps transforming them even more when he returns to his own home to compose his work. While we might like to imagine him sitting at a desk surrounded by books where he can freely copy sections of text at will, we are imagining a scene from a later point in the medieval world.[14] Instead, our very best image of Cassiodorus writing is likely that of Ezra the scribe from the Codex Amiatinus. This biblical pandect, which we encountered back in chapter 2, appears to have been based on the *codex grandior* that Cassiodorus mentions in the *Institutions*. The fact that the image of Ezra at work shows a cupboard behind him with nine volumes—the complete Old and New Testaments

Jean Miélot (d. 1472) at work some eight hundred years after Cassiodorus. (Paris B.n. Fr. 9198, f. 19r)

[14] http://gallica.bnf.fr/ark:/12148/btv1b8451109t/f49.item.r=9198.zoom.

Ezra—or Cassiodorus?—at work (Codex Amiatinus, f. 5r)

bound in the nine-volume arrangement Cassiodorus advances in the *Institutions*—has led scholars to wonder whether or not this is actually an image of Cassiodorus himself writing in Vivarium.

Running the Numbers

If Cassiodorus was intending to create an abridgement of Augustine, then an obvious question is how well Cassiodorus succeeded in his task. Let's explore the three works on the Psalms with roots in Augustine that we've discussed up to this point: Augustine's *Enarrations on the Psalms*, Prosper of Aquitaine's *Exposition on the Psalms*, and Cassiodorus's *Explanation of the Psalms*. First, we need a sense of how long these works are in Latin. Fortunately, all three are printed in Migne's massive Patrologia Latina, a series that brings together nearly one thousand years of Latin theological texts from Tertullian (d. 240) through Innocent III (d. 1216). Because Migne used a consistent font size and layout, we can count the number of columns that each text occupies in Migne and use that as a standard of comparison. Second, as luck would have it (and this is rather extraordinary!), the monastic library at St. Gall in Switzerland owns copies of all three works in manuscripts from the ninth century that share a common size. All three works are found in books with parchment leaves that measure around 320mm x 240mm. Thus, each leaf is a bit larger in both height and width than a standard piece of printer paper. The size is significant because a prepared sheep hide measures around 720mm x 525mm: we can get four of these leaves out of one sheep hide leaving room for trimming to get the correct shape. By running the numbers, we arrive at the following chart:

Editing Augustine and Reading the Scriptures   193

Contents	Manuscript	Printed Columns in PL	Manu-script Leaves	Writing Density (Columns/Leaf)	Sheep
Augustine, vol. 1	Cod. Sang. 162	288	187	1.54	46.75
Augustine, vol. 2	Cod. Sang. 165	355	151	2.351	37.75
Augustine, vol. 3	Cod. Sang. 163	383	250	1.532	62.5
Augustine, vol. 4	Cod. Sang. 164	305	202	1.51	50.5
Augustine, vol. 5	Cod. Sang. 166	303	217	1.396	54.25
Augustine, vol. 6 (missing)	*[Cod. Sang ?]*	*370*	*222*	*1.666*	*55.5*
Totals		**2004**	**1229**	**1.631**	**307.25**
Cassiodorus, vol. 1	Cod. Sang. 200	348	252	1.381	63
Cassiodorus, vol. 2	Cod. Sang. 201	332	199	1.668	49.75
Cassiodorus, vol. 3	Cod Sang. 202	351	184	1.908	46
Totals		**1031**	**635**	**1.624**	**158.75**
Prosper, Pss 100-150	Cod. Sang. 184	148	94	1.574	23.5
Prosper, Pss 1-99(never existed)		*269*	*167*	*1.6*	*41.75*
Totals		**417**	**261**	**1.6**	**65.25**

Based on these figures, we can see that a complete edition of Augustine's commentary, using the format of this surviving set from St. Gall, would require an investment of over three hundred sheep. Cassiodorus's commentary was almost exactly half the length of Augustine's and fits well into three volumes. Prosper's is short. In its incomplete state, it fills part of a volume; it is just over a fifth of the size of Augustine's work. Had Prosper completed the other one hundred psalms in the same way that he did the final fifty, his commentary would have required only sixty-six sheep altogether.

Conclusion

It is not true that Cassiodorus's work on the Psalms is simply an edited version of Augustine's. On the one hand, Cassiodorus is telling us a half-truth, but, on the other hand, it's a very important half-truth for him to tell. As part of a culture that revered the received tradition, Cassiodorus is sending the proper signals of respect. He is paying homage to Augustine despite his departures from him. There is also, however, a sense in which his departures from the *Enarrations* are for the sake of introducing a whole new level of fidelity to the Augustinian vision; he introduces new material and fundamentally alters the structure of the text to be even more faithful to Augustine's grand project.

Reading the Scriptures

Reconsidering the Received Wisdom

In the chariot racing scene from 1959's *Ben Hur*, Charlton Heston whips around a chariot driven by four horses: this is the type of chariot known as a "quadriga." In addition to being the name of a chariot, this was also the Latin shorthand for a popular ditty on Bible interpretation also driven by four things: *Littera gesta docet; quid credas allegoria; moralitas quid agas; quid speres anagogia* ("The letter teaches what happened; allegory, what you should believe; morality, what you should do; anagogy, what you should hope for"). This line was written by Augustine—but not the one we're thinking of. This was written not by Augustine of Hippo but by Augustine of Dacia who died in the year 1285. The fourth Dominican provincial prior for Dacia—the region circumscribing Scandinavia and the Baltics—this Augustine wrote a manual to teach Dominican friars the fundamentals of theology, Scripture interpretation, and the sacraments. Because they were preaching crusades against the church's foes in the north, the training included how to identify schismatics, heretics, and sorcerers—all types, from necromancers to mathematicians!

The conventional wisdom teaches that the formula encapsulated in the quadriga is how medieval Christians interpreted the Scriptures. This perception is reinforced by the great work of de Lubac, *Medieval Exegesis*. In this massively learned work, he traces the fourfold method of reading all the way from Origen into the main writers of the medieval period, teasing out the four senses of Scripture and how they were used. But de Lubac was not a historian of biblical interpretation; nor was he writing for that purpose. He was a theologian. Writing in an age when theology of the Roman Catholic Church had been, in his eyes, overly focused on the writings of Thomas Aquinas, he and his comrades sought to remind the Roman Catholic theological world of Aquinas's own sources of theology—the church fathers—and of their relevance to modern theology. As a result, when he wrote regarding these four means of interpreting the Scriptures—the literal, allegorical, moral, and anagogical—his purpose was to recover them as useful categories with which to do theology.

Here's the problem. Origen laid out a theory of reading with multiple levels of meaning, and John Cassian picked up on that. Augustine even lays out the same kind of fourfold scheme at the beginning of his *On Genesis Literally Interpreted*. This scheme conjures up an image of interpreters sitting down and working through a passage in a mechanical fashion, first applying the literal sense, then going back and applying the allegorical sense, then using the moral sense, and finally going back over it with the anagogical sense and writing all of these out in order. But this isn't the way they worked at all—at least not at this point in time. Most of the church fathers were like Augustine—they were preachers. We just can't preach like that: it simply doesn't work! Even a monastic audience isn't going to pay attention to this kind of an exposition of a text. We don't find this kind of mechanistic application of the four senses to the reading process until scholastic theology in the High Middle Ages—and those are in books for students or scholars that are intended to be read, not preached or heard.

While Origen and Cassian named these senses and Cassian demonstrates them in a fourfold example regarding Jerusalem, the actual sermons and commentaries are far more fluid. These senses are modes of reading and listening: at this point, at least, they are not sequential steps to be applied. As de Lubac demonstrated, they can be effective categories for analysis after the fact, but these are not compositional modes in the way that many people seem to assume.

Cassiodorus and the Augustinian Paradigm

One of the most important choices that Cassiodorus makes as an interpreter and as a teacher of interpretation is in following the Augustinian paradigm for spiritual reading rather than the Alexandrian. In a sense, this is puzzling, because it seems to cut against his nature and the way that he operates with regard to secular learning. The Alexandrian method identifies various strategies of spiritual reading later formalized into the four steps of the quadriga: historical readings, allegorical readings, anagogical meanings, and moral readings can all be differentiated from one another. Augustine goes in the other direction both in *Christian Instruction* and in practice in his *Enarrations on the Psalms* with a simpler two-step pattern: there is a literal reading and then there is a figural reading. While he explicitly called out the fourfold senses in *On Genesis Literally Interpreted*, that's not how he writes in practice. If he must determine boundaries between modes of reading, this is where he will draw them, simply noting a spiritual or mystical or figurative meaning. Cassiodorus chooses to follow him in this regard. As a result, he will refer to a spiritual or mystical meaning of a text—these terms mean the same thing. There is not a mystical sense that is different or apart from a spiritual sense, they are two different ways of saying the same thing.

Cassiodorus frequently uses the term "allegory." This is not because he is differentiating between an allegorical meaning and other kinds of meaning; rather, he is identifying an allegory that is a specific kind of figure of speech and thought. Similarly, he does the same thing with simillitude and parable—and throwing in allegory along with them, these are three of his favorite figures to identify. But these are figures used in spiritual reading; they are not a separate sense of reading for him.

The reason I am belaboring this point is that there is tendency to shoehorn patristic and early medieval readers into a fourfold model of reading based on the later notion of the quadriga and using Cassian's fourfold reading of Jerusalem as evidence. But this is not what we see in the texts themselves.

For Cassiodorus, spiritual reading is not a science; it is not a method. Cassiodorus was aware of the tradition of Origen and his pupils, if only through Cassian's *Conferences*. He could have turned it into a method. After all, this is Cassiodorus we are talking about: the man who obsessively points out the fifteen distinct types of definitions as he runs across them in the psalms. Had he wished, he could easily have called out a moral use of the text, an allegorical use, and an anagogical use and even assigned them unique marginal signs. But he didn't. Instead of communicating spiritual reading as a science, it turns into prayer. We will take a look at how this happens in steps. First, we will discuss how figurative reading plays out in the *Explanation of the Psalms* and then how spiritual meaning shades into spiritual reading; finally we will examine the *Explanation* as an important text in the communication of the practice of *lectio divina*, a monastic form of praying with Scripture that emerged within the early medieval period.

Figurative Reading

The first thing to note about figural reading is that Cassiodorus understands it as a natural extension of the reading process. A spiritual or mystical meaning is not something extra that is tacked on; it is an intrinsic part of the text. As an extension, it grows out of the standard methods for reading literary texts properly.

When a regular text is read, an informed reader needs to identify the figures of speech and thought in order to understand it correctly. For those of us who are from literate societies and have read most of our lives, we do this without a second thought—and sometimes without a first thought too. If a line in a mystery novel says something like, "The sun set on the horizon, the red light looking like blood on the clouds," our brains would process that we have just read a figure of speech: a simile, a comparison using "like" or "as." In fact, we probably wouldn't be consciously aware of the fact that we've just processed a simile, and we do this all the time, without even knowing the names of the various figures of speech we encounter. Most of us wouldn't be confused by this or wonder if there was literal blood on the clouds.

If this line did show up in a mystery novel, there's a pretty good chance that there's a figure of thought at work here too: there's probably foreshadowing going on. Foreshadowing, of course, is when a writer leaves clues or gets us thinking in a certain way that will lead up to what happens next or maybe even some point later in the story. If we're reading a line like that in a mystery with direct reference to blood, it's quite likely that someone in the story is about to die—or already has!

Some figures of speech are more complex and move into what we'd consider ornamented language. For instance, if the line used a metaphor (a comparison that doesn't bother with a "like" or "as") it might read "A bloody sun set." The metaphor may grab our attention more, be more evocative, but it also requires the reader to do more work: What does the author mean by "bloody"? Is it a reference to the color of the sun? Or the character of the day over which the sun is setting? Or is the narrator English and they're using a minor curse word to describe the state of affairs? The more ornamented language gets, the more ambiguity is present and the more the reader has to work. To go one more step in the same direction, consider the multitude of meanings in U2's lyric "Sunday, bloody Sunday."

One of the consistent characteristics of poetry is specialized vocabulary tied to a higher frequency of ornamented language, and the Psalms are no exception. As the ornamentation gets more rich, more interpretive work is required to get a full sense of what is going on and the various ways the poem is trying to affect the reader. Just like a blood-red sun in a mystery novel, one phrase may have multiple figures of both speech and thought that have to be teased out to get at the full meaning of the passage.

Part of Cassiodorus's task is to teach readers to encounter the Psalms as ornamented language, to cull out when figures of speech and thought are at play, and to help them recognize and name what these compositional strategies are. But he also goes one step further than that. Cassiodorus and the broader tradition behind him and informing him understand the Scriptures generally and the Psalms in particular to be not just ornamented language but deliberately veiled language. This is what Cassiodorus is alluding to in his preface when he writes:

> Now the holy depth [*sancta profunditas*] of divine Scripture is expressed in such common language that everyone immediately

takes it in. But buried within it are hidden senses of truth [*sensus . . . veritatis arcano*], so that the vital meaning [*vitalis sententia*] must be most carefully sought out.[15]

This is what Hilary and Origen taught with the image of the beautiful city filled with locked buildings. In fact, hiddenness is a major theme throughout the commentary. While words referring to hiddenness are fairly rare in the Psalter—words based on the root *arcana* or *occultus* show up only nine times throughout the thirty thousand words used—Cassiodorus uses a term translated "hidden" over 170 times!

There are two reasons why the meanings of Scripture are veiled as Cassiodorus reminds his reader in his analysis of Psalm 98:

> We have often remarked that divine Scripture uses diverse images so that the meaning of the words may be hidden from the unholy, and also so that the faithful may be more earnestly fired to seek out that meaning. So here too he states by manifold allegories that we must sing to the Lord. Allegory means saying one thing while meaning another.[16]

The first reason is so that outsiders who are not part of the faith will not hear, understand, and profane the mysteries of God. The church fathers did not just make this up; they saw it proceeding directly from the words of Jesus himself. In the Sermon on the Mount, two things are linked together, an injunction to secrecy regarding holy things and the need to ask, search, and knock:

> [Jesus said:] Do not give what is holy to dogs; and do not throw your pearls before swine, or they will trample them under foot and turn and maul you. Ask, and it will be given you; search, and you will find; knock, and the door will be opened for you. For everyone who asks receives, and everyone who searches finds, and for everyone who knocks, the door will be opened. (Matt 7:6-8)

In interpreting this text, Augustine—in line with the main body of patristic tradition—reads the holy things and pearls as the inner

---

[15] Cassiodorus, *ExplPs* Pref.15, p. 1.37.
[16] Cassiodorus, *ExplPs* 98.8, p. 2.435.

meanings of the Holy Scriptures,[17] to the point of invoking the need for allegory:

> By pearls, again, are meant whatever spiritual things we ought to set a high value upon, both because they lie hid in a secret place, are as it were brought up out of the deep, and are found in wrappings of allegory, as it were in shells that have been opened. We may therefore legitimately understand that one and the same thing may be called both holy and a pearl: but it gets the name of holy for this reason, that it ought not to be corrupted; of a pearl for this reason, that it ought not to be despised.[18]

Thus, the veiling of Scripture protects its holier meanings from being openly and easily read by those who do not have the right to it through conversion and baptism.

The second reason for the veiling of the Scriptures is the joy of discovery. Augustine goes into detail on this property of Scripture in *Christian Instruction*:

> But many and varied obscurities and ambiguities deceive those who read [the Scriptures] casually, understanding one thing instead of another; indeed, in certain places they do not find anything to interpret erroneously, so obscurely are certain sayings covered with a most dense mist. I do not doubt that this situation was provided by God to conquer pride by work and to combat disdain in our minds, to which those things which are easily discovered seem frequently to be worthless.[19]

Augustine then goes into an explanation, first giving a teaching about the example of holy men then offering the same teaching as an explanation of the imagery of Song of Solomon 4:2 ("Your teeth are like a flock of shorn ewes that have come up from the washing, all of which bear twins, and not one among them is bereaved"). He continues:

> Does one learn anything else besides that which he learns when he hears the same thought expressed in plain words without

---

[17] Compare John Chrysostom, *Homilies on Matthew* 23.3, who interprets this verse the same way.
[18] Augustine, *Sermon on the Mount* 2.10.68 (NPNF[1] 6:56).
[19] Augustine, *Christian Instruction* 2.6.7 (ChrDoc, p. 37).

> this similitude? Nevertheless, in a strange way, I contemplate the saints more pleasantly when I envision them as the teeth of the Church cutting off men from their errors and transferring them to her body after their hardness has been softened as if by being bitten and chewed. I recognize them most pleasantly as shorn sheep having put aside the burden of the world like so much fleece, and as ascending from the washing, which is baptism, all to create twins, which are the two precepts of love, and I see no one of them sterile of this holy fruit. But why it seems sweeter to me than if no similitude were offered in the divine books, since the thing perceived is the same, is difficult to say and is a problem for another discussion. For the present, however, no one doubts that things are perceived more readily through similitudes and that what is sought with difficulty is discovered with more pleasure. Those who do not find what they seek directly stated labor in hunger; those who do not seek because they have what they wish at once frequently become indolent in disdain. In either one of these situations indifference is an evil. Thus the Holy Spirit has magnificently and wholesomely modulated the Holy Scriptures so that the more open places present themselves to hunger and the more obscure places may deter a disdainful attitude. Hardly anything may be found in these obscure places which is not found plainly said elsewhere.[20]

Thus, even though Scripture lays out the teachings of the faith clearly and plainly, there is a joy of discovery in finding a truth of the faith hidden among a shadowed metaphor. Using figural reading is a kind of intellectual play: "pleasure" and "delight" are the words that keep showing up in Augustine's passage. Like a spiritual Sudoku puzzle or chess problem that engages the mind, each mystery within Scripture provides a thrill of discovery when it is unraveled. The obscurities don't teach anything that isn't said openly in Scripture—but it's a lot more fun to find them within the obscurities! This angle is frequently overlooked or underappreciated by modern readers; after all, we're not used to thinking of the reading of Scripture as a solemn and sacred game in the same way that they were.

A central strategy for veiled reading is an over-application of figures of speech and thought. That is, Cassiodorus will identify the normal

---

[20] Augustine, *Christian Instruction* 2.6.7–8 (ChrDoc, pp. 37–38).

figures of speech and thought in a passage but then goes on to identify the presence of additional figures of speech and thought beyond what a modern reader might identify as the author's intent. Cassiodorus, however, understands the text of the Psalms to be prophecy, "an outstandingly splendid and truthful form of utterance composed not by man's will but poured forth by divine inspiration."[21] Whatever can be found that is in accordance with the creeds, is taught elsewhere openly in Scripture, and builds up the church in love he would consider a legitimate reading and part of God's own self-revelation through the words of Scripture and the Holy Spirit at work in the reader. An example is his treatment of Psalm 93:3.

The text of the psalm reads: "The floods have lifted up, O Lord, the floods have lifted up their voice; the floods lift up their roaring."[22] I would interpret this as a case of personification, more specifically, a form of anthropomorphism, where an inanimate object is given the characteristics of a human being. Cassiodorus reads it like this:

> Here the prophet, elated by his vision of God's love, says that the rivers well forth the praises of the Lord. This figure is called *prosopopōeia*, when words are attributed to inanimate things; it is found very frequently in the divine scriptures. But it is good for us to seek out the nature of these rivers which lift up their voices and cry out. They are surely the apostles, who have drunk of the holy Spirit. The Lord Himself, the Source of the rivers and the Fount of the waters, bears witness in the gospel: *He that believeth in me, out of his belly shall flow rivers of living water* (John 4:14). So the very rivers welled forth watering words, and lifted up their most holy voices in their preachings. They are rightly said to be *lifted up*, since these rivers offered their saving praises to the Creator, whereas earthly rivers do not direct their courses upward but rather flow downhill.[23]

Cassiodorus is clearly identifying the figure of personification; he is just calling it by its Greek name. What he does next, though, is to establish exactly whose voice the rivers are said to be possessing. It's not

---

[21] Cassiodorus, *ExplPs* Pref.2, p.1.28.

[22] The Latin text will have "rivers" (*flumina*) rather than "floods." "Rivers" is arguably a more common translation of the Hebrew *nahar* which the Greek renders *potamoi* (rivers).

[23] Cassiodorus, *ExplPs* 93.3, p. 2.397.

that he does not see the personification; rather, he sees it and moves an additional step beyond it, treating it as an allegory and linking it with the place where he sees this truth plainly taught in Scripture and connected by a shared word (*flumina*).

It's worth noting here that if we are going to read Cassiodorus on his own terms (as I argue we should), we have to recognize that his assumptions are in opposition to some deeply held modern beliefs. In particular, these two notions about veiled language, that divine revelation is hidden to keep it from the unworthy and that the character of Holy Scripture is intentionally obscure, run counter to modern mainline Protestant understandings of Christianity. The notion that Scripture is intentionally closed to outsiders feels very exclusive, and the appearance of exclusivity is something that many churches avoid like the plague. Furthermore, an important part of the Protestant heritage is the notion of the perspicuity of the Scriptures, that is, the Scriptures are fundamentally open and intelligible and that special forms of reading are not necessary in order to grasp its meaning. We need to recognize that these two beliefs were not held by Cassiodorus and the majority of the church fathers in the way that many modern readers hold them, and we should not prejudge his reading based on anachronistic standards. That is, we need to investigate his way of reading with an open mind before jumping too quickly to if, whether, or how modern readers might use them.

The Nuts and Bolts of Cassiodorus's Reading Strategy

Cassiodorus will use several techniques and strategies to read the Psalms, techniques that he shares in common with Augustine, Jerome, Hilary, and many other interpreters of the early church. The fundamental concept that connects these strategies is pattern recognition. Augustine mentions it in *Christian Instruction*: "When a figurative locution appears, the words of which it is composed will be seen to be derived from similar things or related to such thing by some association."[24] This principle of association is operative in all of the major strategies that we will look at in one way or another.

In *Sanctified Vision: An Introduction to Early Christian Interpretation of the Bible*, John J. O'Keefe and R. R. Reno make some very valuable

---

[24] Augustine, *Christian Instruction* 3.25.34 (ChrDoc, p. 99).

observations about reading strategies of the church fathers that apply directly to the kind of work that Cassiodorus is doing. They broadly identify three chief strategies: intensive reading, typology, and allegory. Obviously, these were applied to Scripture, but there are all kinds of texts—both literal and metaphorical—to which they can be applied.

Intensive reading is about the level of detail at which the fathers work, exploring the words themselves very closely. We saw Cassiodorus doing this with the word "boy" (*puer*) and especially with the verb "to love" (*diligere*) in our glance at Psalm 18. Connecting Scripture references by means of shared words—chaining— is another kind of intensive reading we saw him doing. O'Keefe and Reno write:

> By and large, modern readers distrust the ways in which words are easily connected simply on the basis of verbal echoes and patterns. . . . Modern readers shrink from the purely verbal nature of the link, and they are more careful to restrict themselves to discussing discrete historical periods and literary contexts. Ancient readers had the opposite reaction. They positively relished the way verbal associations can motivate leaps from one context to another. The same sensibility that makes us chuckle when we hear a clever pun was given much freer rein in patristic exegesis.[25]

Notice their choice of words here—"relished," "chuckle," and "clever" are pointing to the spirit of intellectual play we saw Augustine celebrating earlier. Because of the church fathers' underlying belief in the inspiration of the entire text, down to the particular Latin words on the page, none of it was without meaning. Any connections that could be found were found because the Holy Spirit was leading readers to find them as part of God's self-revelation through the text.

Typology is a reading strategy where a pattern in a narrative is recognized as a pattern lived or experienced by scriptural figures, preeminently Christ. In typology, the pattern both prefigures Christ and teaches the reader something deeper about who and what Christ is or what his actions mean. O'Keefe and Reno name it as "the most important interpretive strategy for early Christianity."[26] In explaining

---

[25] John J. O'Keefe and R. R. Reno, *Sanctified Vision: An Introduction to Early Christian Interpretation of the Bible* (Baltimore: Johns Hopkins University Press, 2005), 63.
[26] Ibid., 69.

it for modern readers, they point to the helpful example of Martin Luther King Jr.'s final "mountaintop" speech. When the civil rights leader said that he had been to the mountaintop and seen the Promised Land, he was creating an associative connection between the civil rights movement and his role within it and the exodus of the children of Israel from Egypt and Moses who died before entering the land itself. This is typology. The power of this figure depends on recognizing the connection between the two patterns: the pattern in the biblical text and the unfolding pattern of the civil rights movement. Identifying the link, pointing out that the link exists, is the work of typology. It doesn't have to draw out a specific point-by-point explanation of why the link works, of how the two (or more) patterns cohere. The observation itself that they do is usually sufficient.

O'Keefe and Reno identify three different kinds of typology that frequently appear in patristic writings.[27] First, most common, and most important for our purposes, is the prefiguring of Christ in the Old Testament. For instance, Cassiodorus will constantly see patterns in the events of David's life—particularly those noted in the psalm headings—that he will apply to the Christ. He will also see them in many of the historical events narrated by the Psalms. Second, typology was used to "establish the Scriptural basis for the practices of the early church."[28] In the psalms, statements about animal sacrifice will frequently be transformed typologically to refer to the inner spiritual life of the Christian or to the rites of the church. Too, Cassiodorus will usually find some way to tie references to "water (or rivers or floods or seas)" back to the sacrament of baptism. Third, typology was used to connect community experiences into the scriptural experiences. This is the connection we saw above between the struggle for civil rights and the exodus; the experience of African Americans is understood in light of the patterns of Exodus. In Cassiodorus's work, Israel beset by enemies will commonly be read typologically as the church under assault from heresies.

Allegory has been defined for us by Cassiodorus himself: "Allegory means saying one thing while meaning another."[29] O'Keefe and Reno

---

[27] Ibid., 73.
[28] Ibid.
[29] Cassiodorus, *ExplPs* 98.8, p. 2.435.

helpfully separate allegory into three subcategories. "First, allegories can help make sense of texts that seem to make no sense at the literal level."[30] The most obvious example here is the headings of the psalms. The headings contain Hebrew phrases that are obscure. Modern scholars believe that they refer to tune names. Cassiodorus didn't even have the benefit of seeing them in their original language but rather encountered them as a Latin translator had tried to make sense of what a Hellenistic Jewish translator had rendered into Greek—who himself apparently did not understand what the headings meant. Hence in the chapter on psalm headings in the commentary's preface, Cassiodorus tells us that since they make no literal sense, they must have a spiritual and figural meaning:

> Some psalm-headings where they make similar allusions must clearly be understood in the spiritual [*spiritualiter*] sense, for if you ponder the literal [*litteram*] meaning the heading is irrelevant [*extraneum est*], since you do not find in the psalms the content indicated by the headings. But if a figurative interpretation [*tropicum intellectum*] is applied to them, they seem totally appropriate. For example: *When he fled from the face of Absalom* denotes a historical situation; *When he was in the desert of Edom*, a locality; *On the day before the sabbath*, a date; *For Idithun*, a Hebrew name; *When he changed his countenance in the presence of Abimelech*, a comparison of attitudes; *For the winepresses*, a comparison with similar situations.[31]

What Cassiodorus is suggesting here is that the terms in the headings provide an associative context through which the psalm should be read. Thus, when Cassiodorus sees "For the winepresses" at the head of Psalm 84 (appearing as "according to The Gittith" in the NRSV), he—following Augustine—understands the winepress to be a symbol of affliction. Just as a grape is crushed in a winepress and thereby produces its sweet liquid, "In the same way when God's Church is crushed by afflictions and persecutions, the merits of the saints, hitherto unrealized in tranquil times, become clear."[32] Therefore, because of this

---

[30] O'Keefe and Reno, *Sanctified Vision*, 73.

[31] Cassiodorus, *ExplPs* Intro. 10, p. 1.32.

[32] Cassiodorus, *ExplPs* 84.1, p. 2.313. Just to be clear, in referring to the "merits of the saints," Cassiodorus is talking about virtues acquired by members of the community, not about supernatural benefits accrued to particular holy individuals

heading, the reader should assume that the psalm will be discussing how virtue comes out of affliction for the church.

The second kind of allegory is not caused by an issue at the literal level of the text. "Instead, the interpreters press the literal sense to draw out additional meaning.... The interpretation does not doubt or question the literal sense; instead, the reader sees a surplus within the literal sense, and the interpretation is designed to draw it out."[33] In a secular example, Sigmund Freud read the Oedipus myth as a story about a tragic Greek figure and also as a narrative about how children relate to their parents psychologically as they mature. The psychological reading does not alter or change the meaning of a story about a hero but finds additional meaning within it.

O'Keefe and Reno suggest that with this level, the allegorical meaning lies latent within the text. In the New Testament, the parables offer themselves as clear examples. These short pithy stories can be read as vignettes of Mediterranean peasant life that have meanings embedded in them and also can be read allegorically where the various agricultural images can represent something else. Indeed, the authors of the Synoptic Gospels—Matthew, Mark, and Luke—all show Jesus interpreting the Parable of the Sower as an allegory where there is an additional meaning behind the parable intended by the author.[34] In the Psalms, allegories where the meaning is latent are harder to come by and, when they do appear, the allegories usually look like typology. Psalm 72 is an obvious and easy example. This psalm praises a messianic king who will rule Israel in a state of peace, righteousness, and fertility. There can be no surprise whatsoever that Cassiodorus, Augustine, and all of the church fathers will read it with reference to Christ.

Similarly, Psalm 80:8-18 ("You brought a vine out of Egypt; you drove out the nations and planted it") offers an allegorical account of the history of Israel, using images that draw on the Hebrew poetic tradition and are repeated several times in Scripture. The image of the people of Israel as a vine and the land of Israel as God's vineyard appears in the ancient Song of Miriam (Exod 15:17: "You brought

---

to be shared among the church in the way the phrase is used in later medieval theology.

[33] O'Keefe and Reno, *Sanctified Vision*, 92.
[34] See Matthew 13:1-15; Mark 4:1-12; Luke 8:4-10.

them in and planted them on the mountain of your own possession") and is used to great effect in Isaiah 5, where the image of a vineyard left to be engulfed by the wilderness becomes an oracle of judgment against the sins of the people. Cassiodorus reads the allegory and then applies a typology as well:

> *Thou hast brought a vineyard out of Egypt: thou hast cast out the Gentiles and planted it.* He passes to the second section, in which he recounts the historical events [*gesta*] by means of allegorical utterances [*mysticas figurationes*]. This figure is called *metabole*, the frequent repetition of the one thing with a variety of words. The vineyard is described throughout these six verses up to the third division. The vineyard stands for the Jewish race, clearly denoting a type [*in typo*] of the Church; from it was sprung the gathering of the faithful. Vineyard [*vinea*] gets its name from vines [*vites*]. This vineyard He led out of Egypt by means of great and notable miracles, and then, having driven out the Gentiles (that is, the Hethites, Jebusites, and their other neighbours), the wonder-working Husbandman planted it there. This is the testimony offered, as mentioned in the heading, of the transformation of the Jews, for here too the vineyard is being most splendidly compared with the Church. Just as the vineyard bears vital fruit amidst the foliage doomed to fall, so the Church is adorned with the fruit of the saints amongst the overhanging crowd of sinners.[35]

Thus, Cassiodorus reads the story of the vine as the history of Israel but then also interprets it as representing the church.

The third style of allegory that O'Keefe and Reno identify is "allegory that can be used to negate the literal sense and redirect the reader's attention."[36] This is where allegory takes over the meaning and replaces it with something else that is contrary to the literal meaning. These are the passages that Origen might identify as not having a true literal sense to begin with. The classic example for this kind of allegory is Psalm 137. Despite the first part being used in a pop song in the 1970s, the whole text represents a psalm of trauma, a response to the destruction of Jerusalem, and the exile of the Jewish elite into Babylon. The infamous final verses ("O daughter Babylon, you dev-

---

[35] Cassiodorus, *ExplPs* 80.9, p. 2.287.
[36] O'Keefe and Reno, *Sanctified Vision*, 92.

astator! Happy shall they be who pay you back what you have done to us! Happy shall they be who take your little ones and dash them against the rock!"; Ps 137:8-9) are a cry for vengeance by a people who had seen their own children butchered before their eyes. It is almost surprising that Cassiodorus serves up a standard interpretation for this psalm. As a man himself in exile from a country that had seen bitter war, he gives no indication that the literal sense holds any significance to him personally. Rather, he follows Augustine's interpretation closely throughout the psalm. Babylon represents the city of the earthly world; Jerusalem is the heavenly country where the psalmist wishes to be. Giving the psalm a moral meaning throughout, Cassiodorus takes the abhorrent verse 9 and cuts against the literal meaning of the text:

> *Blessed be he that shall take and dash thy little ones against the rock.* They are still addressing the flesh, stating that the person who takes hold of his little ones, meaning his harmful vices, is blessed, because he has already made progress towards controlling them; for when we hold something we take it in our power, and it ceases to be free since it has begun to be enslaved by us. He added: *And shall dash them against the rock,* so that he does not linger in holding them, in case their enticing pleasure creeps over him. *He shall dash them against the rock* means against none other than the Lord Saviour, of whom it was written: *The rock was Christ* (1 Corinthians 10:4); thus the impulses which fired us with the foulest emotions are at once shattered and dispersed.[37]

In such a way the literal meaning of the text is subverted and converted into a morally satisfactory message.

Thus, O'Keefe and Reno see three varieties of allegory: one that makes sense of a nonsensical literal text, one that amplifies the literal meaning of the text drawing out latent meanings intended within it, and one that cuts against the literal meaning of the text. The issue here is that these three do not adequately cover the range of allegorical styles that Cassiodorus uses. O'Keefe and Reno—like de Lubac—are trying to describe styles of reading that can be used for theological purposes and thus are trying to present allegorical methods in the best possible light to modern readers. In addition to these three,

---

[37] Cassiodorus, *ExplPs* 137.9, p. 3.364.

Cassiodorus uses an additional style that takes a concrete image, item, or concept from the passage and, by verbally or conceptually analyzing that image, constructs a relationship that proceeds from it. An example is his interpretation of the Latin rendering of Psalm 17:8a ("Keep me, O Lord, as the pupil of your eye").

English renderings tend to preserve the Hebrew idiom that is being used here; the NRSV reads, "Guard me as the apple of the eye." The Septuagint translated the idiom and passed a more literal sense into the Latin, offering "pupil" rather than "apple." Cassiodorus seizes upon the notion of the pupil. Working with it, he discovers a theological meaning hidden in the phrase:

> By the figure of *icon*, in Latin *imaginatio*, the Lord compared himself with the pupil of an eye, the pupil being the conspicuous part of the eye set at the centre which enables us to distinguish the colours of objects of different kinds. It is called a pupil [*pupilla*] because it is small [*pusilla*]. The comparison of Christ with it was apt, for His allotted task at His judgment is to separate the just from sinners; hence it is most fitting for Him to be guarded as the pupil of an eye, for it is through the pupil that we discern visible objects, and no more excellent faculty is found in our bodies.[38]

Cassiodorus does begin by conveying the literal sense of the passage, the sense that the pupil of the eye is something that should be carefully guarded or kept (he gets an assist from the Greek since *fulaxo* means both "keep" and "guard" and enters Latin as *custodio*), but he also gives an allegorical reading. Note that the etymology here (*pupilla* coming from *pusilla*, totally wrong linguistically) is simply part of his regular reading process; he does not try to make any interpretive hay out of it. Rather, he determines that the pupil is the part of the eye that does the work of judging or discerning; just as the pupil is the judge of the eye, Christ too is the judge of humanity.

Some interpreters attempt to fix the meaning of the more common images and symbols; in the introductory work of Eucherius, he attempts to establish set meanings for a host of words. Augustine and Cassiodorus reject such an approach. Augustine does so program-

---

[38] Cassiodorus, *ExplPs* 17.8, p. 1.171.

matically in *Christian Instruction*, devoting all of chapter 25 of book 3 to expounding this point. He starts by warning, "We must not think it to be prescribed that what a thing signifies by similitude in one place must always be signified by that thing."[39] Instead, he lays out a couple of possible scenarios. In one, a given thing can be interpreted in either a good or a bad sense; context will determine which sense will fit better. In the other, no such binary is possible: there are some things—he gives the example of water—that can have many different significations.

Cassiodorus, as is his custom, accomplishes the same thing through inductive means rather than deductive; Psalm 11:1b ("Flee like a bird [Lat., sparrow (*passer*)] to the mountains") provides an opportunity for him to lay out Augustine's two scenarios by demonstrating them by means of two images that appear right next to each other:

> In the divine Scriptures, *mountain* is ambivalent, being applied in comparison to very different things. It is often used in both good and bad senses. When it is used in a good sense, its strength and notable height are regarded; when in a bad sense, its inner stolidness and lofty pride. So the one term is aptly applied to different objects after reflection on their qualities. There are also several types of *sparrow*. Some take pleasure in holes in walls, while others make for dewy valleys, and others haunt scaly mountains. But here the psalmist speaks of those whose most random inclination bears them off to the loftiest region of earth. So those who in fickleness of wavering mind turn to most wicked doctrines are rightly considered similar to them.[40]

Here, "mountain" signifies the kind of object that can be taken in either a good or bad sense while "sparrow" demonstrates a more ambiguous range that requires greater discernment. Even the idea that "mountain" is a binary breaks down after a while. By just the end of his first volume, Cassiodorus has already interpreted mountains as the preoccupations of the rich (Ps 18:7), justice (Ps 24:3), the apostles (Ps 36:6; 46:2), and Christ (Ps 48:1).

---

[39] Augustine, *Christian Instruction* 3.25.35 (ChrDoc, pp. 99–100).
[40] Cassiodorus, *ExplPs* 11.2, p. 1.135.

Keeping the Goal in Mind

If the goal of reading the Scriptures is to gain information—data about God, about doctrine, about what to do and what not to do—this process of figurative reading would be very frustrating. If things keep changing their meanings, how are we supposed to know what any given thing means? How can we rely on what is found? Indeed—this was one of the consistent criticisms of allegorical reading in the West from the rise of scholasticism in the twelfth and thirteenth centuries, reaching a fever pitch in the sixteenth century with the Reformation, and even to the present day. If Cassiodorus had been asked this question, particularly with reference to the Psalms commentary, he likely would have been confused by the question. His disagreement would be with the fundamental premise. He is not teaching people how to discover data or to gain information about the Scriptures. Rather, he is teaching them how to read in order to initiate them into the practice of prayer.

This is the goal of reading for him. This is the proper target of interpretation. Scripture in general and the Psalms in particular aren't just read: they are prayed; they are sung. Furthermore, as he frequently likes to say, singing alone is insufficient:

> Singing entails uttering the Lord's words with the lips, and praising means fulfilling with constancy the divine commands by good works. These are the two things demanded of us in every way: faithfully to sing the Lord's praises with our lips and to carry out His commands by our deeds.[41]

Prayer is fulfilled in action. Praying the Scripture brings forth virtues that lead to godly living. Going back to the *Variae*, and in particular to the letter that he sent to the Senate announcing his appointment as praetorian prefect, we can already see this logic in place. Cassiodorus, writing in the voice of King Athalaric, tells us:

> [Cassiodorus] showed goodwill to all, was moderate in prosperity, and knew no anger, unless when gravely wronged. Although he is a man of strict justice, he does not refuse, in his severity, to forgo his wrath. He is remarkably generous with his goods, and,

---

[41] Cassiodorus, *ExplPs* 21.14, p. 1.214.

while incapable of pursuing others' property, he knows well how to be a lavish giver of his own. Now this disposition his studies in divinity have confirmed [*Hos igitur mores lectio divina solidavit*], since affairs are always well conducted if the fear of heaven is opposed to human impulses. For thence is derived the clear understanding of every virtue; thence wisdom is seasoned with the flavour of truth. Thus, the man imbued with the discipline of heaven is rendered lowly in all things.[42]

Whether Cassiodorus had attained all of these virtues (particularly humility) at that time is entirely immaterial. What this letter demonstrates is what virtues he saw as desirable even for a man still in public service and the means by which to acquire them. Sacred reading was itself an efficacious manner of acquiring the virtues and godly character. Obviously, there was more to it than that, but it was certainly a cornerstone of an effective regimen.

Saint Benedict was also convinced of both the importance and efficacy of *lectio divina*; sacred reading was the third leg of the monastic tripod alongside the singing of the Offices and the manual labor. Reading and meditation on what had been read, memorization, and internalization were essential parts of the monastic life. Despite the importance of sacred reading and the amount of time given over to it daily in the monastery, we possess from that time no texts or guides directing monks how sacred reading ought to be done. The earliest guide that we possess is the *Scala Claustralium* (Ladder of Monks) of Guigo II, a Carthusian monk and the ninth abbot of the Grande Chartreuse who died around 1188. That's a gap of some 650 years between Cassian, Benedict, and Guigo. What did monks do to learn how to do sacred reading before Guigo wrote his manual? While a big piece of the puzzle is obviously oral instruction handed down from monk to monk, Cassiodorus's *Explanation of the Psalms* offers a clear example of how reading turns to prayer. Rather than providing a deductive manual on how to pray with Scripture, Cassiodorus demonstrates it with his inductive method. He lapses into prayer, showing how prayer spontaneously arises from the practices of reading and how this natural prayer works, what it looks and sounds like. The further

---

[42] Cassiodorus, *Variae* 9.25.11 (Barnish, 129–30).

into the commentary we go, the more the summaries turn into prayers rather than conceptual summations.

As one of the first full books apart from Scripture a monk would encounter, Cassiodorus's commentary was central for teaching early medieval readers the intermediate and advanced arts of reading; he was also their first great guide into the art of prayer through reading. Cassiodorus didn't just teach them how to read as sophisticated readers; he taught them what prayer in and through a text felt like.

That's why the apparently random nature of the allegorical interpretation in the text would not have been a problem for him or his contemporaries. His spiritual identifications are part of the act of prayer, the act of listening intently to a text to see what word from God might be in them, what hidden revelation might be waiting to shape the reader's character more perfectly into the mind of Christ. This is also why Cassiodorus frequently steps back from a logical explication and uses the terms "apt," "fitting," or "proper."

On Aptness

This idea of "apt"-ness is an interesting one; it is a favorite term and technique of Cassiodorus. All sorts of images and interpretations are identified as being "apt" or "fitting" (which is usually translating some version of the Latin term *aptus*). This is, essentially, an aesthetic category. That is, Cassiodorus sees the world as a grand vision of coherences. There are all sorts of things that align in order to point to a variety of vast hidden truths. One of the ways to see how all of these things are pointing to the truth about God, Christ, and humanity is to notice points of congruence, points of overlap, the associative connections, where one truth suggests another; the confirmation that the two are aligned is that our solution or connection is elegant or beautiful.

Sometimes we make a distinction between two different kinds of knowing: logic and intuition. The widely known Myers-Briggs Type Indicator uses a dichotomy between "sensing" and "intuition" to distinguish the two ends of a spectrum that identifies how a person prefers to gather and interpret information. The first wants to see formal chains of logic where A leads to B which leads to C which leads to D in a clear and linear progression. The second will intuit an answer, looking at a problem and jumping from A to D and then sometimes filling in the steps from B to C to D only after the fact (if at all). Cassiodorus's "fittingness" or "aptness" is an intuitive mode of analysis. He perceives a relationship between two things. He doesn't necessarily show the logical steps between them. Instead—he puts the congruence out there and provides an opportunity for his reader to do that work if that is in one's personality. Thinking spiritually, every time he makes an intuitive leap and connects two disparate concepts, he is offering a riddle or a koan for the reader to tease out over hours of meditation on why or how a certain connection is fitting and illuminating.

In the same way that an intuitive mathematician might look at a problem and recognize a correct solution because of its elegance and then work back to identify the correspondences that make it so, Cassiodorus is an intuitive interpreter. He finds correspondences that fit his aesthetic vision of how the world fits together beautifully and coherently. All beauty and all truth point to God, and he leaves the details about exactly how the logic works to be worked out later.

This space that he leaves is space for the Holy Spirit to do its work: to lead, direct, teach, and—ultimately, in line with John 16:13—guide the readers into all truth.

The end of reading is not information—it is transformation, and that comes only through prayer and contemplation. This is what Cassiodorus is ultimately aiming for: teaching his monks to read in order that they more deeply pray the truths that they find in Scripture. What they find there will enable them to grow into the full stature of Christ. In learning how to read the Psalms—to pray the Psalms—they learn how to read and pray the rest of Scripture as well.

Is Veiled Reading Legitimate Reading?

The final question to tackle before heading back into the Psalms commentary itself is to consider this strategy of reading. Is this veiled reading that Cassiodorus champions a legitimate way to read the biblical text? Is Cassiodorus doing a proper reading of the psalms?

The simplest answer is just this: that's not our call.

Cassiodorus belongs to a community of readers, a community grounded in the organic continuity of the church. Drawing from Origen, from Hilary, from Augustine, and from Jerome, Cassiodorus reads alongside these giants and a host of others whose names we will never know. He has learned to read and exercises his habits of reading within this community of readers. They are the ones who have established the rules of engagement with the text. We can judge the degree to which Cassiodorus reads within his own community, but we cannot judge how he or his community have chosen to read, expecting to stand as independent arbiters of meaning apart from our own reading contexts and intellectual currents. Because we can't—we don't—we aren't.

Gallons of ink have been spilled over the question of where meaning is located within a text. Is the meaning of a text what its author intended it to say? Does the text itself have a meaning entirely independent of its author and its readers? Or is the meaning of a text negotiated among communities who read it—especially when we are talking about texts that certain communities have selected as being foundational to who they are and how they choose to be in the world?

Texts have limits. The words, the grammar, the narrative structure limit what any given passage can mean. But the people who read it together are the ultimate arbiters of how they understand that they will read it. We cannot tell them how to read; we can only inform our own communities within which we read how we believe we should read.

As a biblical scholar, I follow certain canons that have shaped the academic community regarding how texts should be read. Within that community, authorial intention, the cultural and historical context, and the compositional practices of the people and language who produced the text take pride of place. As a student of the history of interpretation, I see Cassiodorus as an exemplar of his tradition: he pulls together the major strands of interpretation that energize how the early medieval Western church read and understood the psalms. As a believing Christian, I follow the historic creeds of the church and the tradition of the church as informed by my own reason and by my experience of the sacraments, trusting in the guidance of the Holy Spirit.

None of this gives me the right to judge Cassiodorus on how he reads. What it does give me is the right to decide whether his reading practices would be appropriate in the overlapping reading communities of which I am a member. As I see it, I have at least three options: yes, no, and yes-but. As a biblical scholar, I have to say no. Cassiodorus does not read the psalms in the way that modern scholars do. He displays a marked lack of respect for authorial intention and no sense that his culture is different from that which produced the text. As a historian of the interpretation of Scripture, Cassiodorus represents primary evidence as to how people read and believed in the complex clash of East, West, and barbarian that characterize the Italian sixth century. I must say yes that he is a faithful exemplar of his time and place. As a believing Christian, I must say yes-but. The reading strategies that Cassiodorus offers are rich, and yet they bear within them a strain of anti-Semitism and anti-Judaism that has born deadly fruit over the centuries, most notably in the twentieth-century attempt to exterminate European Jews by Nazi Germany and most recently fanned by outbreaks of anti-Semitism across the United States and Europe.

Naming Supersessionism

The two deep problems that haunt the reading of Cassiodorus and the early church more broadly are an oppositional image of the Jewish people and supersessionism. I have said before that with reference to Origen some of the strategies that were used that seem puzzling or unusual to modern readers are precisely because they took the text very seriously and were intensely close readers of it. Origen, Augustine, and Cassiodorus are not coming up with this on their own; they are learning it from the pages of the New Testament.

The earliest church was a Jewish phenomenon. Jesus and his followers were all Jewish. So far as we know, all of the writings of the New Testament were written by Jewish authors with the possible exception of Luke and Acts; there is debate around whether Luke was a Gentile or a Hellenized Jew. Obviously, earliest Christianity existed in a contentious relationship with the late Second Temple Judaism from which it emerged, all the more so because of the turmoil around the three unsuccessful Jewish revolts and subsequent wars with Rome that rocked the province of Palestine, including the destruction of the temple in Jerusalem in the year 70 and the expulsion of Jewish people from Jerusalem by Hadrian in 136.

John, Paul, and Revelation all draw a hard and sharp contrast between early Christian communities and the Jewish communities with which they related. The language they use for Jewish believers who do not recognize Jesus as the Messiah is frequently inflammatory. John's gospel records Jesus telling a group of Jewish leaders, "You are from your father the devil, and you choose to do your father's desires. . . .

Whoever is from God hears the words of God. The reason you do not hear them is that you are not from God" (John 8:44, 47). Modern scholars read these words as the bitter reaction of Jewish Christians who had been kicked out of their home communities and remind us that this dialogue and others like it are part of an intra-Jewish conflict. Once Christianity became a largely Gentile movement, though, it becomes frighteningly easy to read these words as divine sanction for anti-Semitism. One of the reasons why the church fathers display a shocking streak of anti-Semitism is because they have taken these passages vilifying the Jewish people at face value.

The other danger is supersessionism. This is the belief that the church has both displaced and replaced the Jewish people as the true people of God. This was a widely accepted understanding through much of Christian history. Reading all references to Israel, Jerusalem, and Zion as references to the church buy into this notion. A strictly allegorical interpretation of these terms that substitutes the church whenever the Jewish people are mentioned in the Scriptures serves to write the Jewish people out of the text of Scripture, leaving only the condemnations found in the gospels. A tall stack of books has been written detailing the precise issues here and problems that this way of reading has caused and does cause. For our purposes, it is sufficient to say that references to Israel, Zion, and Jerusalem can be read as references to the church as long as they are read in an additive fashion. That is, as Paul says, the church is grafted onto the tree of Israel (Rom 11:17-24). The church has been privileged to receive God's self-revelation to Israel, and Christians participate within the broader scope of God's redemptive activity alongside—not instead of—their Jewish brothers and sisters.

Conclusion

Cassiodorus offers a rich and complex strategy for reading the Psalms and making sense of them for the monastic readers of his time period. He regards the Psalter as a repository for a wide array of divine wisdom and teaches his students how to read the text as ornamented language. Passing beyond the straightforward grammatical sense of the text, Cassiodorus distinguishes between two fundamental levels of reading, the literal and the spiritual. While the allegorical interpretations that Cassiodorus presents may be far-fetched to modern readers, the end goal of Cassiodorus's reading project is not information or even a correct interpretation—it is prayer. Taken as a whole, Cassiodorus's *Explanation of the Psalms* represents an in-depth example of the practice of *lectio divina*, the form of spiritual reading as meditation that would dominate monastic spiritual life for centuries to come.

Summary

Cassiodorus's *Explanation of the Psalms* is deeply indebted to Augustine's *Enarrations on the Psalms*. Nevertheless, the borrowing from Augustine is neither as simple nor as direct as it might have been. One reason for this can be found in the means by which Cassiodorus accessed Augustine's work, probably encountering it as an oral text from which he took notes rather than a manuscript lying on his desk. Another reason is that Cassiodorus was doing something different from what Augustine was doing; Augustine was preaching on the Psalms to an assembled congregation while Cassiodorus was realizing an Augustinian vision for Christian study and instruction. Grounded in the Psalms, imbued with classical learning, Cassiodorus was demonstrating how Scripture study ought to be accomplished and how it attained its final end through prayer.

CHAPTER EIGHT

A Thorough Reading of Psalm 87

Getting Ready to Write

Let us imagine, for a moment, Cassiodorus getting himself ready to write. It's early afternoon in Constantinople. He has prayed with monks at the household or at a church around the corner upon rising, then made some morning visits. He went to the Imperial Library where one of the librarians read for him Augustine's commentary on Psalm 87. Then, for good measure, he asked the man to read to him Jerome's homily on the psalm as well. As he listened, he took notes on a set of wax tablets. After returning home, a light meal, and more prayers, he is ready to begin his work. The morning's wax tablets are sitting next to him now. He's in a well-lighted space, maybe on a balcony overlooking a walled garden. A reading stand is in front of him with an open Psalter. He's sitting in a chair, his feet are up on a footstool, and a fresh tablet is in his lap, stylus poised above it. He pauses for a moment and ponders where to go from here.

The text is Psalm 87. It's not a long psalm. The focus is on Zion and a variety of peoples from the Near East and Africa. He thinks about the men for whom he is writing, his collection of monks at Vivarium. While some of them may have come from North Africa, which is just across the Mediterranean, after all, and culturally more similar than either the East or even barbarian-plagued Gaul, none of them would likely visit Jerusalem or Tyre or Babylon. What to say, then, to these men about the places that were just so many names in manuscripts?

Augustine had to deal with the same issue. In his preaching on the north coast of Africa, the people to whom he spoke would likely never leave the town of Hippo, unless it was to see Carthage. Places like Jerusalem and Tyre were just names of far-off places to them. Jerusalem had been in ruins at the time that Augustine was writing—he said as much in his commentary—but the last century had seen much rebuilding in Jerusalem, enough that the Eastern general Belisarius had to move troops south in 542 to dissuade Persian forces from helping themselves to its riches.

Thinking back over what he had heard and flipping through his notes, Cassiodorus notes that Augustine had spent a significant amount of time talking about buildings. In particular, there was a great deal of discussion around the apostles and prophets as the foundation of the city, and Jesus as the chief cornerstone. But hadn't Paul also said that Jesus was the foundation of the building? How could he be in both places at the same time? Cassiodorus couldn't help thinking about the building he had just seen by the library, the towering new church dedicated just a few years ago to Holy Wisdom. Talk about a keystone that holds everything in place—the great dome of the church had to have just such a keystone in order to hold the entire dome suspended in the air, and it was truly an architectural wonder of the world!

Of course, Augustine read Zion as the church, the new Jerusalem, and as it is the holy city of the world, so Babylon represents the unholy city of the world. All of the other cities represented the various parts of the world that had been incorporated into the church through faith and baptism. God had chosen princes, yes, but first had chosen fishermen—choosing the foolish to humble the wise—before choosing orators (like Justin Martyr and Augustine himself) and then princes (like Constantine and the other emperors). And then, indeed, princes from the worldliness of Babylon came to Rome to stand before the tomb of the fisherman. (Cassiodorus knew the church that Augustine referred to well; he had attended services at the church of St. Peter on the Vatican Hill during his time in the city.)

Finally, Augustine spends a fair amount of time praising rest, the quiet rest of peace. It is part of a great joyfulness that the eye has not seen, nor ear heard, nor heart conceived. Indeed, after the career he has been through, a life consisting of songs of praise and a deep quiet sounds like heaven to Cassiodorus as well!

Pausing yet again to summon his copy of Jerome's work on Hebrew names, Cassiodorus prepares to begin his version.

The Psalm Heading

First, Cassiodorus addresses the title: "For the sons of Core. A psalm of a canticle." Although he's addressed these items before, he identifies them briefly. The sons of Core refer to Christians. He had already written on the sons of Core in Psalm 42, where the name first appears, and, following Jerome, had noted that Core means Calvary, the place where Jesus was crucified, and thus children of the cross, Christians. A psalm is a song, but it is a song that raises the mind to the higher parts because the musical instrument called a psaltery produces the sound from its upper and therefore higher part. Both the sons of Core and the psalm are, however, among the earthly tents only able to contemplate the heavenly city. Augustine (and Jerome in his treatment) had signaled a link to Hebrews 11:8-16 where Abraham, dwelling among the tents of a pagan people, raised his eyes and followed a hope of faith toward a more permanent homeland in a city yet to be. Cassiodorus fits this in but without an explicit link. Some will catch it; some won't. At least not now.

The Division of the Psalm

Cassiodorus divides the psalm into three pieces according to his usual pattern. The diapsalms in the text indicate breaks that seem to signal a shift of topic, a shift of speakers, or both. Since there are two in this psalm, he goes with three sections, even if the last one is only one line long.

Although it may seem a bit awkward to have a one-line final section, it does work out with the way that he hears the different speakers in the psalm. The chief and first speaker is David, the Prophet. David speaks the first section from the beginning through verse 3 as he tells the faithful of the wonder of the holy city. The second speaker is Christ, and he speaks from verse 4 through verse 6, announcing the nations who will come to believe in him. Then David concludes with the final line, considering the joys of the heavenly city. In this way Cassiodorus satisfactorily negotiates the tricky pronoun situation: The "me" in verse 4 certainly can't pertain to David—someone else must be speaking it. But whoever speaks that "me" is unlikely to then use "you" in the final verse. Since the final part picks up the theme started first, it seems most logical that the speakers are the same. Having made these dispositions, Cassiodorus is ready to move into the phrases of the psalm itself.

The First Section

New Revised Standard Version	Latin of Cassiodorus	Douay-Rheims (adapted)[1]
¹On the holy mount stands the city he founded; ²the LORD loves the gates of Zion more than all the dwellings of Jacob. ³ Glorious things are spoken of you, O city of God. Selah	Fundamenta eius in montibus sanctis ²diligit Dominus portas Sion super omnia tabernacula Iacob ³gloriosa dicta sunt de te civitas Dei DIAPSALMA	THE foundations thereof are the holy mountains: ² The Lord loveth the gates of Sion above all the tabernacles of Jacob. ³ Glorious things are said of thee, O city of God.

There are a couple of issues here with the first verse that Cassiodorus has to deal with. First, this psalm seems to start out of nowhere. Foundations—of what? What holy mountains are we talking about, anyway? Second, Augustine spends a great deal of time wrestling with where parts of this building are located. Is Christ the cornerstone, the keystone, or the foundation? What of the apostles and prophets? The complication here is that St. Paul speaks on good authority with two contradictory points. Ephesians 2:20 clearly refers to the apostles and prophets as the foundation of the spiritual temple; 1 Corinthians 3:11 says there is no other foundation than Jesus Christ.

---

[1] The Douay-Rheims is an English translation of the standard medieval Latin Vulgate text. As a result, it is widely used by medievalists and historians to understand how the Vulgate text differed in meaning from what they might find in a modern-language Bible translated from the Hebrew and Greek sources. I have made occasional adaptations to bring this Douay-Rheims text into conformity with Cassiodorus's Latin text.

Cassiodorus, following Augustine, solves the first problem in two ways. First, by introducing the theme of the heavenly city at the beginning of his discussion of the superscription and carrying it through his summary in the division, he takes the opportunity to set before his readers what the psalm will be about. By the time the reader encounters a sudden "foundation" at the start of the first verse, a context has already been provided for it. Second, he borrows Augustine's understanding that someone pondering a topic may hold forth—starting in the middle where their thoughts are—rather than beginning with a logical beginning.

Rather than agonize along with Augustine over what is Christ and what is the apostles, he devises a better solution. The foundation of the heavenly city is without a doubt Jesus Christ. The apostles and prophets are none other than mountains on which it is located! Nor is this a novel interpretation: already in five previous psalms he has interpreted the mountains in this way. The apostles and prophets are like mountains because of the solidity of their faith and their towering holiness.

A note added into the text several years later allows Cassiodorus to point out two additional things. In speaking of the structures of the holy city, he is able to plug an important history that he has had translated from Greek into Latin, *On the Antiquities of the Jews* by the Jewish author Josephus. Its circulation in the Latin West seems largely due to the efforts of Cassiodorus. He also recommends to the monks of Vivarium an image of the tabernacle that was the precursor and model of the temple that was painted and inserted into one of the pandects—the big one-volume Bibles—created at Vivarium. In an odd quirk of transmission, we know about this painting not just from this note but also because the pandect itself traveled to England and was seen and commented on by the great English biblical scholar Bede.

Passing to the next verse, Cassiodorus recognizes the verse that should have been placed first: here, a name has been offered and a context provided. If this had been the first verse, the start of the psalm would have been much clearer. Accordingly, he identifies this as a kind of rhetorical figure, called *anastrophe* in Greek, or an inversion, because something has been placed out of order. What ought to have been the first line has been inverted to be second.

Cassiodorus clarifies that "Zion" is a mountain within Jerusalem. By this time, his readers are quite familiar with it because it has been named almost twenty times already by this point in the Psalter; it is not only a mountain but also the holy mountain on which the temple stands. Throughout his interpretation, "Zion," "temple," "city," and "Jerusalem" will become increasingly interchangeable terms for him. When he reads "Zion"—or even "Jerusalem"—he is thinking about it not as the literal, historic city but as the future consummation of the church, the glittering edifice that descends from heaven like a massive jewel as described in Revelation 21–22 that will be the true and pure bride of Christ. "Zion," he informs his readers, means "watchtower" (cribbing from Jerome again) and that is because it is only from the holy mountain that the church can catch sight of the Jerusalem-that-is-to-come that outshines and is the true reality of which the current physical Jerusalem is a shadow.

The gates of Zion that the Lord loves are the means by which a person enters that wondrous Jerusalem-to-come: thus, they are faith, love, hope, baptism, repentance, and anything else that draws the soul into the true practices of the faith. They are the means of entering into the heart of true religion. Jerome had suggested that the gates were the virtues, and this seems right to Cassiodorus and fosters the kind of reading that he wants his monks to learn.

Not wanting to leave Augustine out of it, though, Cassiodorus then provides a second interpretation of the gates that draws from the African bishop: since there are twelve gates to the city (he assumes his readers will remember this detail from Rev 21:12-13) the gates themselves might be the apostles since their preaching is what originally drew people into the church—and still does through their letters and their doctrine that the church preserves.

When it comes to the "tabernacles of Jacob," Cassiodorus has a fixation on a particular kind of meaning. If we're not talking about the first place of worship that the Israelites established when leaving Egypt, then Cassiodorus understands tabernacles to be campaigning tents. These are the sorts of temporary structures that armies live in when they are on the move. From that definition, he sees "tabernacles" as referring to the Catholic Church and has mentioned this in at least two psalms before this one because the church on the march has taken over the whole of the known world (as far he's concerned). The church is always on campaign against the forces of the world that oppose it and keeps itself fit and ready to fight. The problem, then, is why the Lord would love something more than the dwelling places of the church? Cassiodorus solves this issue by assuring his readers that the Lord certainly loves the church now but that he will love the future Jerusalem more because it will be at rest and at peace, no longer needing to be constantly at war. It will be the permanent dwelling where God and the church will be united in blessed peace.

The next verse that closes out this first section is a transition. Here, David utilizes a grammatical sleight of hand to move into past tense what actually ought to be in the future tense. That is, he says, glorious things "are said" or "have been" said, when what is properly intended is that glorious things "will be spoken" of the new Jerusalem—and Jesus is about to say them in the next section.

The Second Section

New Revised Standard Version	Latin of Cassiodorus	Douay-Rheims (adapted)
⁴Among those who know me I mention Rahab and Babylon; Philistia too, and Tyre, with Ethiopia— "This one was born there," they say. ⁵And of Zion it shall be said, "This one and that one were born in it"; for the Most High himself will establish it. ⁶The LORD records, as he registers the peoples, "This one was born there." Selah	⁴memor ero Raab et Babylonis scientibus me ecce alienigenae et Tyrus et populus Aethiopum hi fuerunt in ea ⁵ Mater Sion dicet homo et homo facius est in ea et ipse fundavit eam Altissimus ⁶ Dominus narravit scripturas populorum et principum horum qui fuerunt in ea DIAPSALMA	⁴I will be mindful of Rahab and of Babylon knowing me. Behold the foreigners, and Tyre, and the people of the Ethiopians, these were there. ⁵The Mother of Sion says: This is a man, and he was born a man in her, and the Highest himself hath founded her. ⁶The Lord has told of the writings of peoples and of princes, of them that have been in her.

Since the psalm has crossed over a diapsalm, it has moved to a new speaker and new set of topics—or is at least addressing the former topics from a different angle now. Jesus Christ is now the speaker and discusses those who know him.

In the first verse of this section, though, there is an issue of terminology. "Rahab" can refer to three different things in Hebrew. By far the most familiar is the prostitute of Jericho who sheltered the spies of Joshua. This will be how Augustine, Jerome, and Cassiodorus all read this text: as referring to her. But Rahab is also a poetic expression for the great dragon of the deeps, a chaos monster whom God conquers as order-bringer in epic moments of the Psalms and Job. Then, the prophets, Isaiah in particular, give it a third meaning by transferring the name of this watery chaos beast to Egypt, the great, ancient, and dangerous serpent of the Nile. This is what prompts the Hebrew name in the psalm—this is an oblique and poetic reference to the nation of Egypt, which is why we find it in the NRSV among the other names of places.

But the church fathers never know any of this. The Septuagint translates away the name of Rahab in its second and third uses, leaving it solely as the name of the heroine of Jericho who will later be included in Matthew's genealogy of Jesus. Jerome is the only one of the church fathers who had the competence in Hebrew to make this catch—but even he doesn't.

Hence, Cassiodorus—like Augustine and Jerome before him—goes into some detail on Rahab and why she appears here. Starting with the basics, he identifies her as the prostitute who took in Joshua's spies, hid them, and enabled them to escape the city once they had completed their scouting. Etymologically, her name means "pride" and she represents the proud people who are nevertheless able to be converted to God's mercy and embrace the Gospel. She points to the church because the church is able to convert the proud and, teaching them humility and obedience, can lead them into the way of salvation.

Babylon is the city of the world that is set opposite to the city of heaven; its name means "confusion." These are the people who were trapped in idolatry until the proclamation of the church taught them a better way. Christ says that these people—the proud and the confused—came over to him, once they knew and recognized him. Just so Christ stated in the gospel openly when he told the Pharisees that the tax collectors and harlots would enter the kingdom of God before they would.

The next part of the verse continues in the same vein. More nations represent more kinds of people who are gathered into the church.

"Foreigners" are the outsiders, the Gentiles who believed and were included in the promises of God. Tyre refers to the anguish of penitents. Cassiodorus doesn't explain how he derives this explanation—he may be borrowing from Jerome here, but even that is uncertain. Jerome gives just a one-word meaning for Tyre: tribulation. Finally, Cassiodorus interprets the Ethiopians as those who were black with sins who, having been washed clean, are now in the church. Cassiodorus betrays here an implied whiteness in his readership. That is, he assumes that normal is not black and that skin color can and ought to be read in moral terms: dark-skinned people represent the sinful. While Jerome provides this same interpretation, it's significant that Augustine, the African bishop of Berber stock, chooses not to make this interpretive move.

This verse in the mouth of Christ becomes for Cassiodorus a literal fulfillment of the prophecy foretold by David in the previous verse. David had promised that glorious things would be spoken of Zion. Here, Christ lays out what these glorious things are: that peoples from across the earth from a host of moral conditions have been converted and gathered into the church, which will be the heavenly Jerusalem.

In moving to the next verse, another linguistic conundrum confronts Cassiodorus. This one Jerome calls out. Greek has a way of signaling rhetorical questions by means of a grammatical particle added onto the beginning of the sentence. Jerome notes that the Septuagint version of this verse starts off with one of these—it signals a rhetorical question ("Shall not Sion say a man . . . ?"). The problem is—as both he and Augustine noted—most of the translators had more piety than Greek and assumed that a letter had dropped out and that the Greek meant "mother." Hence Augustine refers to "Mother Zion," as do most editions of the Latin text. Even Jerome grudgingly interprets "Mother Zion," even though he knows that it is wrong, because it is popular and how people know the verse.

Cassiodorus needs to complicate the text even more. A lot of grammatical decisions in Latin are based on the word endings. Foreign words, however, often get away with getting no endings at all, which means we can sometimes project grammatical meanings onto them without any support from the letters on the page. Cassiodorus goes this route and translates "Mother *of* Zion" (projecting a genitive meaning onto an ostensibly nominative noun, for those who want the technical details).

He does this because of the way he has assigned his speaking roles and what he is going to do with the text. Augustine wants "the man" to be Jesus; Cassiodorus sees the problem here. If Mother Zion is the church, Jesus is not born into the church. If Mother Zion is the city of Jerusalem, Jesus was not born in Jerusalem either. He threads the interpretive needle by his grammatical sleight of hand. He maintains that "Zion" is the Catholic Church. The "Mother of Zion" therefore must be the synagogue—the Jewish faith—because the church was born out of it. In this way he can affirm that the "man" referred to here is Jesus because he was born as a Jewish man into the practice of the synagogue.

Cassiodorus isn't done messing with the grammar, though. He needs to alter the structure of the sentence a bit to get it to say what he wants. Many words that we take for granted in English can be implied in Latin, so the Latin has a certain flexibility to its meaning. The best way to take the Latin here is to render it "this man and that man were born in her" but the "this" and "that" are implied. Cassiodorus strains the grammatical possibilities a bit by taking the first "man [*homo*]" as a sentence unto itself: "this is a man." The first three words are all implied. The "and" becomes not a conjunction between nouns but a conjunction between two clauses or sentences. Yes, it's grammatical cheating, but, yes, Cassiodorus is pretty sure that he can get away with it.

The result of this verbal manipulation is that Cassiodorus has the synagogue, the mother of the church, asserting that Jesus is just a man, a christological fault that he points out to his readers to underscore the proper doctrine. But then he also has a new, true, sentence: "he was born a man in her," which is now correct in a way that it would not have been had he not made his manipulation. Now he can set this phrase off against the next, "the Highest himself hath founded her," in order to present a favorite kind of christological paradox. Yes, Jesus was born as a Jewish man, but—simultaneously—he is also the Most High God who created the synagogue and Zion and everything else to begin with. This way, Cassiodorus can shut down both Jewish and heretical Arian understandings of the nature of Christ that saw him just as a creature and not participating in divinity. That's a lot of interpretive gymnastics, but it ends up just the way Cassiodorus wants it: locating orthodox Christology in the psalm text against both Jewish and Arian claims.

The final verse of the section cements the christological claim: here, Cassiodorus sees Jesus referring all doubters of his incarnation back to the Law and the Prophets in which they can find abundant promises and prophecies regarding his true nature. Moses and the prophets, then, are the "peoples" and "princes" mentioned here. The odd "of them that have been in her" simply clarifies who these people and princes are—that they also were members of the synagogue and the Jewish faith; it's not intending to refer to outside princes and people at this point.

The Third Section

New Revised Standard Version	Latin of Cassiodorus	Douay-Rheims (adapted)
[7]Singers and dancers alike say, "All my springs are in you."	[7]sicut laetantium omnium nostrum habitatio est in te	[7]The dwelling in thee is as it were of all rejoicing.

We'll just start out by noting a great gulf between the Greek and the Hebrew in this verse; it's hard to see that the Greek has anything to do with the Hebrew at all; there's a chance that it may be drawing on a different textual tradition entirely. In any case, the Latin faithfully renders the rather jumbled Greek.

The key point here that all of the early Christian interpreters focus on is that we are talking about dwelling at last in the new Jerusalem, the ideal, heavenly city, and that there's a whole lot of rejoicing going on. Augustine will point out that there are no more pains, no more prayers, only songs of praise. Cassiodorus reverts this verse to David. He was the one talking about the heavenly city before, so he is going to round out the discussion here as well. Cassiodorus starts off by noticing that this is a very short verse and identifies it as a figure of speech called *brachylogy* which is the technical rhetorical term for cramming a whole lot of things into just a few words. Following Augustine, he cites Paul from 1 Corinthians 2:9, saying that no eye has seen nor ear heard nor heart known what God has prepared for those who love him. Thus, since we don't know it and can't express it, we can assume it's packed in here. Affliction ceases; prayer turns to praise;

tranquility abides forever because there is nothing to disturb it. There is nothing but joy.

Summary

Psalm 87 is a representative example of how Cassiodorus goes about his interpretive work. While he begins with Augustine and other interpreters like Jerome, he frequently goes in his own interpretive directions. While he maintains contact with the interpretive tradition, he makes his own decisions about how and when to apply their readings. He brings out classical techniques of reading in order to interpret what he finds, and, in some cases, he tends to over apply these techniques in order to achieve a reading that he sees within the text. He tends to do this the most when he believes a point about Christology is at stake. Finally, prayer and praise play an important role in Cassiodorus's art of interpretation as he sees these as the truest intention of the biblical text and its revelation of the triune God.

CHAPTER NINE

Five Psalms—Short Takes

Psalm 1 and the Christological Psalms[1]

Looking at Psalm 1

Psalm 1 is a relatively short psalm—only six verses in the NRSV. It pronounces blessings on those who do not do what the wicked do, on those who meditate on the Lord's law. A metaphor announces that these righteous will be like well-watered trees that flourish and bear good fruit whereas the opposite will happen to the wicked; dried up and shriveled, they will blow away like chaff in the wind. The Lord will watch over the righteous but will frustrate the wicked.

It is important to know that modern inclusive-language translations of the Psalms like the NRSV, the Grail Psalter, and the Psalter in the *Book of Common Prayer* make this psalm inclusive by moving to a plural subject: "Happy are those." The classical texts, following the original Hebrew text, all have "Happy is the man." This matters because, as we have noted, the intensive readers of the patristic age would often seize on certain small details of the text to construct a systemic understanding of the psalm. Sure enough, this word at the start of the psalm will become a major interpretive point of decision that we would be blind to if we were not aware of the underlying words.

How Cassiodorus Reads It

Since Psalms 1 and 2 are the only psalms in the Vulgate Psalter that do not have titles, Cassiodorus can't use his usual protocol by

---

[1] The Christological Psalms are an informal group that include Psalms 1, 2, 8, 21, 72, 82, 108, 110, and 139.

explaining what the title means and how it applies to the psalm. Not one to be daunted, however, Cassiodorus begins with an initial section explaining why Psalm 1 does not have a title! Christ himself is the head and the title not just of the psalm but of the whole book of Psalms. He notes that commentators are split on the identity of "the man" who is called happy or blessed. Is this a generic righteous person or Christ? He asserts that such righteousness belongs to Christ alone and that therefore the psalm must be in reference to him.

Having established Christ himself as the meaning of the psalm and the title over the whole Psalter, he launches into an instructive metaphor before moving on:

> What a marvellous sequence, a truly heavenly arrangement, since in our interest the beginning of the psalms has sprouted from Him who is clearly the moving Gate to heaven! So let us hasten to enter with the utmost joy where we observe our Advocate himself as the open Gate. As the apostle says: *For we have not a high priest who cannot have compassion on our infirmities*, and a little later: *Let us go therefore with confidence to the throne of his grace, that we may obtain mercy and find grace in seasonable aid*. Now let us insert the keys which can unlock the psalms, so that with the Lord's help we may deserve to enter the palace of our King.[2]

Just as Hilary wrote in his preface, paraphrasing Origen, Cassiodorus understands Christ himself as both the door (thinking of John 10:7-9) and as the key (thinking of Rev 3:7) who can unlock the meanings of the psalms and open the way into the celestial palace.

After making a twofold division of the psalm (separating vv. 1-3 from vv. 4-6) and identifying the speaker of the psalm as the prophet, Cassiodorus works on the verses themselves. He applies the specific activities mentioned of the righteous man to Christ and sets up an opposition between Christ and Adam along the lines of Romans 5, following Augustine. His first task, though, is to establish proper Christology. This he does while taking up once again the term "man":

> You should not doubt that he calls the Lord Saviour a man, for the prophet Isaiah also says of Him: *Behold a man, the orient is his*

[2] Cassiodorus, *ExplPs* 1.Title, pp. 1.45–46.

> *name*. But remember that whenever this definition occurs, the humanity which He assumed is revealed, for man describes sex in the flesh which is wholly absent from divinity. Since human nature had to be assumed by the Lord for our redemption, the psalmist aptly called Him man so that we might believe Him to be one Person with two natures.³

First, he makes a reference to another biblical passage to secure his point (Zech 6:12 actually, not Isaiah) and then presents the orthodox position on Christ: "one Person with two natures [*utriusque naturae . . . una persona*]."

Remember, at this time the controversy around the Three Chapters was a major topic of conversation in Constantinople. Pope Vigilius had been brought there under duress specifically because of arguments over the natures and Person of Christ. Cassiodorus is adamant on his christological doctrine, particularly against the part of the Monophysites, who denied multiple natures within Christ (*mono-* meaning "one"; *-phys-* meaning "nature"). The phrase "one Person" with reference to Christ appears twenty-one times throughout the commentary; "two natures," thirty-eight times. Thus, Cassiodorus consistently locates material that he uses to reinforce orthodox Christology against heretical beliefs.

Taking the three actions of the wicked that the righteous person does not do, Cassiodorus reads them christologically. He provides a framework for the text, first, by identifying the three figures of speech to refer to the three ways in which humans sin: by thought, by word, and by deed. Taking up first "the advice of the wicked," which therefore corresponds to thought, he argues thus:

> First he says: *He hath not departed to the counsel of the ungodly.* So he first excludes any abominable thoughts such as human beings claim intimate acquaintance with, but which had no place whatever in the Lord Christ. We need no extraneous proofs of this, for Psalm 40 fully attests that we must interpret the passage as referring to the Lord Saviour when it says: *Then said I: Behold I come. In the head of the book it is written of me. Departed* means forsaking the right path and sliding on to crooked ways.⁴

---

³ Cassiodorus, *ExplPs* 1.1, p. 1.48.
⁴ Cassiodorus, *ExplPs* 1.1, p. 1.48.

Cassiodorus is denying that Christ could have any sinful thoughts as the one person who did not sin (Heb 4:15 is in the background here but is not explicitly quoted). Rather than needing to confirm that Christ did not sin, he moves to strengthen his position that Christ is the one being spoken of here. Psalm 40:7 provides a solid connection; this verse is already read with reference to Christ in Hebrews 10:5-7. Furthermore, the phrase with which it begins, "Behold, I come [*ecce venio*]" appears in the mouth of the risen Christ in Revelation 16:15; 22:7, 12. Once these three New Testament uses establish the identity of the speaker, the phrase "head of the book [*in capite libri*]" is understood as a reference to the head or beginning of the book of Psalms and thus Psalm 1. In this way, even though the reference to Psalm 40:7 may seem unusual or out of place, it relies on both a thorough knowledge of Scripture and careful attention to the Latin text.

Moving on to the next figure and connecting it with deeds, "tak[ing] the path that sinners tread" is interpreted as the world itself, because it is the place where sinners dwell. The difference is that Christ did not linger there but moved through it without being affected. Here, Cassiodorus is able to add another reference to the incarnation. Nor should this be a surprise—with some two hundred uses of "incarnate" or "incarnation" this is a concept that he returns to constantly; he works it into almost every psalm. (This is of particular importance in refuting the Arians, the dominant tradition followed by the Goths.)

Cassiodorus connects the third and final figure, the "seat of scoffers" ("seat of pestilence" in the Latin), with sinful words and reads it as referring to those who teach heresies. The interpretation of "seat" as a place of teaching is grounded with a reference to Matthew 23:2-3a ("The scribes and the Pharisees sit on Moses' seat; therefore, do whatever they teach you and follow it"). Those who teach heresies spread contagious pestilence through their harmful words; Cassiodorus insists that the opposite is true of Christ: "for by His healing teaching He cured the wounds of the whole world."[5]

If we jump to Cassiodorus's discussion of the tree metaphor, this is a fruitful one, both in looking at Christ and the contrast—borrowed

---

[5] Cassiodorus, *ExplPs* 1.1, p. 1.48.

from Augustine—with Adam. In Romans 5, Paul had already set up a contrast between the first Adam and Christ, the new Adam: where the first Adam had condemned humanity to death through his disobedience, Christ, the new Adam, offers humanity a restoration of life through his obedience. Thus, Cassiodorus sees the "tree planted by streams of water"—an image recalling the well-watered garden of paradise—as a reference to the cross, "the wood of life [*lignum vitae*]," and mentions too that Jesus had told the repentant thief on the cross that they would be together in paradise (Luke 24:43). The connection between the cross, paradise, and the tree of life (*lignum vitae*) planted in paradise is sufficient for Cassiodorus to see in this psalm a parable of Christ on the cross undoing Adam's sin in paradise.

In addition to the reading with Adam, the "tree planted by streams of water" is likewise for Cassiodorus a sign of the sacrament of baptism: "Just as the running water of the earth is the life of living trees, so spiritual water washes over the sign of the cross which is acknowledged to be the salvation of faithful souls."[6] Cassiodorus will frequently find the sacraments of the church in the psalms; far and away he refers to baptism much more than the Eucharist. Almost any time that water imagery appears in the psalms, Cassiodorus will seek a connection with baptism. This is entirely in keeping with his overall theological vision: if the psalms are largely a trio played by the prophet, Christ, and the church, then baptism—the gift given by Christ that produces the church—is going to take a central place.

The conclusion of the psalm reinforces that Christ is set at the head of the Psalms as the single source of all else; he goes into a bit of Neoplatonic numerology on the glories of the Monad before arriving at a full conclusion. At this point, however, Cassiodorus lays out a summarization of how he intends to read the rest of the book:

> I think that we should note also that all the ensuing psalms mount in a marvellously prearranged scheme. In the first, the bodily life of our Lord Christ is described, and next the almighty nature of His divinity is subtly revealed. Thirdly, the psalmist mentions the numerous people who strove to destroy Him; then seven psalms of penitents purify the hearts of the faithful. The subsequent

---

[6] Cassiodorus, *ExplPs* 1.3, p. 1.51.

action [*drama*] hastens on in parables [*parabolis*] and figurative allusions [*tropicis allusionibus*], with almost everything pointing by allegorical similes [*per allegoricas similitudines*] to the Lord Saviour, as I shall duly explain at the appropriate places. Then the prophet celebrates the praise of the Lord Christ with wondrous variation, and to the end of the book never ceases to utter the proclamation of His holiness. So in this sense everything is acknowledged to be a revelation of Him for whose sake this commentary was undertaken.[7]

Thus, Cassiodorus sees Psalm 1 as setting the tone for the rest of the book. Jesus Christ is at the heart of it and is the true meaning within it. Locating Christ within the psalm is an essential part of the reading endeavor.

Christological Themes

Our look at Psalm 1 will not be complete, though, without also a glance at the conclusion Cassiodorus writes to Psalm 3. He understands the first three psalms to represent an interpretive model that ought to be deployed by a careful reader whether he draws attention to it or not:

> Let us now consider how the true order of heavenly wisdom is deployed. Psalm 1 contains the Lord Christ's moral aspect; Psalm 2, His natural aspect, that is, His human and divine being; and Psalm 3, by speaking of His resurrection, His reflective aspect; the rationale of these runs through the whole of the divine Scriptures. So the patriarch Isaac dug three wells, thereby showing that the Lord's commands are contained in threefold teaching. Wisdom too warns us to describe them in our hearts in three ways, and so on. As you read subsequent psalms you will be able easily to recognise these three aspects, individual or combined, even if you are not reminded of them. You must not demand such notification repeatedly, for I have numerous points to make which are new to you.[8]

Thus, the moral character of Christ, the doctrine of the two natures that understands Christ as both human and divine, and the resurrection

---

[7] Cassiodorus, *ExplPs* 1.concl, pp. 1.56–57.
[8] Cassiodorus, *ExplPs* 3.concl, pp. 1.72–73.

of Christ are the three basic aspects that will appear again and again in this means of reading.

This christological reading of the Psalms is central to Cassiodorus's project. It is not unique to him; in doing so, he is relaying how the church has read. He is continuing a tradition of teaching handed down by Origen, Hilary, Jerome, Augustine, and countless other writers and teachers—some of whom we know, others who have been lost to history. As he writes his commentary, Cassiodorus will understand himself to be in conscious continuity with them. Even when he produces new material, writes new thoughts, creates new interpretations, he will see them not as novelties but as the logical implications of the traditional means for reading the text.

Glancing at the Sources

Hilary rejects the notion that Christ is the speaker of this psalm on logical grounds. The idea that the very author of the Law would need to meditate on it is ridiculous; furthermore, he disdains the notion that the Lord of Creation could be profitably compared with a tree. For him, the speaker is the prophet, and he is referring to any person who is striving toward righteousness. Jerome agrees in his sermon on the psalm, rejecting the christological move. In doing so, it is pretty clear that both are relying on the opinion of Origen. While Jerome suggests that Joseph of Arimathea may be the topic because he was righteous and did not go along with the Jewish rulers in their plans regarding Jesus, he too falls back to the position that the psalmist is speaking of any just person.

Augustine confidently asserts at the head of his material on Psalm 1 that it refers completely to Jesus Christ. He also sets up the parallel with Adam immediately thereafter, but otherwise Cassiodorus does not follow him very closely. Thus, while Cassiodorus follows him in the identification of Christ and in using Adam, he is otherwise independent from his interpretation. Augustine's exposition of Psalm 1 is only three columns long in the Patrologia Latina; Cassiodorus's treatment is nine columns long—three times longer than Augustine's! Far from shortening Augustine's verbosity, Cassiodorus is the long-winded one here.

Psalm 6 and the Penitential Psalms[9]

Looking at Psalm 6

Psalm 6 is an individual lament psalm of the kind frequently found in the first half of the Psalter. The psalmist speaks mostly to God, detailing how his woes are impacting him in bodily terms; his emotional pains are expressing themselves in physical effects. We never get a clear sense of what these woes are. It's not until the last portion, verses 8 through 10, that "enemies" enter the picture. They are the agents of the psalmist's oppression, and all we learn is the psalmist's confidence that God will deal with them as they deserve.

Recasting Rhetoric

Rhetoric had a specific purpose in late antiquity: winning court cases. As a result, a certain amount of rhetorical theory didn't have much application as the era turned into the early medieval period. While there were certainly law codes under the various tribal rulers, the proceedings didn't have the same kind of formality or require the same kind of rhetorical polish prized in the Greco-Roman courts. One of the signature experiences of reading through Cassiodorus's commentary is seeing the ways that the learning of late antiquity gets repurposed for an early medieval monastic world. Nowhere is this more evident than in the Penitential Psalms.

Cassiodorus, being the fusion of Greco-Roman legal thought and monastic piety that he was, reads the Penitential Psalms as legal briefs drafted in order to beg for mercy from the Judge of all in the most proper and orderly way possible. Indeed, "Judge" is one of the chief titles for God in the *Explanation of the Psalms*. The interpretation of Psalm 6 is a matter of dividing the psalm into the component parts of a Roman brief, applying stasis theory in order to determine what kind of case is being argued, and then describing how each section is being used to achieve the correct effect in the mind of the listener.

Cassiodorus's section on rhetoric in the *Institutions* provides a helpful overview of classical rhetoric. First, in order to construct an argument, we have to know what we are arguing for or against. This is where stasis theory comes in. The various legal arguments are broken out into a tree diagram structure to help the person arguing

---

[9] The Penitential Psalms are Psalms 6, 32, 38, 51, 102, 130, and 143.

decide which course of action to take. There are some obvious courses: maintain that the client is innocent, or maintain that the client did act but that what he did was not against the law, or that what he did may be against the law but that the law is not correctly applied in his case. While all of the options get laid out, there are some possible options that are only rarely chosen—they're generally not a good way to go. This includes the grouping that falls under "acknowledgment" (*concessio*), where guilt is admitted. Foremost among the bad ideas within "acknowledgment" is the "plea for mercy" (*deprecatio*). Cassiodorus, quoting Cicero, writes: "The *plea for mercy* arises when the defendant confesses the crime and premeditation, and yet seeks pardon; this type can rarely occur."[10] That is, it's possible but not a good option if we'd like more clients in the future or if we're trying to get ourself out of a jam!

After the discussion of stasis theory and borrowing heavily from Cicero's *On Invention*, Cassiodorus lays out the six parts of a fully constituted judicial speech: introduction (*exordium*), statement of the facts (*narratio*), division into logical parts (*partitio*), proof (*confirmatio*), refutation (*reprehensio*), and the conclusion (*conclusio*). These are defined and applied as follows:

> The *introduction* is speech that suitably prepares the mind of the listener for the rest of the discourse. The *statement of facts* sets forth the events that have occurred or might have occurred. The *division* is that part of a speech that, if it is correctly handled, makes the whole speech clear and apparent. *Proof* is that part which by setting out the argument gives credit, authority, and a foundation to our case. *Refutation* is the section in which our opponents' proof is weakened or damaged by the presentation of arguments. The *conclusion* ends and closes the entire speech sometimes with a tear-jerking recapitulation of the main points.[11]

The parts laid out here are the central ones. There are other parts that other kinds of speeches sometimes use, but this is the standard template for a normal trial argument.

---

[10] Cassiodorus, *Institutions* 2.2.5, p. 182.
[11] Cassiodorus, *Institutions* 2.2.9, p. 183.

How Cassiodorus Reads It

Turning to Psalm 6, Cassiodorus located the psalm within its proper category of stasis theory:

> [F]or among other types of arguments which orators have attached to developing lawsuits they included admission [of guilt] and prayer for pardon [*concessivam deprecationem*] in which the defendant refrains from defending what has been done, but begs for pardon. Though this type of argument seems without resort and bereft of human force in court-trials here on earth, before God it is invested with invincible protection. Only confession of faith can acquit the man whom no arguments defend. Such a course is permitted to those who truly repent, who in seeking pardon for themselves strive instead to condemn their own actions.[12]

While it may not be that helpful in the courtroom, the plea for mercy is ideal in the monastic cell.

In the division portion of the exposition, Cassiodorus identifies the component pieces of the psalm and relates them to the four pertinent sections out of the six possible parts of a rhetorical address. He begins with a general statement and then moves right into explaining the structure and how it functions:

> In this psalm the man of piety who confesses his sins prays in four ways. In the exordium, he makes the Judge well-disposed to him; the exordium is a prayer which aptly prepares the listener's mind to hear the rest of what he has to say. . . . In the second section he recounts his own hardships by which he is seen to be afflicted and worn. The narration [*narratio*] is the clear and careful explanation of events to have his case approved. Next follows the correction [*correctio*], for he separates himself from the wicked, a gesture which he knew was most welcome to the good Judge, so that his mind might be alienated from those who clearly regarded justice as foreign to them. There remains the conclusion, in which a definite statement is now made that nothing further is being solicited, for he confounds and rejects all the wicked, as he refused in any sense to share with them.[13]

---

[12] Cassiodorus, *ExplPs* 6.2, p. 1.92.
[13] Cassiodorus, *ExplPs* 6.div, p. 1.91.

Three of the four parts listed here match the usual six-section formula. The odd one out is the "correction," which stands in the place of the division, proof, and refutation. Because the penitent is throwing himself on the mercy of the court, these three sections are unnecessary. Instead, the correction lays out what the penitent has done to begin making amends for his crime; this will not exonerate him of his guilt. It should, however, demonstrate that his repentance is sincere and that he intends to amend his ways and lead a new life.

Assigning these four sections to verses in the psalm, the first section encompasses verses 1-5, the second, verses 6-7, the third, verses 8-9, and the fourth is the final verse. While this division may seem a little arbitrary at first, note the way that Cassiodorus is leveraging the basic grammar of the text to make his divisions. The first section that will "prepare the mind of the listener" (*Institutions* 2.2.9 and *ExplPs* 6.div) is the section that is in the form of direct address. That is, verses 1-5 involve direct address, where the psalmist is speaking directly to God. Looking at the translation in the NRSV, we know this because "Lord" appears in the vocative case for direct address (saying "O Lord") five times in this section and none at all in the rest of the psalm, and because the speech involves the term "you" connected with the vocative. Thus, verses 1-5 do address God directly just as a judicial exordium would.

From there, the psalm makes a shift. Verses 6 and 7, which Cassiodorus pulls out as the narration, are spoken by the psalmist, confirmed by the repetition of "I" and "my." There is no sense of the person or people to whom the psalmist is speaking. Is the psalmist speaking to God or to a hitherto unmentioned group (like a chorus in a Greek play)? Verses 8 and 9 clarify to whom the psalmist is speaking. Although it is ambiguous in verses 6 and 7, the use of direct address in verse 8 clears things up: "all you workers of evil." This shift provides license to identify this as the correction. The final verse is again a shift of addressee; instead of talking to workers of evil, the psalmist is now talking about them with the reference to "my enemies." Presumably, the conclusion is once more addressed to God the Judge as a closing argument of sorts. Thus, Cassiodorus is reading the shifts between who the psalmist is addressing as signals for where to begin new sections.

The final summary of the psalm emphasizes that the work done here carries through all the penitential psalms:

> Though we should apply our eager intelligence to all the psalms, since the greatest resources for living are sought from them, yet we ought to pay particular attention to the psalms of the penitents, for they are like suitable medicine prescribed for the human race. From them we obtain most health-giving baths for our souls, from them we are restored to life when dead through sins, from them when grief-stricken we attain eternal joys. They form a sort of judicial genre, in which the defendant appears before the sight of the Judge, atoning for his sin with tears, and dissolving it by confessing it. He offers the best type of defence by condemning himself. Here there is no outside person acting as prosecutor; he is his own accuser. He merits pardon because he does not excuse himself from blame. No other approach is possible before such a Judge, for before Him no man can deny his sins. Here inference [*conjectura*] gives place, definition [*finis*] is not sought, other aspects of the nature of the case are not in evidence, since the whole situation is exposed by the brightness of truth. So the only approach necessary is that called concession [*concessio*], in which the defendant does not defend what has been done, but asks to be pardoned. How immeasurable is the Creator's fatherly love! The defendant caused sentence to be passed in his favour because he accused himself more fiercely. Yet in vain could the cleverest of orators have sought to obtain from the Judge what the psalmist deserved to get from Him out of the fullness of his simplicity.[14]

All seven of the Penitential Psalms are thus classed as judicial orations of this kind. Cassiodorus does carry this theme through them, continuing to analyze the other Penitential Psalms according to this judicial rubric.

No treatment on Cassiodorus's take on the seven Penitential Psalms can be complete, though, without including the memorable mnemonic that he provides as to why there are seven of them:

> Remember that this is the first of the penitents' psalms. It is followed by Psalms 32, 38, 51, 102, 130, and 143. We shall discuss each of these in its due place as opportunity allows. Do not believe that there is no significance in this aggregate of seven, because our forbearers said that our sins could be forgiven in seven ways: first

---

[14] Casiodorus, *ExplPs* 6.conc, p. 1.98.

by baptism, second by suffering martyrdom, third by almsgiving, fourth by forgiving the sins of our brethren, fifth by diverting a sinner from the error of his ways, sixth by abundance of charity, and seventh by repentance. We must further add the sharing of the blood of our Lord Jesus Christ, provided that it is received worthily. Perhaps other ways of forgiveness can be found, for it is fitting that God's kindness should rise higher than the number of our prayers.[15]

With that summation, he earns the last word.

Glancing at the Sources

This psalm is a fairly straightforward text; there are not a lot of items that need to be explained or that call for deeper investigation. It is clear that Cassiodorus is influenced by Augustine's reading and that he has it in mind. In particular, he borrows a number of scriptural cross-references that aren't necessarily obvious from the context. Nevertheless, Augustine does not have judicial rhetoric anywhere on his radar. Thus, once again, Cassiodorus is setting his own interpretive agenda but is making reference to Augustine's work. Just as he indicated in the *Institutions*, he is dipping into Augustine's interpretation to provide glosses on phrases and to fill out the cross-referential texture of his exposition.

The two treatments of Psalm 6 are almost exactly the same length, both taking up roughly seven and one-third columns in Migne.

Psalm 22 and the Psalms of the Passion[16]

Looking at Psalm 22

I still remember the first time I ran across Psalm 22. It was probably in my early teens or so. I was sitting in church—the sermon was probably going long or something—and I was flipping through the Lutheran hymnal and had landed in the section containing the psalms. As I glanced at the words, I was astonished; I recognized the things that the psalm was talking about but had never expected to see them

---

[15] Cassiodorus, *ExplPs* 6.Title, pp. 1.90–91.

[16] Cassiodorus identifies the Passion Psalms as 22, 35, 55, 69, and 109. Later traditions would include Psalms 2, 38, 59, and 88 as well.

there! "My God, my God, why have you forsaken me? . . . Gangs of evildoers circle around me; they pierce my hands and my feet . . . they divide my clothes among themselves, and for my clothing they cast lots" (Ps 22:1, 16, 17, BCP).[17] I had just discovered what the church fathers had known long before me. All allegory aside, there are some psalms that have an uncanny connection with the events narrated in the gospels—including the crucifixion. Psalm 22 is chief among these.

Psalm 22 is a fairly long one, coming in at thirty-one verses according to the NRSV's reckoning. It begins with an individual's cry of abandonment and a request for God to deliver the speaker from the current situation of torment. It alternates between praise toward God and a depiction of the dire situation the psalmist is in. It recounts the history that exists between the psalmist and God and gives vivid descriptions of the body's pain because of what is happening to it. After asking for vindication, the psalm ends with the confidence that deliverance will come and that the psalmist will yet again praise God in the congregation, having passed through these present struggles.

How Cassiodorus Reads It

Cassiodorus divides this psalm into three parts. The first, verses 1-11, is Christ's prayer for deliverance to the Father. The second section, verses 12-22, recounts the events of Christ's crucifixion and death (the passion, from the Latin word *passio* ["suffering"]). In the third section, verses 23-31, Christ calls on the church to praise God for the salvation accomplished through the crucifixion. In commenting on the shift from the first to the second section, Cassiodorus draws attention to a parallel narrative structure: just as this psalm begins with a prayer and then moves to the events of the crucifixion, so too do the gospel narratives begin with a prayer from Jesus and then move to the events of his crucifixion. In particular, Cassiodorus has John's gospel in mind; the last third of John focuses on the night of Jesus's betrayal. Jesus prays a long prayer that spans all of John 17, and then he goes out to his betrayal in chapter 18. As Cassiodorus concludes his division of the psalm, he notes: "Though many of the psalms briefly recall

---

[17] This was a Lutheran church and hymnal but that hymnal used the same version of the Psalms created for the 1979 *Book of Common Prayer*.

the Lord's passion, none has described it in such apt terms, so that it appears not so much as prophecy, but as history."[18] This is the first of several comments that will draw the reader's attention to a careful consideration of the plain sense of the text. Despite that, Cassiodorus will follow his usual pattern and even when the plain sense of the text has a most obvious connection to the narrative of the gospel, he will go deeper still to expose the spiritual meaning he finds under it.

Cassiodorus's interpretation of the first section—the starting prayer—focuses on two interrelated questions of significant spiritual import to his readers: Why would Jesus pray the words that this psalm places in his mouth (words of fear and abandonment), and what does this teach about whether and how God answers prayer? He begins with a christological answer: these words should be seen as a clear statement of and from the humanity of Jesus. He asks to be spared as any person would, even though he knows what must occur: "The Son most dear in a double address invoked Him who He clearly knew would afford him not safety in this world, but the brightness of eternal majesty."[19] This reading is reinforced in the interpretation of the next phrase:

> Next comes: *Why hast thou forsaken me?* The word *why* is known to introduce a question; so the Master of consubstantial wisdom, the Spokesman of the Father is so confused by the impending death of His flesh that in apparent ignorance He asks the Father why He has been abandoned by Him. These and similar expressions seek to express His humanity, but we must not believe that divinity was absent to Him even at the passion, since the apostle says: *If they had known, they would never have crucified the Lord of glory.* Though He was impassible, He suffered through the humanity which He assumed, and which could suffer. He was immortal, but He died; He never dies, but He rose again.[20]

Thus, Cassiodorus understands Jesus to be expressing his human fear of death. The use of the epithets "Master of consubstantial wisdom, the Spokesman of the Father" paired with the phrase "apparent igno-

---

[18] Cassiodorus, *ExplPs* 22.Div, p. 1.216.
[19] Cassiodorus, *ExplPs* 22.2, p. 1.216.
[20] Cassiodorus, *ExplPs* 22.2, p. 1.217.

rance" feels ironic; Cassiodorus is casting scorn on the idea that Christ would not know what is in store for him. Throughout his commentary, Cassiodorus portrays a Jesus fully equipped with divine omnipotence. In contrast to modern theologies of a kenotic or self-emptying Jesus who willingly relinquishes all knowledge but that of a normal human person (including all supernatural knowledge of things past and future), the Jesus Cassiodorus finds in the text is well aware of what will happen—both in the crucifixion and in a subsequent resurrection. Despite this knowledge, Christ is expressing his own human emotions, "broadcast[ing] the experiences of the humanity which He assumed."[21] Cassiodorus is quick to note that this does not in any way discount the divinity of Christ and points to the paradoxes inherent in the situation, bolstering them with citations from Cyril and Ambrose.

Cassiodorus then takes up the difficulty of verse 2: How should his readers understand the problem of unanswered prayer when it is coming, not from a common sinner, but from the lips of the Son to the Father? Cassiodorus explains that the fulfillment of prayer is often delayed in order that the purposes of God might be fully worked out. Hence, Paul's prayer that he be freed from the thorn in his flesh (2 Cor 12:7-9) was not answered to give him more glory, whereas the devil's prayer to torment Job (Job 2:1-6) was granted swiftly because it would end badly for the devil. He then counsels his readers to distinguish properly between two different kinds of prayer:

> When we ask for distinctions, riches, vengeance over enemies and other things of this kind, our requests are foolish because we long for worldly things. But when we demand to be freed from dangers so that eternal life may be granted us, our request is not stupid; rather, our prayer is appropriate. So Christ, Mediator between God and men, petitioned not foolishly but wisely, yet clearly went unheard because this was how the world's redemption was to come through the Lord's dispensation.[22]

Cassiodorus teaches his monks that not all prayers will be answered; foolish prayers should be avoided and, instead, wise prayers relating to the salvation of the soul are those that must be embraced.

---

[21] Ibid.
[22] Cassiodorus, *ExplPs* 22.3, p. 1.218.

Moving down to verses 4 and 5, Cassiodorus walks a careful line in order to represent faithfully both the words of the biblical text and also the experience of the church. With verse 4 ("In you our ancestors trusted; they trusted, and you delivered them") he affirms that God performed mighty acts on behalf of the Children of Israel to save them from bodily harm; he mentions the three young men cast into the fiery furnace of Daniel 3 and Daniel's own episode in the lion's den as particular examples. These acts do not, however, preclude God's own decisions especially in this case: "But though He granted or grants these great concessions in answer to men's prayers, *He did not spare his own Son, but delivered him up for us all* [Rom 8:32], clearly so that the scriptures might be fulfilled and that through His passion the salvation of the world might emerge."[23] While God can and does answer these kinds of prayers, God's freedom to act is not constrained by them. Too, they may be carried out in a way not visible to the unbelieving world.

Thus, interpreting verse 5 ("To you they cried, and were saved; in you they trusted, and were not put to shame"), Cassiodorus denies that this always happens on the bodily level:

> The belief which expresses the outcome leaves no room for doubt; he who cries to the Lord is invariably heard for his advantage. Think of the stature of the martyrs who infidels thought were not being heard while physical torment was consuming them; on the contrary, they were indeed heard, for they deserved to obtain the crown of martyrdom. So the Lord always listens to His just ones, but with awareness of their interests.[24]

By invoking the martyrs within a prayer put on the lips of Christ immediately before his crucifixion, Cassiodorus is making it abundantly clear that Christians should not rely on prayer for deliverance from physical death and mortal danger; indeed, he understands death itself to sometimes be the pathway to greater glory and the fulfillment of the Christian's hopes. Everything is carried out with reference to eternal salvation, spiritual safety, not mortal security and bodily safety.

Not even Christ can pray his way off the cross.

---

[23] Cassiodorus, *ExplPs* 22.5, p. 1.219.
[24] Cassiodorus, *ExplPs* 22.6, p. 1.219.

Cassiodorus takes a turn toward the passion itself with verses 7-8—especially 8 ("Commit your cause to the Lord; let him deliver: let him rescue the one in whom he delights!")—noting that the events and words were to take place just as recorded:

> These words are in fact an exact gospel-text, for when Christ hung on the cross the Jews said: *He hoped in the Lord: let him deliver him, since he will have him.* How unchanging is the divine dispensation! We surely seem to be reviewing the gospel here rather than a psalm, since these things were fulfilled so authentically that they seem already enacted rather than still to come.[25]

This is but the first of several passages that will receive similar comments.

Cassiodorus then moves into the second section of the psalm, which he identifies as a full revelation of the passion: "in which he reveals the secret [*arcanum*] of His crucifixion by allegorical comparisons [*allegoricas comparationes*]."[26] The first few verses of this section ("Many bulls encircle me, strong bulls of Bashan surround me; they open wide their mouths at me, like a ravening and roaring lion" [Ps 22:12-13]) are easily applied to those crucifying Christ; the next few verses take what might be an unexpected tack. Verses 14-15 describe the physical suffering of the psalmist's body. Since Cassiodorus sees the words as Christ's, he interprets these passages with reference not to the embodied flesh of Christ as he suffered on the cross but to the Body of Christ, the church. Hence, when the psalmist prays, "I am poured out like water, and all my bones are out of joint" (Ps 22:14a), Cassiodorus interprets this as an allegorical reference to the church; the bones are identified as the apostles, who were scattered and sent out into the world to cleanse it with the water of baptism. The second part of the verse ("my heart is like wax; it is melted within my breast") becomes an elaborate metaphor where Christ's heart—his will—is revealed in the Scriptures as the fires of the passion melt the wax that had been obscuring its true meaning so that it is now evident within the church—his breast. Cassiodorus aligns this meaning with the tearing of the temple veil at the crucifixion (Matt 27:51), another sign that the Lord's passion reveals the formerly hidden things of God.

---

[25] Cassiodorus, *ExplPs* 22.9, pp. 1.220–21.
[26] Cassiodorus, *ExplPs* 22.13, p. 1.221.

In his discussion of verse 16 ("a company of evildoers encircles me. My hands and feet have shriveled ['been dug' in the Latin]"), Cassiodorus begins with the shape of the cross, caused by the stretching out of the pierced hands and feet: with the stretching out of the arms it embraces the whole world. He notes here too the paradox of the cross:

> I speak of the Lord's cross, which from being the punitive source of ill for sinners became their blessed redemption. What had for long brought death later bestowed the blessing of salvation. It is the gibbet of salvation, the death denoting life, the lowliness announcing God's loftiness. So by the figure of the cross you may realise that Christ is in heaven, on earth, throughout the world, and even in the realms below.[27]

From death comes life and in the extension of the arms of the cross, Christ embraces the entire cosmos.

Cassiodorus does not stop at this point, though, but goes deeper as well: "Though there seems to be here simply and literally an account of the Lord's passion, this action indicates something which we should interpret also on the spiritual level."[28] He takes the Latin verb *fodere* ("to dig or stab"), which is applied to the hands and feet of Jesus in verse 16. Among other meanings the earth gives life to plants when it is dug, so too in the case of Christ's body: "For when it was fastened with nails and pierced by a lance, it yielded for us fruit which would abide for ever."[29] He then maintains by a variety of quotations from Augustine and Paul the foolishness of the proclamation of the cross; the saving foolishness, though, is not what we might expect: "For the Lord's incarnation is the wondrous height of His mercy, a gift beyond calculation and a mystery beyond understanding. From it either salvation sprouts for right-thinking minds or death is begotten for perverted intelligences."[30] Note this—this is significant. Even in the midst of a psalm about the passion, the ultimate sacrifice of Christ on the cross for the sins of humanity, Cassiodorus still places the greater weight on the importance of the incarnation. While he will in no way

---

[27] Cassiodorus, *ExplPs* 22.17, p. 1.225.
[28] Ibid.
[29] Ibid.
[30] Cassiodorus, *ExplPs* 22.17, p. 1.226.

discount the crucifixion, resurrection, or ascension of Christ as being essential to the salvation of humanity, it is the contested doctrine of the incarnation that receives pride of place.

Similarly, when he addresses verse 18 ("They divide my clothes among themselves, and for my clothing they cast lots"), he intimates secrets here as well: "Though the Lord's entire passion contains great mysteries, some greater secret is brought forth here."[31] The garments are the writings of the prophets which have been separated and split by the poor interpretation of heretics. The shirt, in contrast:

> For which lots were drawn, which compassed His holy body and which the evangelist says was *woven from the top throughout* [John 19:23], is clearly the Catholic Church, which is certainly not allowed to be torn by human discretion, but by God's kindness is always bestowed whole and inviable as if by lot on every man. It is woven from the top because no man parts or tears it. With the greatest of strength of enduring firmness, it abides with the power of its unity. Of it Truth himself says: *Thou art Peter, and upon this rock I will build my church, and the gates of hell shall not prevail against it* [Matt 16:18].

Let's take a step back for a moment and remember the context for this. Cassiodorus is in Constantinople. He's there because orthodox troops have routed the Arian government he has served his entire life after years of brutal war. He is attending Pope Vigilius, who was kidnapped during the celebration of the Eucharist and hauled off to Constantinople to be "persuaded" to condemn the Three Chapters on one side and Origen on the other at a council called by Justinian for the purpose of playing nice with the Monophysites. The image that Cassiodorus presents here of the Scriptures torn and parted by heretics, yet the church remaining whole and inviolate, is not offered from a position of triumphalist superiority. Rather, this is the fruit of ardent faith—the conviction of something most certainly not seen—that the mystical Body of Christ will pull through no matter what.

Jumping down to the end, Cassiodorus's conclusion falls into three sections. The first is an observation on the spiritual teaching of the psalm:

---

[31] Cassiodorus, ExplPs 22.19, p. 1.227.

> This is the psalm which the Church solemnly chants at the paschal service, so that we obtain the salutary teaching that in human affairs even the blessed are for a time abandoned by the Lord to some degree, though by the strength of His protection He leads them to eternal joys. As we listen to it, we happily weep, for we can be refashioned by it if after fixing our minds on it, we merit a similar affliction.[32]

For Cassiodorus, one of the most important aspects of this psalm is what it teaches about prayer. Even Jesus, the righteous Son of God, expressing his humanity in a prayer of anguish, is not guaranteed the instantaneous bodily results one might expect. Instead, Cassiodorus reminds his readers that proper prayer is directed toward obtaining eternal joys, not material rewards or even bodily safety.

The second part of the conclusion enumerates the psalms of the passion but also reveals their dark side as well:

> How hard were the hearts of the Jews, how foolish their minds, bereft of all belief! Ought not this psalm alone to have been enough to inspire belief in the passion which Truth so obviously proclaimed about himself? So that no excuse should be left to those of extreme hardness of heart, among succeeding psalms are others composed on this subject in clear and most obvious prophecy, namely, Psalms 35, 55, 69, and 109. So what was proclaimed by heralds of such eminence ought to be doubtful to none.[33]

The early church consistently read the passion psalms as a condemnation of the Jews. There are two issues here that both caused this state of affairs and exacerbated it.

The Psalms and Christian Anti-Semitism

First, the rhetoric of the Psalter is quite stark. When it portrays people there are no shades of gray: there are simply the righteous and the wicked, the poor and the rich, the humble and the haughty, the wise and the fools, the good and the bad. It is a world cast in binaries.

---

[32] Cassiodorus, *ExplPs* 22.Conc, p. 1.234.
[33] Ibid.

Once one group has been positively identified—like Jesus or the prophet or the church—then anyone opposing or set in conflict with it is vilified, thanks to the narrative structure of the poems themselves. There are no parties who are mistaken; there is no one who holds sincere beliefs but with whom one disagrees on points of interpretation. There are only the righteous and the wicked. This binary perspective is reinforced by dualistic tendencies within the Scriptures (like the light/dark imagery in the Gospel of John) and within the philosophy of the age that formed part of the interpretive lens (like the matter/spirit split in Neoplatonic thought).

Second, once Christ as the interpretative key has been established as normative, the church asks precisely what Cassiodorus expresses here: since Christ and events of his life—even specific details—are proclaimed so clearly in the Psalms and in the Prophets, how could Jewish readers not see the evident truth: that Jesus is the Messiah? While the readers of the early church were open to a wide variety of meanings in the biblical text, and while they were comfortable with a host of reading strategies, all of these assumed Jesus as the Christ and any reading that would deny or even question that assumption was deemed illegitimate. As a result, Christian anti-Semitism was not challenged by their readings of the Hebrew Bible but inflamed by it.

When the two are put together, things get even worse. When Jesus is identified as the speaker of a psalm, when the meaning of the psalm is identified as his passion and death, and when the assumption is made that the Jewish people recognized the identity of Jesus as both Messiah and incarnate God and still executed him, then the anger against the "opponents" in the psalm is pointed directly at the Jewish people as those who willingly and knowingly murdered God. It is no surprise or accident that many of the European pogroms against Jewish communities corresponded with Holy Week—the ritual remembrance of the death of Christ and the use of texts like these psalms fueled Christian violence.

Cassiodorus was just as complicit in this abhorrent practice as the other church fathers—perhaps more so. Theologically speaking, the Gothic administration was fairly tolerant regarding religious differences. This was a wise policy since, as Arians, they were themselves a theological minority within broadly orthodox Italy. In the *Variae*, Cassiodorus preserves three letters that refer to Jewish communities;

two are to synagogues, the third to the Roman Senate on behalf of a Jewish congregation in Rome. In all three, the Jewish communities have suffered violence at the hands of Christians: a synagogue needed rebuilding in Genoa having somehow lost its roof (in a fire?), a synagogue in Trastevere was burned down by a mob of Christians, and a synagogue in Milan is under attack and is suffering some kind of legal encroachment from the Christian population. Within this correspondence the official line is toleration:

> We cannot order a religion, because no one is forced to believe against his will. . . . The propriety of manners which is characteristic of the City of Rome must be upheld. To fall into the follies of popular tumult and to set about burning their own City is not like the Roman disposition. . . . For the preservation of *civilitas*, the benefits of justice are not to be denied even to those who are recognized as wandering from the right way in matters of faith.[34]

Despite the official line, the tone of the letters is hostile; the first line quoted above—sometimes cited to demonstrate the tolerance of the period—is expressed almost regretfully and comes after a condemnation of the Jewish faith. The passage in full runs as follows:

> Why do ye desire what you ought to shun? In truth we give the permission which you craved, but we suitably blame the desire of your wandering minds. We cannot order a religion, because no one is forced to believe against his will.

This is not true tolerance but a grudging acceptance that the protection of the law extends even to religious dissenters.

Moments like this remind us that Cassiodorus is neither a modern person nor a modern reader. As a sixth-century reader, Cassiodorus lumps together pagans, Jews, and heretics (as in his treatment of Ps 31) as opponents of the church and the Gospel. He understands this to be a religious duty commanded in the psalms themselves as he writes in his preface: "For true love of the Lord lies precisely in regarding His foes with perfect hatred,"[35] this passage itself a reference to Psalm 139:21-22 ("Do I not hate those who hate you, O Lord? And do I not

---

[34] Cassiodorus, *Variae* 2.27; 4.43; 5.37.
[35] Cassiodorus, *ExplPs* Intro.14, p. 1.36.

loathe those who rise up against you? I hate them with perfect hatred; I count them my enemies"). Taking Cassiodorus on his own terms means wrestling with difficult texts like these and acknowledging this darkness that stains the history of Christian interpretation and nurtured hatred that flared out against Jewish communities across Europe and America for centuries after.

Glancing at the Sources

In his commentary for this psalm, Augustine, the African bishop, provides two texts. The first is a quick paraphrase that reads as a set of exegetical notes from which to prepare a sermon; the second is a sermon preached on a Good Friday at some point after the year 394 during the controversy with the Donatist schismatics. Rather than targeting his interpretation against the Jews, he attacks the Donatists.

Augustine's second text draws largely from the first. That is, it looks like he referred to his own notes when considering what he was going to say. Nevertheless, he does depart from it at points. Cassiodorus is clearly influenced by these works and in particular uses the exegetical notes more than the sermon itself. Cassiodorus goes into more detail, however, especially with the spiritual meanings. Cassiodorus follows Augustine's lead on the initial cry of abandonment and on God hearing prayer but expands it greatly and moves in directions Augustine never gets to. Augustine is also the source of the allegory on the melting wax but when it comes to the events prefiguring the crucifixion, Augustine reads these literally in both the notes and the sermon. He does interpret the division of the garments and tunic allegorically, but for him they represent the sacraments and love—he has the Donatists in mind here, that they have fractured the meaning of the sacraments from the rest of the church but have lost hold of love in doing so. Thus, Cassiodorus takes some details from Augustine and extends some of his thoughts; he clearly used Augustine's works, but they were not determinative for his reading.

Cassiodorus's text occupies almost fifteen columns in Migne's edition; Augustine's first exposition takes up four columns, and the second, eleven columns. Since Augustine's sermon effectively duplicates his notes, on the balance, Cassiodorus has written more and given a more in-depth reading.

Psalm 66 and the Liturgical Environment

Looking at Psalm 66

Psalm 66 is a psalm of praise to God, a communal thanksgiving. It opens with the praise of God, then invites the community to join in praise. It uses allusive language to refer to God's saving acts in the past performed on behalf of Israel; it relates trials that the people have suffered yet insists that God has brought the people through these trials. An individual voice then promises to bring sacrificial offerings to the temple with which to honor God and calls on the community to follow suit.

How Cassiodorus Reads It

In this quick glance at Psalm 66, I am not looking at it because it stands out in any particular way. Instead, it is a fairly ordinary psalm that—unlike the others I am considering in this chapter—does not belong to a specific grouping of psalms. I am selecting it for closer examination because it neatly illustrates in four different interpretive moments the way that Cassiodorus both relies on and informs the liturgical environment within which his monks dwelt. His treatment of this psalm demonstrates the degree to which biblical interpretation, liturgical experience, and spiritual development are intertwined throughout Cassiodorus's commentary. Thus, I highlight this psalm because it is representative, not because it is exceptional.

The first point I want to highlight appears in the interpretation of the first part of the third verse. The NRSV renders it: "Say to God, 'How awesome are your deeds!'" (Ps 66:3). Cassiodorus's rendering, following the translation choices of the Vulgate, is more like this: "Say unto God, How terrible are thy works, O Lord" (Douay-Rheims, adapted). Cassiodorus frames this verse as what the church is telling the nations to sing: this is their libretto. He gives it significant weight, though, and provides insight into his understanding of religious consciousness: "Let us hear what the Church teaches the nations to say in a single phrase and to encapsulate in short compass the great motivation of religion [*magnum causam religionis*]. How terrible are thy works!"[36]

---

[36] Cassiodorus, *ExplPs* 66.2, p. 2.108.

Modern psychology frowns on the use of fear as a chief motivating factor for most anything; the view from late antiquity was rather different. This appeal to fear is not, however, as obvious or simplistic as modern prejudices might lead us to believe; Cassiodorus takes some time developing exactly what he means here.

Cassiodorus starts to develop this idea by qualifying the sense of "terrible":

> Though [the church] says that the works of the Lord are terrible, she did not proclaim the degree of terror which they contain. My view is that the works of the Lord are to be feared on this count: we are to consider what can befall us if the Majesty which looked with pity on the world were to become hostile through the action of our sins.[37]

The fear of God spoken of here is what a grammarian would refer to as a statement contrary to fact. Cassiodorus essentially invites us into a thought experiment. God is, he asserts, loving and looks on humanity with compassion. But—contrary to this current state of reality—what would be the result if God didn't regard us with this favor but rather held us liable for our sins? His next step is to anchor the proof of God's love for humanity. His prime evidence for the love of God is the truth of the incarnation. He states, "God deigned to become man for us," and notates this in the margin with the sign for a doctrine.[38] He then quotes a section from Pope Leo's Letter *28* that emphasizes the self-empty character of the incarnation, that Christ willingly "cloaked the boundlessness of His majesty" because he "sought to be understood."[39] The logic then moves in a reflexive direction: this is what Christ has done for humanity; what, then, has humanity in general and the reader in particular done to respond to a love of this depth?

Cassiodorus anchors this notion with a citation of Habakkuk 3:2 ("O LORD, I have heard of your renown, and I stand in awe, O LORD, of your work"), which reflects the proper attitude. This is more than

---

[37] Ibid.
[38] Ibid.
[39] Ibid. Quoting from Leo, Letter 28.4 (NPNF[1] 12:40). This letter of Pope Leo is also known as "The Tome" and is famous for being sent to the Council of Chalcedon and helping to define the church's doctrine of the two natures in Christ.

just a simple quote, though. A monk would immediately recognize what he was getting at here and hearing the beginning of this line would kick off a cascade of music in the monk's head. The passage Cassiodorus cites is the first line of the canticle sung among the psalms of Lauds on Friday mornings. The canticle *Domine audivi audiotorem* (Hab 3:2-20) is one of the canticles that was always bound into the back of early medieval psalters after the psalms and before any hymns that might appear. The text describes the fearful appearing of God in a storm theophany (much like Ps 18); peoples and natural landscape features shudder and cower in terror at the passing of God and his train but the purpose for the divine expedition is "for the salvation of thy people: for salvation with thy Christ" (Hab 3:13, Douay-Rheims). The speaker experiences embodied fear ("I have heard and my bowels were troubled: my lips trembled at the voice. Let rottenness enter into my bones, and swarm under me"; Hab 3:16, Douay-Rheims) but ends with a proclamation of joy ("But I will rejoice in the Lord: and I will joy in God my Jesus [*in Deo Iesu meo*]"; Hab 3:18, Douay-Rheims). With just a few words, Cassiodorus is able to call up a rich cross-reference, tapping into monastic memorization for another resource that wrestles with the psychological complexities around fear, awe, and wonder.

He concludes this exploration into religious fear with a final note that emphasizes the theological virtues: "But this fear is loving and devoted, with the character of sweetness not bitterness. It begets hope rather than creates doubt. It intensifies desires and does not extinguish the flame of charity."[40] Theologians in later centuries will tease out definitions and make a distinction between servile fear (a fear that motivates good behavior borne out of fear of punishment) and filial fear (a fear that motivates good behavior lest any missteps cause pain to or disapproval from the beloved). While Cassiodorus doesn't use these terms, he's got the future filial fear in mind. This isn't a fear of punishment but a fear that the reader's love will fail to even recognize all of what God has done for it.

The second point appears in the interpretation of verse 6 ("He turned the sea into dry land; they passed through the river on foot. There we rejoiced in him"). The first part of the verse is a reference to the mighty acts of God on behalf of the people of Israel, and Cas-

---

[40] Cassiodorus, *ExplPs* 66.2, p. 2.108.

siodorus rightly explains these as references to the crossing of the Red Sea (Exod 14), the crossing of the Jordan at the entrance into the Promised Land (Judg 3–4), and the crossings of the Jordan by Elijah and Elisha (2 Kgs 2). Turning to the second part of the verse, though, Cassiodorus draws out some typological implications that he sees all of these wonders ultimately pointing to:

> [The Church] now hastens to reveal the mysteries of these works, because the Christian people subsequently took joy in the prefiguration of them. The crossing of the Jewish nation over the seas announced Christ's future baptism. The fact that they crossed rivers without hazard from the deep waters and with dry feet showed that they could traverse the billows of this world untroubled, and attain a most safe haven of repentance. So it was vital that the Church and her holy people should say that they would rejoice at this event, from which sprang the source of our joy and the origin of our eternal salvation.[41]

Baptism is an important theme throughout the commentary and his mention of it here is characteristic of his work. The baptism of Jesus in the Jordan and the subsequent establishment of this rite in the church is, in the view of Cassiodorus, the fundamental truth that all of these earlier encounters with God's people and water were pointing to. He does not make explicit reference to 1 Corinthians 10, but Paul makes the same point—that the crossing of the Red Sea was a foreshadowing of baptism.

Cassiodorus continues in that same vein as he comes to verse 8; the "voice of praise" heard by the nations is the announcement from heaven at the baptism of Jesus as recorded in Matthew 3:17:

> There follows: And hear the voice of his praise, in other words "Accept with trusting belief what the Father says of the Son." The voice of praise is: "This is my beloved Son in whom I am well pleased," and it must be listened to with unsullied and devoted minds, so that we may believe that the one and the same Lord Christ who was sprung from the Father before time began and is consubstantial with Him, was born of the virgin Mary and deigned to become like us when He took on human nature. Holy Church

[41] Ibid.

lives in this faith and advances in this faith, our belief that in the Lord Christ there is no humanity without true divinity, and no divinity without true humanity.[42]

His interpretation of the voice of praise becomes a creedal passage that reinforces an orthodox Christology; Cassiodorus emphasizes the full humanity and full divinity of Jesus as agreed at the Council of Chalcedon.

Having established the miracles of God in Israel's past that he says point to and are fulfilled in the baptism of Jesus, Cassiodorus moves to the implications of baptism for current believers in his interpretation of the next piece: "Who hath set my soul to live: and hath not suffered my feet to be moved" (Ps 66:8b, Douay-Rheims). The two clauses within this passage are the reasons for the church's proclamation of mercy:

> These are the two mysteries of our liberation: first that He leads us through the gift of baptism to life (for we do not reach that goal through our own merits, but are drawn to it by the kindness of His mercy), and second that He does not allow us to be expelled from it though we are clearly burdened by grave faults. The One who sets us in life is He who said: "I am the way, the truth and the life." He who does not allow our steps to be moved is He who offered His hand to Peter so that he would not drown.[43]

The first point is that baptism thus draws Christians into life by joining them into the Body of Christ and plugging them into the life of God. The second addresses a problematic point that the church had been working with for a while: everyone agreed that baptism wiped away sins, but what happened if one sinned (especially a big one) after being baptized? Cassiodorus does not provide an answer but declares his conviction that even grave faults will not expel the baptized from the mercy of Christ. He secures these points with two references, the first a direct citation of the words of Jesus from John 14:6, the second a reference to the story of Jesus assisting Peter as he attempted to walk on the water in Matthew 14:28-31. Jesus confirms with both his words and works that he will not abandon those in trouble but will assist the struggling even in their doubts.

---

[42] Ibid.
[43] Cassiodorus, *ExplPs* 66.9, p. 2.111.

The third point for us to explore turns on the unusual interpretation of the trials related in verses 10-12. Cassiodorus understands these events as the travails of the martyrs! They pass through these trials successfully not because they survived them but because their faith and souls remained intact despite their bodily sufferings and death.

The end of verse 12 concludes this section. The NRSV renders this text: "yet you have brought us out to a spacious place." The Latin uses a different phrase: *et eduxisti nos in refrigerium* ("and thou hast brought us out into a cool refreshment"). This is the way Cassiodorus renders it:

> There follows the blessed promise of the world to come: And thou hast brought us into cool refreshment, so that you might realise that all the Church's sufferings in her members have been imposed on her not as execrable punishment but to bring the blessedness of rest; for cool refreshment after burning troubles is that delightful and pleasant freedom from care which those who have deserved to suffer for the Lord's name obtain by that repayment.[44]

The promise of which Cassiodorus speaks is the peaceful rest of death after the trials of the martyrs. This reading is reinforced in the text of the Mass. One of the prayers that makes up the Western eucharistic canon is the *Memento etiam* that offers prayers for the departed, saying, "To [the departed faithful], O Lord, and to all who rest in Christ, grant, we entreat thee, a place of cool repose (*locum refrigerii*), of light, and peace."[45] To the monks familiar with this prayer—and to what degree it was spoken audibly in the time of Cassiodorus is an open question—the mention of *refrigerium* in the psalm would be mentally connected with the peaceful rest of the faithful dead in the *locum refrigerii* of the Mass.

Fourth and finally, Cassiodorus goes on to invoke another reference to the Mass. In verse 13, *introibo in domum tuam in holocaustis reddam tibi vota mea* ("I will go into thy house with burnt offerings: I will pay thee my vows"), Cassiodorus makes another grammatical observation, then provides a summary of what will unfold in the next few lines:

---

[44] Cassiodorus, *ExplPs* 66.12, pp. 2.112–13.
[45] Bard Thompson, *Liturgies of the Western Church* (Philadelphia: Fortress Press, 1961), 77.

At this point Christ's members revert to the singular; His body says that she will happily go into His house, that is, into the Jerusalem to come, in which are sought not holocausts of cattle but purity of souls. Note that just as in the three previous verses she spoke of the pains of martyrs, so now in the next four up to the end of the section she recounts the good fortunes of the blessed, so that she could strengthen in their grim tribulations the faithful to whom she promises these great rewards.[46]

So, if the last three verses were about the trials the martyrs had to endure for their purification, the next four will speak of their heavenly rewards.

In an unusual twist on the typical understanding, Cassiodorus reads the "holocaust," the whole burnt-offering sacrifice, that the church offers as the souls of the martyrs who have been purified by fire that were spoken of in verses 10 and 12. They have been wholly burnt through their trials and so the church is offering her own cleansed soul to God.

Passing to the next line, *reddam tibi vota mea* ("I will pay thee my vows"), he offers first an expansive paraphrase, then an interpretation:

> [This] means "sing Your praises for ever, and always hymn Your mercy in the company of angels, powers, thrones and dominations." These are the prayers of the faithful, the longings of simple Christians, that those aligning themselves with the holiness of faith and good works may be received into that fellowship with Him.[47]

The church affirms her continuity in praising God alongside the whole angelic order. Powers, thrones, and dominations refer to specific ranks or different kinds of angels; this was an aspect of Jewish tradition mentioned in Paul's writings (Eph 1:21; Col 1:16) and was a topic of great interest in the sixth century. Gregory the Great's Gospel Homily 34, from the generation after Cassiodorus, goes to great lengths speaking about all of these angelic ranks. His discussion is indebted to a work devoted to the topic *The Celestial Hierarchies* by an anonymous mystic writing under the name Dionysius the Areopagite in Syria in the

---

[46] Cassiodorus, *ExplPs* 66.12, p. 2.113.
[47] Cassiodorus, *ExplPs* 66.13, p. 2.113.

530s. This was exactly the same time that Cassiodorus was writing the *Explanation of the Psalms* in Constantinople. Cassiodorus's mention of these specific angelic groups is interesting because the interpretation again points back to the Mass.

A portion of the eucharistic liturgy called the common preface—for use on days that do not have their own appointed preface—invokes the congregation to join in the praise of the whole church and the whole celestial realm by saying, "It is through [Christ] that thy majesty is praised by Angels, adored by Dominations, feared by Powers, through him that the heavens and the celestial Virtues join with the blessed Seraphim in one glad hymn of praise. We pray thee, let our voices blend with theirs as we humbly praise thee."[48] In fact, all prefaces end with this invocation for the congregation to join with the angels because what follows is the *Sanctus* (Holy, Holy, Holy), a hymn adapted from the words of angels from Isaiah 6:3 and Revelation 4:8. As Cassiodorus works with this language of sacrifice and offering in reference to the martyrs, he instinctively makes reference to the central Christian experience of sacrifice in the Mass.

The Psalms and the Liturgical Life

The presence of liturgical references in the *Explanation of the Psalms* would not have seemed unusual at all to monks. Chances are, they might not even see a conceptual distinction between the words of Scripture and the words of liturgy. There is a great deal of overlap between the two—much of the monastic liturgy was drawn directly from Scripture or imbued with its grammar and vocabulary. The act of explaining the Scriptures, its vocabulary, and grammar was frequently an act of explaining the liturgy as well. Nowhere is this more true than in the psalms. Since the psalms existed at the intersection of Scripture and liturgy for the early medieval mind, the blending of the two categories is entirely natural.

As far as the monks were concerned, it was the psalms themselves that defined the shape of their worship; both the Rule of the Master and the Rule of Benedict accept without question that the statement in Psalm 119:164 ("Seven times a day I praise you for your righteous

---

[48] Thompson, *Liturgies*, 71.

ordinances") combined with Psalm 119:148 ("My eyes are awake before each watch of the night, that I may meditate on your promise") were intended as programmatic for monastic worship. Benedict never explains why the psalms formed the backbone of monastic prayer—it was enough that they were. To the monastic mind it was completely self-evident. As the scriptural book of praises, there was no other book more perfectly suited to monastic liturgy. The liturgy and the psalms flowed one into the other.

Glancing at the Sources

Augustine's interpretation of Psalm 66 does not contain any of these four motifs. This is largely a function of purpose. Again, Augustine's purpose was preaching to the laypeople and clergy attending the Mass at his cathedral. A deep dive into the language of the liturgy would not have meant as much to those listening to him in the church at Hippo as it did to the monks of Vivarium.

Psalm 131 and the Gradual Psalms

Looking at Psalm 131

Psalm 131 is a short psalm, just three verses long in the NRSV. In the first verse, the psalmist speaks directly to God, portraying an attitude of humility. The second verse invokes a vivid metaphor: the psalmist's soul has been quieted like a child with its mother. The final verse calls for Israel to put its hope in the Lord forevermore. Scholars largely regard the Psalter as an anonymous collection of liturgical poems, written and collected over a period of centuries. Likely, we will never learn the identity of the people who wrote the specific psalms that survive in our collection. Nevertheless, the unusual image in the second verse has led some to speculate that the author might have been a woman.

Psalm 131 is one of a block of fifteen identically named psalms, running from Psalm 120 through Psalm 134, known as the Songs of Ascent or the Gradual Psalms. The former comes directly from their Hebrew title; the latter from their Latin title, *Canticum graduum*, as translated from the Septuagint. In English, one might call them the Stairclimbing Psalms. These were likely part of an earlier collection that was incorporated into the Psalter as a whole when it was edited. As several of these psalms make reference to Jerusalem and the temple, these have been tentatively identified as pilgrim songs sung by travelers on the way up to Jerusalem.

In the centuries after Cassiodorus, Benedictine monks chanted all of the gradual psalms sequentially as a prefatory devotion before beginning the Night Office. Thus, getting a sense of how Cassiodorus read one of these with reference to the whole will help us understand how the monks conceived of this early morning devotion.

Regarding the Songs of Ascent

Augustine, and Cassiodorus following him, sees the Songs of Ascent foretold in Psalm 84:6-7. The connection is harder to see in the English than it is in the Latin:

New Revised Standard Version	Latin of Cassiodorus	Douay-Rheims (adapted)
⁵Happy are those whose strength is in you, in whose heart are the highways to Zion. ⁶As they go through the valley of Baca they make it a place of springs; the early rain also covers it with pools. ⁷They go from strength to strength; the God of gods will be seen in Zion. ⁸O LORD God of hosts, hear my prayer; give ear, O God of Jacob! Selah ⁹ Behold our shield, O God; look on the face of your anointed.	⁵beatus vir cuius est auxilium abs te, Domine ascensus in corde eius ⁶Disposuit in convalle lacrimarum in loco quem disposuit etenim benedictiones dabit qui legem dedit ⁷ambulant de virtute in virtutem videbitur Deus deorum in Sion ⁸Domine Deus virtutum exaudi orationem meam auribus percipe Deus Iacob DIAPSALM ⁹protector noster aspice Deus et respice in faciem christi tui	⁵Blessed is the man whose help is from thee, O Lord: in his heart he hath disposed to ascend by steps, ⁶Set in the vale of tears, in the place which he hath set. For the lawgiver shall give a blessing, ⁷they shall go from virtue to virtue: the God of gods shall be seen in Sion. ⁸O Lord God of hosts, hear my prayer: give ear, O God of Jacob. ⁹Behold, O God our protector: and look on the face of thy Christ.

Augustine goes to great lengths in his commentary on Psalm 84 to connect this psalm with the gradual psalms: "Let there be these steps in your heart, then, these steps set up by God through his grace. Climb them by loving. While you are climbing, the song of ascent rings out."[49] These are two key points for Augustine's understanding of these psalms (and the broader Psalter as well): first, that the Psalter provides a method of ascent from tears to perfect love; second, that this is possible because of steps carved into the heart through God's grace.[50] The place where the steps lead is none other than the heavenly temple where one meets God face-to-face. At the successful completion of the path, God will be seen and experienced as perfect love.

Jerome reads this text like Augustine. He makes the same fundamental moves, noting that the text begins with the notion of a pilgrimage, moves in steps from low, cursed, place of tears up until it finally reaches the height where God is seen. Here, Jerome appeals directly to the Sermon on the Mount: "Blessed are the pure in heart, for they shall see God" (Matt 5:8). The fathers see this section of Psalm 84 as a road map for the important function of the Gradual Psalms, an unfolding journey from penitence to the fullest possible revelation of God.

Cassiodorus makes the connection between Psalm 84 and the Gradual Psalms in his discussion of the title of Psalm 120:

> A series of new and remarkable headings is now inaugurated, though the words have been encountered in our explanation of the previous psalm. Their purpose is to unfold in fifteen ordered steps the blessedness of the faithful people, celebrated in that previous song in which their wide-ranging merits are assembled, to elucidate the mystery of the New and Old Testaments. The number seven, as has often been said, denotes the week occasioned by the sabbath of the Old Testament; the number eight signifies the Lord's day, on which He clearly rose again, and this is relevant to the New. When joined together, they are seen to make up the

---

[49] Augustine, *Enarrations* 83.10, p. 4.196.

[50] See Gerard McLarney, *St. Augustine's Interpretation of the Psalms of Ascent* (Washington, DC: The Catholic University of America Press, 2014), 128–30. Unfortunately, this work came out as I was concluding my study and I was not able to incorporate it and its conclusions into this work.

number fifteen. The psalmist begins with renunciation of the world, for he shudders at the worldly ways which constitute the burden of his ills. From this base he mounts by the steps, so to say, of merits, and reaches the perfect and eternal love of the Lord, which as we know is set at the very summit of the virtues. . . . So when we hear the word *steps* in the psalms, we are not to think of anything material to be mounted by physical movement, but we should interpret it as the mind's ascent. The word *canticle* has been placed first so that we may apply it rather to the progress of the soul. *Step* here is the ascent of humility, confession of sins, as was stated in Psalm 84: *In his heart he has disposed to ascend by steps, in the vale of tears*. We shall deserve to mount these steps only if we prostrate ourselves for our sins. So let us continually entreat the Lord.[51]

Here, following Augustine, Cassiodorus transmits an understanding of these psalms as a coherent block of material that serves a particular spiritual function: they provide a map of virtues that literally walk the soul from a place of weeping up into the presence of God Almighty.

At the end of this road, Cassiodorus will look back and once again explain the steps. In his conclusion of the very brief Psalm 134, he surveys the entire staircase just traveled and enumerates them all again:

It is pleasant to recount how these steps have led all the way to the heavenly Jerusalem. On the first step [Ps 120] he denotes loathing of the world, after which there is haste to attain zeal for all the virtues. Secondly [Ps 121], the strength of divine protection is explained, and it is demonstrated that nothing can withstand it. Thirdly [Ps 122], the great joy of dwelling with pure mind in the Lord's Church is stated. Fourth [Ps 123], he teaches us that we must continually presume on the Lord's help whatever the constraints surrounding us, until He takes pity and hears us. Fifth [Ps 124], he warns us that when we are freed from dangers, we must not attach any credit to ourselves, but attribute it all to the power of the Lord. In the sixth [Ps 125], the trust of the most faithful Christian is compared to immovable mountains. In the seventh [Ps 126], we are told how abundant is the harvest reaped by those who sow in tears. In the eighth [Ps 127], it is said that

---

[51] Cassiodorus, *ExplPs* 120.title, pp. 3.259–60.

nothing remains of what any individual has performed by his own will; only the things built by the sponsorship of the Lord are most firmly established. In the ninth [Ps 128], it is proclaimed that we become blessed through fear of the Lord, and that all profitable things are granted us. In the tenth [Ps 129], he inculcates in committed persons the patience which he commands through the words of the Church. In the eleventh [Ps 130], as penitent he cries from the depths to the Lord, asking that the great power of the Godhead be experienced by the deliverance of mankind. In the twelfth [Ps 131], the strength of meekness and humility is revealed; in the thirteenth [Ps 132], the promise of the holy incarnation and the truth of the words spoken are demonstrated. In the fourteenth [Ps 133], spiritual unity is proclaimed to the brethren, and to them the Lord's benediction and eternal life are shown to accrue. In the fifteenth [Ps 134], there is awakened in the course of the Lord's praises that perfect charity than which nothing greater can be expressed, and nothing more splendid discovered. As the apostle attests: *God is love* [1 John 4:8]. So let us continually meditate on the hidden nature of this great miracle, so that by ever setting our gaze on such things, we may avoid the deadly errors of the world.[52]

Cassiodorus is benefiting here from producing a written commentary designed to be read. While Augustine certainly conceived of the Songs of Ascent as a block of material, he could not—did not—loop back to provide this kind of overview at the conclusion of his sermon series on the Songs of Ascent. Again, we see here Cassiodorus's commitment to looking at the biblical text beyond a verse-level frame of reference. He is willing to zoom out from that level where patristic interpretation normally occurs and to take in the big picture.

How Cassiodorus Reads It

Psalm 131 comes on the heels of Psalm 130, the second to last of the Penitential Psalms. As Cassiodorus addresses the title, he begins with a rather unexpected pastoral image. This is not out of the ordinary for him—the *Variae* contain quite a number of pastoral illustrations—but this one seems unusual as there does not seem to be anything

---

[52] Cassiodorus, *ExplPs* 134.concl, pp. 3.340–41.

prompting it. He compares the prophet David, having surmounted the last step of penitence and now bestowing on his readers a sweet song of humility, to a farmer who has completed his plowing and now cuts branches from the treetops to feed to the hungry oxen.

Cassiodorus sees this psalm as a refreshing break after the work of penitence. Having completed that task, a song of humility renews the energy and prepares the reader for the journey onward. The interpretive center point of this psalm is humility, and Cassiodorus cites Luke 14:11 ("For all who exalt themselves will be humbled, and those who humble themselves will be exalted") as a summary of the text that both condemns the devil, the ultimate symbol of pride, and lifts up Christ, the very image of humility.

Despite it being a short text, Cassiodorus divides it into two sections. The first, verses 1-2, teaches humility by appealing to the example of the prophet but also issues a warning. The second, verse 3, reinforces the message of hope.

After identifying the start of the psalm as a dialectical device—a hypothetical syllogism—he breaks it down into four statements that tell the reader what not to do (*anastrophe* being the technical term for this figure). Then, these four negative examples are linked with four biblical people who are not to be imitated. His heart was not exalted: therefore he was not like Pharaoh whose heart was overly exalted. His eyes were not too lifted up: therefore he was not like the rich man in the gospel who ordered his barns to be pulled down to build up bigger ones (Luke 12:16-21). He has not walked in matters too great for him: Pontius Pilate overstepped his bounds when he tried to assert his authority over Christ himself (John 19:10). He is not involved in wonderful things above him either: Simon Magus did when he tried to purchase the Holy Spirit from the apostles with money (Acts 8:18-24). Thus, these four vices to be avoided are tied to concrete examples from the biblical narrative.

The next phrase ("If I was not humbly minded") is read with reference to the arts of biblical interpretation. Cassiodorus attributes heresies and errors to prideful reading of the Scriptures:

> So he informs us that he has pondered the divine Scriptures with a simple and pure heart, unlike Arians, Manicheans, Donatists and the rest who are cut off from the true religion. If they had been willing to be *humbly minded*, they would not have elected

> to defend their depraved views. They would have turned to the truest and holiest teachers, and deserved to obtain understanding of the true faith.[53]

Thus, an important aspect of humility is following the teachings of the church and reading alongside the acknowledged teachers of holiness rather than striking off to find new meanings.

Instead, the soul is exalted when it is lifted up to understand the Trinity or to wonder at the incarnation. "It is lawful to raise the soul in the things which are the source of life, of vigour, of nourishment by the heavenly bread."[54]

At the image of the weaned child, Cassiodorus makes the obligatory reference to 1 Corinthians 3:1-2 ("And so, brothers and sisters, I could not speak to you as spiritual people, but rather as people of the flesh, as infants in Christ. I fed you with milk, not solid food, for you were not ready for solid food") but prefers to center his focus on the mutual feelings between the infant and the mother; the sense of longing and desire that infants show toward their mothers is precisely the feeling of yearning that Christians should show toward God.

The final verse, calling on Israel to hope in the Lord, is a teaching on patience as well as humility. The brevity of the psalm itself is a sign of the psalmist's humility and is itself part of the teaching.

The conclusion is interesting. First, Cassiodorus praises David who, despite being a great king of Israel, has the spiritual wherewithal to write such a psalm on humility. Then, the conclusion turns from exposition directly into prayer. Here is the conclusion in full:

> The humility which is commended at this lofty height is exceedingly wonderful. If some eremite at leisure in his cell uttered such sentiments, he would glow with the great glory of his patience, but it was a prince in the purple, one outstanding among prophets, who uttered them, to ensure that he shunned pride as eagerly as he glowed with the distinction of honours. What then is demanded of us, seeing that such were his meditations? Grant us, O Lord, the humility of the king, the patience of the prophet, for these are truly your gifts in whatever person they reside. Such

---

[53] Cassiodorus, *ExplPs* 130.2, p. 3.318.
[54] Ibid.

virtue is not assumed at large by human will, but is granted by the generosity of Your mercy. This humility rises to a special rank of honour among outstanding virtues, for Your majesty deigned to embrace it. In short, let us ponder how greatly honoured is the humility opposed to pride, the humility set, as we see, on the twelfth step. Pride plunges people into hell, but humility leads them to heaven.[55]

This turn to direct prayer is something that occurs more frequently as the commentary works its way through the psalms. Cassiodorus is not just conveying information here but teaching his readers a method of engagement that certainly includes study and the application of the liberal arts but that is always moving toward and should always conclude with prayer and praise.

A Glance at the Sources

Hilary gives a brief exposition on this psalm (as is fitting given its length). While he is working in similar territory around humility and meekness, his interpretive decisions and directions are not ones taken up by Cassiodorus. Starting with a reference to Psalm 51, the attitude of the heart here is linked to the "troubled heart" there that is the proper sacrifice to God. Hilary prefers to look on David directly as an example of humility, appealing to his status in his father's household before attaining his kingly status; the interpretive focus on exaltation also looks at a balance: the heart is not exalted but the soul is. Thus, the lowering of the heart to facilitate the exaltation of the soul is key to achieving a proper middle course. While Hilary picks up the same passage from 1 Corinthians 3 he also balances it with the feast Abraham threw to celebrate the weaning of Isaac (Gen 21:8); his point focuses on the advantages of reaching spiritual maturity.

Augustine's sermon on Psalm 131 takes a bit to get to the psalm itself, beginning with the metaphor of the church as the true temple, exhorting his congregation not to be among the number whipped out of it with cords. (Could John 4 have been the gospel reading for the day?) Once he does get into the psalm, he starts in the same place as Hilary—connecting the heart mentioned in Psalm 131 with the

---

[55] Cassiodorus, *ExplPs* 130.concl, pp. 3.320–21.

heart of Psalm 51. Discussing the first verse, he touches on Simon Magus as a negative example but spends more time and energy on Paul's metaphor of the church as the Body of Christ, composed of a host of members who perform a variety of functions. Humility and not exalting the self, then, has to do with understanding one's appropriate place within the body as a whole. Peter and Paul were given extraordinary graces that most Christians will never receive. Rather than expecting or hoping for such gifts, Christians should hope that their names are written in heaven. He touches on both Psalm 7 and 1 Corinthians 3 in his discussion of the weaned child but also moves to the problem of heresy. Understanding the core doctrines of the faith are the milk of the faith; they must be absorbed before moving on to other matters. Heretics try to move to the deeper mysteries of faith without adequately grasping the basics. An alternative explanation discusses those who wish to remain at the "milk" level of the faith and not grow beyond it. After discussing this for some time, Augustine reveals that he prefers the first reading.

Cassiodorus borrows a few details from Augustine: he picks up the reference to Simon Magus, he uses the references to Psalm 7 and 1 Corinthians 3, and he also reads the weaned child with reference to heretics. Other than that, he is largely independent of Augustine. His interpretive focus is much more explicitly on the virtues of humility and patience. Rather than following the path of Augustine's sermon, Cassiodorus remains focused on the larger purpose of the Gradual Psalms collection. In essence, he is more faithful to Augustine's larger construction of this set of materials than he is to the course of this psalm's exposition. By maintaining this focus, moreover, he produces a tighter set of thoughts than Augustine's rather wandering foray. While Augustine's text covers almost twelve columns of text in Migne, Cassiodorus uses only three and a half. In this sort of exposition Cassiodorus exhibits much-needed editorial control on Augustine's expansive homiletical rhetoric!

Summary

From this brief look at a series of psalms, we can see how Cassiodorus brought both his learning and faith to bear on his interpretive task. While he was indebted to the tradition of the church—relying on

Augustine, Hilary, and Jerome in particular—he used them selectively and adapted their work for his own purposes. They were sources of inspiration and assistance, rather than authorities who must be mimicked directly. Cassiodorus displays an independence characteristic of a skilled synthesist who is able to remain in contact with an official tradition without being controlled by it.

As we can see from just these few excerpts, Cassiodorus's great contribution to the study of the psalms was his leveraging of the classical arts of reading for theological profit. Taking the wisdom of the fathers, he melded it with the learning of the classical world and put that classical learning in service to the needs of faith. From the rhetorical reframing of the penitential psalms to the over-reading possible through the interpretation of ornamented language to the emphasis on etymology, Cassiodorus demonstrates time and again how intellectual arts can be placed in service of spiritual aims. Underlying all of his work is that consistent focus. The emphasis on correct doctrine, on the appropriate skills of reading, on reading in consonance with the church, is all in service of communicating a pure faith to be believed, followed, and lived. The reading and understanding of the psalms is not enough. Even the praying of the psalms is not enough. For Cassiodorus, the monk is not fulfilling his vocation until the praises and exhortations of the Psalter are lived out in the monk's life and when his every action is as much a hymn to God flowing from his heart as the words and songs flowing from his lips.

CHAPTER TEN

The Legacy of Cassiodorus

Looking at a Legacy

When a man retires around the age of fifty-five, we figure he still has a few good decades before him. If he happened to live in sixth-century Italy—a time of notoriously bad nutrition, a complete lack of antibiotics, filled with touchy people holding sharp implements—we might shrink that estimate a bit and hope for at least one more decent decade. For Cassiodorus, retirement proved quite a surprise. Almost four decades later, he was still writing in his pleasant villa-turned-monastic enclosure. So, what was the legacy of this man, this thinker and writer, patrician and monk?

During his life Cassiodorus established two monasteries. We've talked about Vivarium quite a lot because it has figured directly in our story. It was the place of his retirement. It's where he wrote the *Institutions* and where he located, in that work, certain bookcases that held certain books bound into particular volumes. The other one, we don't know so much about. We know that it was in Sicily—territory governed by Cassiodori—so it's no surprise that they would have holdings there that Cassiodorus Senator would have converted into a monastery. What's significant is that we know about it only because it was mentioned in connection with Vivarium by Gregory the Great in a letter shortly before the year 600. That's the last notice we get of either the Sicilian monastery or Vivarium. Two mentions in the letters of Gregory the Great—one about a dispute with a bishop, another on the appointment of a priest to serve in the monastery—then silence.

But that can't be the end of the story.

We're not talking about a modern world here. There's at least one more piece of the puzzle that remains for us to explore: what happened to the books?

Think about that: the *Institutions* tell us of a large library (certainly large for a small Italian monastery) filled with central texts on the Christian faith and practice. This would be a treasure trove for someone, both in the metaphorical sense but also in the literal one. These weren't just disembodied ideas; they were artifacts in leather and parchment and oaken boards that would have taken at least an ox cart or two to haul around. If the words of Cassiodorus survived him, survived his death, survived the collapse of his monastery, it was because someone lifted these words in his arms and carried them off, taking them to a place where they would be copied, circulated, and preserved. That's the last part of our story: the arms that carried, the hands that copied.

The next place where we see the *Explanation of the Psalms* is on the periphery of the old empire: the linked monasteries of Wearmouth and Jarrow in Northumbria, the section of England just south of Scotland. The founder of Wearmouth, Benedict Biscop, was a surprisingly wide-ranging individual who made the long and perilous journey from the empire's edge to its ancient center not once but many times. The monasteries' most famous resident, the Venerable Bede, recorded its history in sermons and a series of lives of its early abbots. In his sermon on Biscop, Bede tells us the purpose of Biscop's many pilgrimages to Rome:

> As often as he crossed the sea, he never returned, as is the custom with some people, empty-handed and without profit, but one time he brought an abundance of holy books, and another time he brought a venerable present of relics of the blessed martyrs of Christ. Another time he had architects come for the construction of the church; another time it was glaziers to cover its windows with ornament; and another time he carried back a letter of privilege sent from the lord Pope, by which our freedom from every outside interference was maintained. Another time he transported pictures of the holy histories which were put up, not only for the

ornamentation of the church, but also for the instruction of those who looked at them, namely so that those who could not read might learn of the works of our Lord and Savior through gazing on images of these [works].[1]

Although this makes it sound like Biscop brought one kind of thing with him each trip, this is not the case and is clarified by details at other points in Bede's accounts. Piecing these together, French scholar Pierre Courcelle writes, "The Abbot Benedict made five trips to Rome, and Bede informs us that at each of his last three trips, in 671, 678, 684, he brought back collections of manuscripts that constituted the contents of his library."[2] We know without a doubt that some of these books came from Vivarium. Twice in his commentaries, Bede refers to illustrations from Cassiodorus that he has seen, pictures that Cassiodorus also mentions in his *Explanation of the Psalms*. As I mentioned in our discussion of the Codex Amiatinus, this book may well be a fusion of two Cassiodorian manuscripts, the Codex Grandior (which was the original source of the pictures) and the other Vulgate manuscript mentioned in the *Institutions* as the text of Amiatinus is the Vulgate, not the Old Latin of the Codex Grandior.

Bede not only refers to the drawings and records their mention in the Psalms commentary but also uses the commentary itself in his writings and proclaims it to be excellent. In addition to these, Courcelle notices even further connections between Bede's reading and Cassiodorus's library:

> Like Cassiodorus, [Bede] possessed Basil's *Hexameron* translated by Eustathius, Ambrose's *Hexameron*, and Augustine's *De Genesi ad litteram*, *Contra Manichaeos*, *Confessiones*, and *Contra adversarium legis et prophetarum*. Knowing that the holdings of Yarrow came from the Lateran and included several Vivarian manuscripts brought back from Rome, is it venturesome for us to think that Bede read

---

[1] Bede, Homily 1.13, in *Homilies on the Gospels: Book One, Advent to Lent*, trans. Lawrence T. Martin and David Hurst, Cistercian Studies 110 (Kalamazoo, MI: Cistercian Publications, 1991), 131.

[2] Pierre Courcelle, *Late Latin Writers and Their Greek Sources*, trans. Harry E. Wedeck (Cambridge, MA: Harvard University Press, 1969), 394.

at least certain of these works in Cassiodoran manuscripts or in copies of them?[3]

Courcelle traces the movement of the library from Vivarium to the Lateran—suggesting that Gregory the Great may have had a hand in it—and from there to the wilds of Northumbria to the home of Bede.

Indeed, the earliest manuscript of Cassiodorus's *Explanation of the Psalms* that we possess is not a complete text but an abbreviation known as the Durham Cassiodorus. Located in Durham, England, it is one of the treasures of Northumbria that, along with the bones of Bede himself, the Lindisfarne Gospels, and other relics, were taken to Durham for safety during the harrowing of northern England through the incessant Viking raids that plagued the region for centuries shortly after Bede's own death.

Thus, it appears that the *Explanation of the Psalms* spread to the wider world not from southern Italy but from northern England. After being laboriously trekked across Europe, it was copied and distributed in northern England to the Irish-held regions in the north and west. From there, it moved south and east across the channel to the continental monasteries. If there were early copies made and circulated within Italy itself, their remnants have not yet been identified.

How do we determine what makes a work successful? What are the metrics to figure out when a work has taken hold of a population or an environment? It's not an easy thing to do, especially when survivals from the medieval period are inherently partial and rely on the vagaries of chance. There are a few easy moves: we can look at the number of manuscripts that survive, whether whole or partial. We can look at where and how and by whom an author is mentioned. We can look at the number of citations where the text itself is used by later authors.

But then there are intangibles, points of influence, points of correspondence where there's nothing hard and fast that we can pin down but where we recognize a common feeling, a common spirit, a certain something that evokes the memory of the original.

---

[3] Ibid., 395–96.

Looking at Manuscripts

Judging by manuscripts, the *Explanation of the Psalms* was a success. Some works from the medieval world survive in one solitary copy. *Beowulf*, anyone? Only one copy. It's arguably far more important to us (given the number of students assigned to read sections of it every year in schools) than it was to early medieval England.

In our discussion of Cassiodorus as an editor we talked about three works on the Psalms—Augustine's *Enarrations on the Psalms*, which was the original source text; Prosper of Aquitaine's abridgement of Augustine; and Cassiodorus's *Explanation of the Psalms*. One of the ways to determine how well a work was received is the number of copies that survive. Now let's just say at the outset that this is a crude measure of how well a text was appreciated. Just because copies did not survive to the present does not mean they did not exist. All we can do at this point is to see what has come down to us and if we can observe any interesting trends in what remains.

One of the standard tools used by medievalists to determine circulations of works like these is Friedrich Stegmüller's eleven-volume *Repertorium Biblicum Medii Aeuii*, which lists the surviving manuscripts of various biblical materials from the medieval period. Fortunately, in addition to editions in most research libraries, this work can now be found online as well and is searchable by anyone (although we do have to reckon with German and Latin to find what we're looking for).[4]

Searching for these three works in the electronic edition of Stegmüller yields a list of surviving manuscripts representing full, partial, or excerpted editions of these particular works. After sorting through to determine which volumes should be linked with one another to make complete sets, I reckon the sets as follows:

- Augustine's *Enarrations on the Psalms*: representative parts of sixty-six sets survive
- Prosper of Aquitaine's *Exposition on the Psalms*: four full texts survive
- Cassiodorus's *Explanation of the Psalms*: representative parts of eighty-five sets survive

---

[4] The resource is currently found here: http://www.repbib.uni-trier.de/cgi-bin/rebiIndex.tcl.

Stegmüller is great but it is a general collection based on lists drawn together by experts who have devoted their careers to some of the individual documents that make up the literary leavings of the Middle Ages. It's a starting point, not an ending point. James W. Halporn, who wrote broadly on Cassiodorus throughout his career, compiled the definitive published list in 1981. Adding in newly cataloged materials from the online Stegmüller, there are 109 sets of Cassiodorus's work from which something survives, or texts that contain large parts of the commentary.

This is almost twice the number of sets of Cassiodorus's commentary than Augustine's.

If Cassiodorus was trying to produce a shorter version that transmitted Augustine's insights but only used half the material, then it's clear that he succeeded. In the process of traditioning that we discussed earlier, Cassiodorus scored by producing something useful because, on the one hand, it was more concise where it needed to be and, on the other, added value to what had been received.

If we dig a little deeper into the manuscript tradition, we can discover some interesting things. One way we can look at the numbers is to evaluate the list based on when the surviving manuscripts were copied. Plotting this by century gives us a graph showing the distribution of manuscripts between the eighth century—our earliest surviving copies—and the fifteenth century. After that point, we move into the age of printing, and the number of surviving copies doesn't matter in the same way.

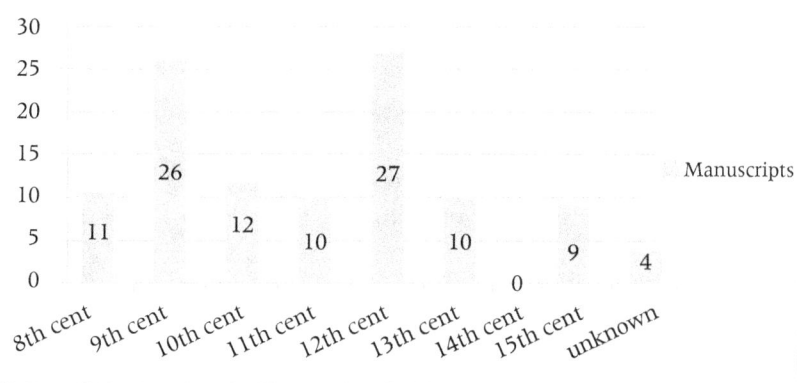

Figure 15: Surviving manuscripts of the ExplPs by century of creation

The graph shows two spikes, one in the ninth century and the other in the twelfth century. These periods immediately jump out to historians of monasticism because they represent two periods of intense monastic reform.

The monastic ninth century began with the Councils of Aachen in 816–817, where reformers under Benedict of Aniane and Smaragdus of Saint-Mihiel established primacy of the Benedictine Rule throughout the Carolingian Empire and territories beyond that were under its cultural sway. This movement brought an increased interest in promoting the core texts of monasticism as the reformers understood it. Ten of the eleven surviving eighth-century manuscripts of the *Explanation of the Psalms* were produced in seven monastic centers of the Carolingian domain: Chelles, Flavigny, Corbie, Reichenau, Lorsch, St. Gall, and Weissenburg; the sole exception is from Northumbria in England, the Durham Cassiodorus that hails from Bede's monastery. From there, the growth in texts in the ninth century is largely within the northern Carolingian regions with only three manuscripts from the area of northern Italy, likely from Nonantola Abbey. The picture that emerges, then, is the commentary arriving from England and diffusing throughout northern Europe through the Carolingian monastic network.

The twelfth century brought a back-to-basics reform driven by groups like the Cistercians, Carthusians, and Camaldolese who pruned the liturgical overgrowth of the Cluniac tradition and tried to return to the spirit of the Benedictine vision as read through Cassian and the Desert Fathers. Many of the manuscripts of the *Explanations* from the twelfth century were copied in Benedictine or Cistercian centers.

The drop-off in manuscript copies, beginning in the thirteenth century, reflects both the growth of scholasticism over monasticism and the increased use of the *Glossa Ordinaria* as a source for biblical commentary. Nonetheless, manuscripts were still being copied in the fifteenth century despite these factors.

Looking at the manuscript tradition, there are a few mutations that are worth noting. One of the manuscripts from the eighth or ninth century is from the library of Reichenau Abbey, a library we've encountered previously. This text is unique because it is an abbreviated version of Cassiodorus's work: for all of the psalms, it preserves his discussion of the psalm heading, the division of the psalm, and the conclusion but skips the internal commentary![5] This method of condensation preserves much of what is original to Cassiodorus that cannot be found in other sources.

Two manuscripts from the fifteenth century transmit only Cassiodorus's work on the seven Penitential Psalms.[6]

Insertions in Bibles and Psalters

We can't just look for Cassiodorus's writing within his own manuscript tradition. Very early on, his work breaks free of these narrow confines and starts appearing in an arguably more useful location: within Bibles and Psalters themselves. Modern study Bibles have material before the start of a biblical book to offer some initial orientation and context. Then, they may have section headings that attempt to summarize the contents in order to help a searcher find a pertinent passage without having to scan all of the text. Furthermore, usually at the bottom of the page, they will have notes that help explain any difficulties or obscurities within the verses. Medieval Bibles tended to have these same three kinds of materials: contextualizing prefaces, summarizing headings, and explanatory notes or glosses. Cassiodorus's work was relied on—along with other patristic authors—to provide all three.

Halporn's great list of manuscript survivals contains not only lists of manuscripts of the full Psalms commentary but also a shorter list of eighteen Bibles or Psalters that he knew of that had portions of Cassiodorus's prefaces inserted in them. Because manuscript catalogers of the past did not necessarily indicate the full span of prefatory material in the kinds of catalogs that Halporn was scanning, there is a far greater presence of Cassiodorian material floating around than one might expect from his list.

For instance, there is a preface to the Psalms attributed to Bede that starts off *In primo libro Paralipomenon legitur* ("In the first book of Chronicles we read"). This is the beginning of Cassiodorus's chapter 2. In some copies of the text, the quote continues for a bit and then it stops,

---

[5] Karlsruhe, Richenau Perg. CLV.
[6] Leipzig, Stadtbib. Rep. I fol. 19 and Wilhering Stiftsbibliothek 122.

acknowledges Cassiodorus, and then offers excerpts from Jerome and Hilary, identifying them by name as well. There is, however, another preface attributed to Bede that begins *Psalterium est, ut Hieronymus ait, in modum deltae litterae* ("A psaltery is, as Jerome said, in the shape of the letter *delta*"). This preface was probably not written by Bede and is, instead, a straight-up compilation of material from Cassiodorus. The opening words come directly from Cassiodorus's chapter 4. Some versions of this preface stop at the end of chapter 4, but in some manuscripts I've seen, it continues without a break through chapter 6 before jumping without warning to a short section from the exposition of Psalm 2 before moving on to another source.[7] As more manuscripts are looked over and annotated as more digital libraries come online, we'll have a better idea how truly widespread these prefaces were and what shapes they took.

Cassiodorus's chapters used as prefaces in Paris, BN 16744, f. 168r.

An example of how Cassiodorus's chapters were used is a twelfth-century Bible now in the French national library in Paris. The book of Baruch ends on folio 165r. Then, a variety of prefaces appear, each set off by a decorated initial to visually mark a difference between them. There is a lengthy prayer attributed to St. Eugenius of Toledo (d. 647), then two prefaces attributed to Jerome, then three exchanges between Jerome and Damasus—two letters and a dialogue of sorts. Folio 168r has two large initials that indicate the start of two prefaces: the first starts a preface labeled "From the book of Saint Isidore." The next initial is simply marked with a red rubric, "On Prophecy," the title of Cassiodorus's first chapter in

---

[7] This is the case in the preface to Rome, Biblioteca Vallicelliana, MS E.24.15v-16r.

his preface. In succession after that are the first twelve chapters of the preface with the exception only of chapter 10, the one that pulls together Cassiodorus's discussion of the psalm headings. The final chapter, on f. 171v, is followed by Jerome's preface addressed to Sophronius and an unattributed discussion of the languages of the Psalter. A discussion from Augustine on the virtues of the Psalms follows, then Origen's words that we heard Hilary quote—seeing the Psalms as a great house filled with many locked doors. After that are the one-line summaries attributed to Origen of all 150 psalms. Finally, after these materials the psalms themselves begin on f. 176r. Thus, in this example of the Paris Bible tradition, there is a lengthy collection of patristic material introducing the Psalter; of this text, a good amount of it was written by Cassiodorus, but unlike Isidore, Augustine, Jerome, and even the lesser-known Eugenius of Toledo, his name is not mentioned.

As is evident in the Paris manuscript, one-line summaries attributed to Origen were placed before the actual text of the psalms as a kind of table of contents. The other place these are frequently found is as section headings introducing each psalm. In fact, the Paris manuscript has a second set of these summarizing headings within the psalms themselves, in this case a set that identifies the speaker of each psalm. Looking across the manuscript tradition, there were six sets of these headings that appear over and over again within medieval Bibles and Psalters. As in the case of the Paris manuscript, it was common to have more than one of these sets of headers. The set identified as Series VI consists of material extracted from Cassiodorus.

These headings are fairly short, usually between twenty and thirty words long, and focus on the speakers and the general interpretive thrust of Cassiodorus's explanation. Thus, the heading for Psalm 4 reads: "The church prays that her prayer would be heard, rebuking the unfaithful, because they pursue vanity; and she generally warns that the sacrifice of righteousness should be rendered from which great benefits will follow."[8] This is a straightforward extract from the "division" section of Psalm 4 that does some summarizing but, for the most part, uses the words of Cassiodorus directly. This set of headings even tries to follow some of the more complicated changes of speakers.

---

[8] Pierre Salmon, *Les 'Tituli Psalmorum' des Manuscripts Latin*, Collectanea Biblical Latina 12 (Rome: Vatican Library, 1959), 154.

For instance, this is the heading for Psalm 18 that we looked at in chapter 4: "The prophet gives thanks to the Lord because he saved him from grave danger; the church speaks because before the advent of the Lord it suffered innumerable calamities; also the voice of Christ is introduced when his power and majesty are described."[9] Again, this is compiled from phrases taken directly from the "division" portion of Cassiodorus's work, but it misses a final twist at the end: Cassiodorus has the church chiming in one more time to praise God.

The modern editor of these headings, Pierre Salmon, identifies this set as largely northern Italian material, pulling together the text from three ninth- and tenth-century manuscripts from Milan and the Abbey of Nonantola. In addition to these, it seems to have left traces in some of the other series of psalm headings; Salmon notes some correspondence with material in Series I as well. He states that this set began circulating by the eighth century and connects it to the psalm commentary associated with Bede that we will touch on below.

One of the most fascinating places where Cassiodorus makes his mark is in a group of books that scholars refer to as the Carolingian glossed Psalters. Here's the problem: generally speaking, the books that survive the centuries are the pretty ones. It's the books with lavish initials, intricate miniatures, and rich owners that have been treasured and preserved to the point that they come down to us through the centuries. By and large, the Carolingian glossed Psalters were not pretty books; they were functional books intended for either students or scholars. For whatever reason, however, Count Eberhard of Ebersburg, who died around 1040, commissioned a deluxe glossed psalter now known as the Eberhard Psalter. This text is rightly described as being "among the most magnificent monuments of Bavarian illumination in the first quarter of the 11th century."[10] This book is, in essence, the pretty version of a kind of book that monastic scholars had worked from for centuries. Once we get past the lavish initial for the beginning of Psalm 1 and flip to the start of Psalm 2, starting on folio 9, we get a sense of what the body of the manuscript looks like. The page is written in two columns; the larger left column con-

---

[9] Ibid., 157.
[10] "Eberhard Psalter," World Digital Library, https://www.wdl.org/en/item/8960/ (online: accessed January 26, 2017).

tains the text of the psalm; the smaller writing in the right column is commentary. That's the "glossing" from which this kind of book takes its name. The text just above the big initial "Q" is the psalm heading—it's from that Series VI of summarizing section headings that comes from Cassiodorus. Not only that, the glossed commentary in the right-hand column is also largely pulled from Cassiodorus. This beautiful book represents an evolution that Cassiodorus would have approved of: a strategic combination of text and commentary that facilitates informed prayer.

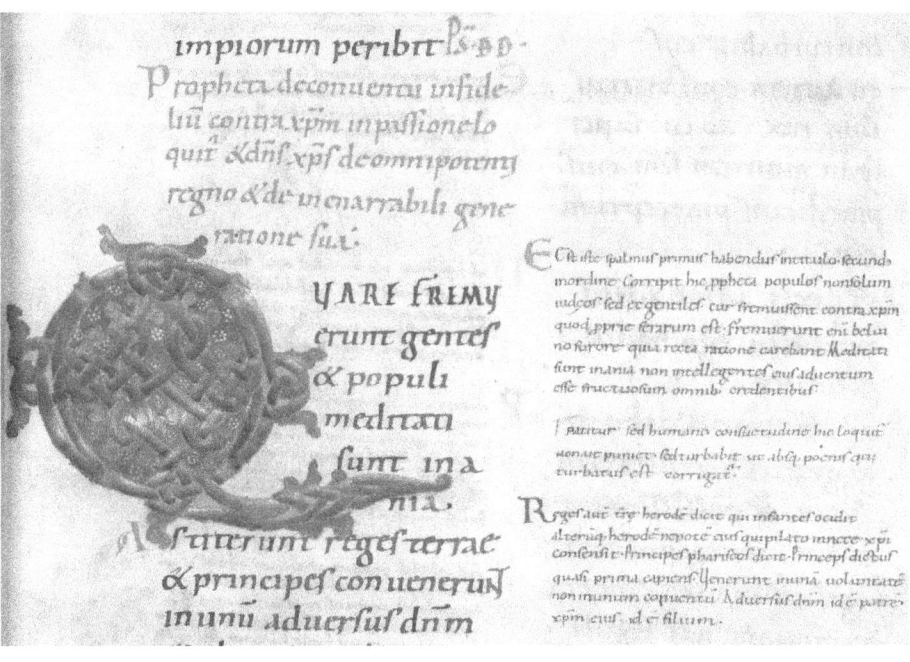

Eberhard Psalter, Psalm 2. BSB Clm 7355, f.9r.

It's clear that this deluxe book didn't appear out of nowhere. Its format had been established over the centuries in functional versions, most of which do not survive. Nevertheless, Margaret Gibson traces the content and layout of the Eberhard Psalter back to a family of manuscripts that integrates the biblical text along with the commentary apparatus to the German monastery of Fulda around the year 800. From there she can discern a German strand and an Italian strand. The German strand is represented by three manuscripts (one now fragmentary) that all came from the Swiss abbey of St. Gall in the mid-ninth century.

The book, still at St. Gall,[11] has the Series VI summarizing headings that we discussed above written in red rustic capitals before the start of each psalm. These summaries and the psalm text proper occupy a central column. The psalm is written in large clear letters—no more than two or three words to a line with generous space around them. Right and left columns around the central column contain blocks of commentary, some clearly original, beginning with large green initials and a highlighted first line, and also black or brown notes added by other hands at a later point. Glosses also appear in small black minuscule letters among the psalm text.

Commenting on the content of the commentaries copied into these Psalters, Gibson identifies them as generally patristic but with a heavy reliance on Cassiodorus:

> [T]he two studies that were genuinely accessible throughout the earlier Middle Ages were the *Ennarationes in Psalmos* of Augustine and the *Expositio Psalmorum* of Cassiodorus. The great anomaly is Jerome. His revision and translations of the Psalter render him the expositor par excellence, yet he left no authentic commentary; the *Brevarium* of Jerome is a work of the mid-seventh century.
>
> During the seventh century this patristic inheritance was reworked in the earliest of the medieval commentaries: the *Glosa ex traditione seniorum* (first half of the seventh century), drawing principally on Augustine; the *Brevarium* of Pseudo-Jerome (mid-seventh century), using the *Glosa* and Cassiodorus; above all the series of introductions to individual psalms which is attributed to Bede (c. 700+). This *'liber de titulis psalmorum'* (as Fischer called it), or *'Titulatio'* (in the language of the St Germain-des-Pres Psalter), consists of excerpts from Cassiodorus, abridged, slightly reordered and deployed as a continuous commentary with lemmata. It circulated well into the eleventh century, both in its original form and as an element in a Glossed Psalter. Finally the commentary in the Mondsee Psalter (pre-778), for which Cassiodorus is again the primary source, is another witness to the systematic study of the Psalter in pre-Carolingian Europe.
>
> All these early commentaries are "continuous": that is, they consist of lemmata of text, each followed by its exposition. The

---

[11] St. Gallen, Stiftsbibliothek, Cod. Sang. 27. See it here: http://www.e-codices.unifr.ch/en/csg/0027/.

more elegant and difficult alternative was the planned text with apparatus: the Glossed Psalter as such. Here the preferred source is Cassiodorus, sometimes in the Bedan *Titulatio*, often quarried directly from the original text. The picture can be drawn in broad outline, although much remains to be explored.[12]

Thus, the post-Cassiodoran tradition used him extensively, even while bringing in material from Augustine and Jerome. This is a completely natural development: it is the ongoing process of traditioning. Later generations assess what they receive and add what will continue to keep the tradition both viable and vital. Then, with this commentary tradition in hand, we turn back to the glossed psalters to see how it gets deployed.

The marginal-glossed commentary of the earliest example, the Frankfurt Psalter from around 800, has three sources: "The Bedan *Titulatio*, direct quotation and adaptation of Cassiodorus, and some new material."[13] From that point, the German tradition was established at St. Gall, and was perpetuated by Tegernsee Abbey, originally a daughter-house of St. Gall. Like the Eberhard Psalter, four deluxe glossed Psalters survive from Tegernsee created in the mid-eleventh century. These alter the contents a bit:

> With or without the Bedan *Titulatio*, it consists of Cassiodorus' exposition freely altered and adapted with extensive new material. It appears to be independent of the apparatus that had already been developed in Fulda. Now the annotation extends through Psalm 150 through the Canticles and the Lord's Prayer to the concluding Athanasian Creed, the *Quicunque uult*. The attribution of the Tegernsee version to Bruno, bishop of Würzburg (*ob.* 1045) may indicate the patron who commissioned a volume rather than the "author" of an already traditional gloss.[14]

So, this is evolution of the material resting on a Cassiodoran foundation. The situation is very similar in the Italian strand of the tradition:

---

[12] Margaret Gibson, "Carolingian Glossed Psalters," in Gameson, *The Early Medieval Bible*, 78–100, at 96–97.

[13] Gibson, "Carolingian Glossed Psalters," 97.

[14] Ibid.

In Vercelli the text already seen as a continuous commentary in Mondsee appears as a marginal gloss in Vercelli 62. As usual, the basic source is Cassiodorus. The Schøyen fragment may testify to an Augustinian tradition, but we need more evidence. Finally, the *Brevarium* of pseudo-Jerome makes an unexpected appearance in Camaldoli as the only element so far identified in the Romuald Psalter.[15]

The two strands that Gibson identifies ground the notion that far more of these ordinary books circulated and have not survived, the beautiful, colorful ones being the lucky representatives of a standard educational tradition. It's not a stretch to suggest that it might even have been a psalter of this type for which Mael Isu composed his love song that we encountered at the beginning of chapter 1.

That Cassiodorus was used is obvious from Gibson's investigation; how he was being used is not as clear and is another point that requires further study. Generally speaking, in my cursory examination of these manuscripts, the commentary picks up on Cassiodorus's interpretation—the way he paraphrases and the allegorical or typological connections that he makes. The grammar, rhetoric, and dialectic is usually not included.

Of course, medieval manuscripts are an idiosyncratic lot, and even this is not a hard-and-fast rule. In the margins of Psalm 1 in an Italian glossed Psalter are three references to figures of thought: *paradyigma*, *metafora*, and *metonomia*.[16] Of these three, Cassiodorus mentions only the first in his commentary. The image from Psalm 1:4 of the wicked being blown away like chaff is a metaphor (a comparison of dissimilar things), however, and the "way of the wicked" castigated in Psalm 1:6 is correctly identified as a metonomy, for this is not truly an objection to the road itself but to the manner of life lived by the wicked.

One possible clue as to how Cassiodorus's work was used in monastic education lies in a pair of books that survives from England. One is the Regius or Royal Psalter. This manuscript has received a great deal of attention among scholars who study Old English and

---

[15] Gibson, "Carolingian Glossed Psalters," 98.

[16] Roma, Biblioteca Vallicelliana, Manoscritti, ms.E 24, f.29r. Accessed online January 26, 2017: http://www.internetculturale.it/jmms/iccuviewer/iccu.jsp?id
=oai%3Awww.internetculturale.sbn.it%2FTeca%3A20%3ANT0000%3ACNMD
%5C%5C0000171876.

the Anglo-Saxon period because of its relationship to the Benedictine Reform in late tenth-century England. Hence, there is quite a bit of secondary literature about it that we will not be going into. The Psalter has the Romanus text of the Psalms, uses the Cassiodoran headings, and contains glosses in both Latin and Old English. The Latin marginal commentary notes are the usual mixed sort that rely heavily on Jerome and Cassiodorus. The use of these sources extends, however, into the Old English glosses as well. One scholar, Evert Wiesenekker, "notes the prevalence of what he calls 'exegetical glosses,' glosses which, often referring to proper names, offer interpretations derived principally from the psalm commentary of Cassiodorus. Some forty glosses may reflect (sometimes indirectly through translation equivalents) the commentaries with interpretive and often allegorical translations."[17] Clearly this was a classroom teaching book rather than a liturgical manuscript.

The other book is an edition of Jerome's commentary on selected psalms that fall in the final third of the Psalter. The dimensions of the book and the handwriting are the same as the Regius Psalter. Clearly, they were designed as companion books. The Jerome text would have been used in the classroom, likely at the same time as the Regius Psalter to complement it. The fascinating part is that we know that the Jerome volume was never intended to be the only companion to the Psalter. The quires—the gatherings of folded manuscript folios that make up the book—are numbered; the numbering starts at twenty-seven and goes through thirty-eight.

> This suggests that it is possible that along with the [Regius] Psalter, with its preliminary glosses and comments in two languages on the psalms, went a set of probably four codices (or 39 unbound quires) of psalter commentary, to be read and ruminated upon after or in conjunction with a study of the psalter text. Given that Jerome's commentary, though in a somewhat confused state, is so carefully provided, it even seems possible that yet another set of quires might have offered Cassiodorus's commentary as well, since both were used in the exegetical glossing of the [Regius] Psalter.[18]

---

[17] M. J. Toswell, *The Anglo-Saxon Psalter*, Medieval Church Studies 10 (Turnhout: Brepols, 2014), 237.

[18] Ibid., 267.

This, then, is what we're after: a glimpse into the monastic classroom. How were these books actually used? Is the gloss in the Psalter the only encounter students might have had with Cassiodorus? This perspective, at least, suggests not. Instead, the gloss is either a pointer to the broader exposition or a reminder of what had been said. Certainly this is the implication of the Cassiodoran rhetorical glosses in the Italian Psalter: formation in Cassiodorus and his methods go beyond more than just what we see on the side of the page.

Learning for a Liturgical Purpose

When we speak of monastic schooling, monastic education, and monastic culture, our account will be inherently incomplete until we return to the monastic liturgy. As Leclercq notes in the final chapter of his study of monastic culture, it was "in the liturgy that their culture found one of its chosen fields for expression."[19] Learning in the monastic world was oriented toward the liturgical life of the community. If Cassiodorus made an impression on monastic life, this is where we would hope to find it. Within recent years, musicologists have begun analyzing the corpus of monastic chant to understand more about it; the results are intriguing.

Musicologist Emma Hornby has analyzed the second-mode tracts of the Romano-Frankish and Old Roman chant corpus. These consist of several musical pieces whose texts come from the Psalms or—in one case—a canticle. Most of these have connections to Lent and Holy Week, the penitential part of the Christian year when the betrayal and death of Jesus are remembered liturgically. By analyzing the music, she has determined that the patterns of the melodies are not random or happenstance but rather follow the grammar of the passage and syntax. There are four standard phrases that predictably occur within these melodies. Sometimes, however, these phrases are used out of place or with changes. She demonstrates that these changes occur in order to underscore or highlight certain passages within the text. Looking at these points of musical emphasis within the second-mode tracts, she compares them with the Psalms commentaries of Jerome, Augustine, and Cassiodorus in order to show that the emphases appear

---

[19] Leclercq, *Love of Learning*, 236.

in the verses and passages that the church fathers likewise emphasize. She concludes her evidence by saying:

> Augustine wrote in *De civitate Dei* that one should apply what one has learned in grammar and rhetoric studies to interpreting and proclaiming scripture. My study of the second-mode tracts suggests that this advice was taken to heart by the chants' creators. Not only is the textual grammar an important determinant of musical form, but the melodies provide rhetorically heightened deliveries of the texts which in turn promote particular interpretations of the scriptural texts.[20]

While Hornby is dealing only with a small slice of the chant repertoire, her findings are both intriguing and quite suggestive. The intersection of the arts of reading—grammar and rhetoric in particular—and theological interpretation applied to the monastic liturgy exemplifies Cassiodorus's intention in his commentary.

Scholar William Flynn likewise analyzes the new developments in chant that arose in the ninth through eleventh centuries: the *prosae* and the *tropi*. He begins by noting that both "prose" and "trope" started out as grammatical terms for ornamented and figural language and then became liturgical ones for ornamented musical pieces. Tropes are sung sections inserted into standard liturgical pieces. In explaining how these pieces function, Flynn shows how a portion of a psalm used as the introit or starting music for the third Mass of Christmas is interpreted allegorically by the introduction of a set of tropes. He writes:

> Liturgical tropes and proses occur specifically at those points of the liturgy where the allegorical interpretation of the rite was most prominent and might require clarification; similarly a grammatical gloss was often occasioned by those portions of scripture that used a grammatical "trope" or traditionally required an allegorical interpretation. However, liturgical tropes and proses have features that distinguish themselves from grammatical glosses and commentaries. Most important, unlike grammatical glosses, they

---

[20] Emma Hornby, *Medieval Liturgical Chant and Patristic Exegesis: Words and Music in the Second Mode Tracts*, Studies in Medieval and Renaissance Music 9 (Woodbridge, UK: Boydell Press, 2009), 112.

themselves are part of what they are commenting on, and as part of the liturgy, they are intending to be sung.[21]

We have seen in the glossed Psalters how interpretive words are arranged around and within the text of the psalms; Flynn demonstrates how these new genres of chant were putting these glosses into aural form.

In addition to the tropes, the proses were modeled after psalms in many ways, including their style, vocabulary, and content. The shift from tropes to proses and change in standards "stems from an increasingly successful grammatical and liturgical pedagogy."[22] Along with liturgist Margot Fassler, Flynn suggests that "later prose repertories show a greater concern with the use of allegorical interpretation through biblical typology; they are increasingly marked by the features of patristic interpretation and preaching."[23] Flynn emphasizes the way that the readings in the Mass and the chants appointed alongside them interacted with one another. The readings were primarily from the New Testament: the gospel reading was, of course, from the evangelists' records of Jesus and his words; the epistles were usually drawn from the other New Testament texts. The chants were primarily drawn from the Psalms and especially in the more important liturgical seasons, the gospels and psalms were designed to interact with one another, the psalms providing a prophetic perspective, the gospel events fulfilling the psalmic predictions. Cassiodorus represents a crucial link in teaching the arts of grammar and rhetoric and initiating monastic composers into the allegorical and typological strategies that would flower in their compositions for the liturgies.

Into the Scholastic Period

Cassiodorus's work was fundamentally created by someone with monasticism in mind and was accordingly received and transmitted by the monastic tradition. But the monastic strand went into decline as time passed, situations changed, politics shifted, and the church

---

[21] William Flynn, *Medieval Music as Medieval Exegesis*, Studies in Liturgical Musicology 8 (Lanham, MD: Scarecrow Press, 1999), 51.
[22] Ibid., 55.
[23] Ibid., 55–56.

found itself confronted by new challenges. While the monastic orders still existed, the energy of the church's intellectual life shifted to scholasticism and the mendicant orders—chiefly the Dominicans and Franciscans—by the thirteenth century. These groups—despite what many people believe—were not monks in the same way that Benedictine or Cistercian monks were. While they did live an austere religious life, they were focused around clergy who wandered about (that's what the root term "mendicant" means). Rather than focusing on stability, which was a big deal in monastic thought, especially in that of Benedict, these orders were focused on preaching and teaching the proper practice of the faith to the laity; buildings, houses, and establishments existed for the purpose of supporting the study and spirituality necessary for the preaching. The great universities of Europe—preeminently the University of Paris—were largely attended and staffed by members of these orders. Monastic ways and monastic formation lacked a certain relevance within these environments. One famous teacher, Peter the Chanter (d. 1197), said, "The study of Scripture consists of three things: reading, disputation, and preaching."[24] Benedict and Cassiodorus would have been equally horrified to hear this; their shared vision of memorization, meditation, and conversion of life was a very different path for engaging the Scriptures. The study of the Bible and the arts of reading were both essential to the new vision and taught in these intellectual centers, but in new and different ways.

The study of the Bible was dominated by the *Glossa Ordinaria*. This was like the glossed Psalters where the biblical text and commentary would appear on the same page, but it covered the entire Bible and became

Glossa Ordinaria on the Song of Songs, Paris, BN Lat. 131, f.6r.

---

[24] Frans van Liere, *An Introduction to the Medieval Bible* (New York: Cambridge University Press, 2014), 164.

standardized by the end of the twelfth century. No one planned or directed this process, and existing glosses were compiled and assembled into a set of manuscripts, often the nine-volume set recommended by Cassiodorus in the *Institutions*. Because it arose organically, the coverage of the Bible was uneven, and some parts received multiple glosses. The Psalms had no less than three different glosses attributed to Anselm of Laon (d. 1133), Gilbert of Poitiers (d. 1154), and Peter Lombard (d. 1160). The last of these teachers, Lombard, was one of the great men of scholasticism and stands second only to Thomas Aquinas in this domain. An electronic search of Lombard's gloss on the Psalms in Migne's edition turns up over two thousand references to Cassiodorus. This number is imprecise for a variety of reasons, not least of which is a point made in the volume's introductory material: discerning between Cassiodorus and Augustine is not an easy task when we get to the level of glossing. Because Cassiodorus borrows many of Augustine's figural interpretations, it becomes very difficult to determine when a passage is from one and not the other.

Since we have turned to the matter of citations and references, it's worth citing O'Donnell's final assessment of the *Explanation of the Psalms*:

> This was the most successful of Cassiodorus' own works. It was known in continental catalogues of every century and used frequently as early as Bede and Alcuin, who spoke of the work highly; Alcuin listed it in the York library. The utility of the work was obvious, since it was the only complete Psalm commentary from the patristic era except for Augustine's bulkier and less well-organized collection of sermons; and Cassiodorus' express purpose had been to produce a more useful work than Augustine's. The passage from Ranulphus Higden cited above shows the priority of mention of this work [among Cassiodorus's other writings]. Adriaen [editor of the modern critical edition] collected testimonia to this work from Bede and Paul the Deacon (in the eighth century); Alcuin, Theodulf of Orleans, Amalarius, Hildemar, Gottschalk, Hincmar of Rheims, Prudentius of Troyes, Angelome, and Notker Balbulus (in the ninth century); Flodoard of Rheims (in the tenth century); Berno of Reichenau, Bruno of Wurzburd, and Durandus of Troarn (in the eleventh century); and Abelard and the Decretals of Gratian (in the twelfth century). The work's popularity faded only with that of its style of exegesis and the rise of the great *Glossa Ordinaria*.[25]

---

[25] O'Donnell, *Cassiodorus*, 244.

This catalog of mentions is not intended to be complete but is only representative. Other authors of equal and lesser renown who used this work do not appear on this list.

Thomas Aquinas does cite Cassiodorus and the *Explanation of the Psalms* a few times in the great *Summa Theologica*, but by this point, the influence of Cassiodorus has passed. Cassiodorus would continue to be cited in materials invoking the Psalms, and the first printed edition of the *Explanation of the Psalms* appeared in 1491, just fifty years after the invention of the printing press. But Cassiodorus's true home and true place of influence was in the monasteries. His culture was a monastic culture. His commentary is not just about understanding what the Psalms are saying; it was about forming readers in a distinct process where the arts of reading—grammar, rhetoric, and dialectic—become pathways to prayer and spiritual truth, all of which leads to conversion of life. As citations of his work grow apart from this environment, Cassiodorus's interpretation loses its potency and potential. He is best read and best understood as a teacher of theology at prayer.

The Formation of Monastic Minds

At the end of the day, Cassiodorus's goal was not to get lots of manuscripts copied or to be cited by important writers. His goal was to form monks—a particular kind of monk who understood reading, writing, and prayer to be inextricably linked, who understood intellectual effort not as a means for self-promotion or to wow the world with a sharply honed intellect but to join him in the work of traditioning: handing on the faith and practice of the contemplative life as he understood it. Cassiodorus is best measured by the minds he formed and the cultures they created. Of course, assessing his success on this point is challenging but, I would suggest, not impossible. As we scan the past, a couple of individuals in particular offer themselves as examples of the template that Cassiodorus strove to create.

Isidore and Bede

Cassiodorus wrote two works that encapsulate his concept of formation: the *Institutions* and the *Explanation of the Psalms*. As a thought experiment, we could wonder what would happen if two brilliant early medieval minds were exposed to one but not the other. It just so happens that this very well may be the case for two giants of the early medieval world: Isidore of Seville and the Venerable Bede. Born in Visigothic Spain around the year 560, Isidore was the younger brother of Leander, archbishop of Seville. Leander established a school at his cathedral that Isidore attended, and Leander taught him the seven classical liberal arts—the *trivium* and *quadrivium*. He assisted Leander in converting the Visigothic court from Arianism back to christological orthodoxy. On the death of Leander in 600, Isidore became the new archbishop of Seville and established himself as a major force, advising the king, presiding over church councils, protecting monasteries from encroachment, and establishing centers of education. In particular, he is best known for his massive tome referred to as the *Etymologies*. This work was, in some respects, the quintessential early medieval text as it attempted to present a synthesis of all classical knowledge in a portable and digestible form. If Cassiodorus attempted to present the seven liberal arts in book 2 of his *Institutions*, Isidore took the notion and ran with it, bringing in all forms of natural history, medicine, and technology that he could manage. It was the first attempt to capture the sum of human knowledge between two covers and proved radically successful. Over a thousand manuscript copies survive into the modern age.

Whether Isidore learned the seven liberal arts from Cassiodorus is an open question. Whether he knew the *Institutions* is not: the first three books of the *Etymologies* on the seven liberal arts rely heavily on the *Institutions*. Indeed, if we wonder why the *Institutions* was not a more widely copied text in the early medieval world, the best answer is that it had already been incorporated into its own successor. Indeed, the very name of the replacement—*Etymologies*—is due to Isidore's habit of constructing a vast number of etymologies (most rather far-fetched and almost fanciful) throughout his work. This is precisely one of Cassiodorus's favorite moves that we see across his writings from the *Institutions* to the *Explanation of the Psalms* to his secular *Variae*.

Isidore, although he was a strong protector of the monasteries within his archdiocese, is not known to have ever taken monastic vows. It is tempting to see him as a man of the mind, a counselor and educator, a collector of Classical antiquities and a preserver of them as he incorporated their wisdom—particularly the works of Pliny—into his own great synthesis. He may well represent a man shaped by the intention and character of the *Institutions*, devoted to the faith, but informed by and invested in classical learning.

The Venerable Bede, on the other hand, was a monk's monk. As noted above, he is the first person outside of Vivarium to mention the *Explanation of the Psalms*. It is entirely possible that, thanks to Biscop's acquisition of Vivarian manuscripts, Bede read a copy of the *Explanations* straight from Cassiodorus's own hands. Whatever the truth of it, the tradition suggests that the Durham Cassiodorus was itself written by the hand of Bede. Although the note alleging this possibility is in a fourteenth-century hand, we do not know whether this was merely a later age's guess or long-standing tradition associated with the manuscript.

What we can say is that Bede exemplifies an early medieval monk's mastery of the Psalms. M. J. Toswell summarizes her account of Bede's scholarship this way:

> For Bede, then, the psalter was a kind of intellectual home base. It was a text he could call to mind at will, probably even without volition, and use as a bridge from the Old Testament to the New, from prophecy to fulfillment, from literal and historical analysis to allegory. Bede made mention of the psalms as part of the ordinary course of his writing, interleaving quotations from the psalter so deeply into his works that at times it becomes difficult to tease out the original text. . . . Psalm reference made understanding Christian doctrine easier for the laity, and Bede used the psalms to encourage devotion and deeper thought on these issues. His lifelong engagement with the psalms was a lifelong engagement with the challenge of understanding and explicating the fundamental text of Christian spirituality. At the same time, Bede is in no way unusual amongst the church fathers. His engagement with the psalms was the engagement of a committed Christian intellectual. It offered a model, and a challenge, to other Anglo-Saxon Christians.[26]

His was a mind fully formed by the Psalms, their study, and understanding.

Nothing demonstrates the commitment to the Psalter in his home monastery better than an episode recorded in the anonymous *Life of Ceolfrid*. Ceolfrid was the abbot of Jarrow and took the young Bede

---

[26] Toswell, *The Anglo-Saxon Psalter*, 63.

under his wing. According to the *Life*, a plague—one of the recurring reinfections of Justinian's Plague of a century previous—slew the entire population of the Wearmoth and Jarrow monasteries, save for two: Ceolfrid and a teenage boy. Given their fraught circumstances, the two attempted to scale back the liturgical round and do only a simplified version of the Masses and Offices but soon gave it up as too difficult: they returned to the full services, complete with all of the antiphons, responds, and other liturgical accoutrements. While the anonymous *Life* does not name the lad, clues that it provides and circumstantial evidence all point to Bede.

Bede helpfully provides for us his own self-understanding of his task. The last chapter of his *Ecclesiastical History of the English People* preserves a brief autobiography and a list of his works—at least those up to that point. While he is known to literature as the Father of English History, he saw himself differently:

> I was born on the lands of this monastery, and on reaching seven years of age, I was entrusted by my family first to the most reverend Abbot Benedict [Biscop] and later to Abbot Ceolfrid for my education. I have spent all the remainder of my life in this monastery and have devoted myself entirely to the study of the Scriptures. And while I have observed the regular discipline and sung the choir offices daily in church, my chief delight has always been in study, teaching, and writing. I was ordained deacon in my nineteenth year, and priest in my thirtieth, receiving both these orders at the hands of the most reverend Bishop John at the direction of Abbot Ceolfrid. From the time of my receiving the priesthood until my fifty-ninth year, I have worked, both for my own benefit and that of my brethren, to compile short extracts from the works of the venerable Fathers on Holy Scripture and to comment on their meaning and interpretation.[27]

After this he provides a list of thirty-six works that are a mixture of commentaries on books of the Bible, chapter headings for Scripture, lives of the saints, homilies, and hymns. Both his commentaries and homilies would be very well received and quickly incorporated into the material read across the Carolingian world in the Night Office; his

---

[27] Bede, *History of the English Church*, p. 336.

fellow Englishman, the missionary bishop Boniface while in the midst of converting the Germans would regularly write to his kinsmen and friends, requesting them to send him more of Bede's books, calling him "the candle of the church."

In addition to his biblical commentary, it's worth noting that Bede wrote a short book called *On Figures and Tropes* (*De Schematibus et Tropis*). The first book on rhetoric written in England, it offers what neither the *Explanation of the Psalms* nor the *Institutions* does—a deductive list of the various figures of speech and thought. While he is following the example of Isidore and the grammarian Donatus, he replaces almost all of the pagan examples in Donatus with examples from the Scriptures, and these are overwhelmingly from the Psalms. Toswell informs us that these selections come "steeped in the exegesis of the early church, and particularly the *Explanation of the Psalms* of Cassiodorus. Bede uses many of the same examples as does Cassiodorus in the *Explanation*, and although the two differ in the way they label particular devices, Bede was certainly aware of the schemes and tropes identified by Cassiodorus in his commentary."[28]

Bede follows the path that Cassiodorus lays down. He exemplifies a monk engaged in the study of Scripture for the sake of the church. He is deeply invested in the project of traditioning, and many of his works demonstrate a desire to fill in gaps in the patristic record. For instance, his commentaries on Mark, Luke, and Acts address previously neglected New Testament books, and it has been noted that there is "a striking lack of overlap" between the homilies he chooses to write and Gregory the Great's Forty Gospel Homilies—between the two there is only one text treated by both.[29]

As a monk, a man of prayer who used his considerable intellectual gifts for the interpretation of Scripture, guided by the fathers and informed by the classical arts of reading, the Venerable Bede is exactly the kind of mind that Cassiodorus was intent on forming. If we seek to count the successes and demonstrate the legacy of Cassiodorus, Bede must surely be among his victories.

---

[28] Toswell, *The Anglo-Saxon Psalter*, 50.
[29] Bede, *Homilies on the Gospels*, xvi.

Smaragdus of Saint Mihiel

Another figure who was informed by the *Institutions*, the *Explanation of the Psalms*, and Isidore's *Etymologies* was Smaragdus of Saint Mihiel. Although today his name is as obscure as that of Cassiodorus, he was one of three men who dominated the ecclesiastical world of Charlemagne and the sweeping religious and liturgical reforms that would establish the theological, liturgical, and social shape of the church in Europe for centuries after them. Alongside Benedict of Aniane and Alcuin of York, Smaragdus was the third figure who not only directed the universal adoption of the Rule of Benedict within the Carolingian Empire and beyond it but also wrote essential texts for its study and practice.

As the abbot of Saint Mihiel, Smaragdus wrote one of the earliest commentaries on the Rule of Benedict as well as *The Crown of Monks*, a set of extracts on monastic topics to be read at the evening gathering of monks just before Compline and the monastic bedtime. In addition, he wrote a commentary on the gospels and epistles appointed for the liturgical year, gathering interpretations out of the writings of the church fathers but also adding his own notions on the texts and how the gospel and epistle corresponded with one another.

Like Bede, as advised by Cassiodorus, much of his work consisted of selections and judicious editing of works from the fathers, chiefly Gregory the Great, Isidore, and Bede himself. He cites Cassiodorus's *Explanation of the Psalms* in *The Crown of Monks* a few times but uses it more extensively in his *Commentary on the Rule of Saint Benedict*. More important than the level of dependence or the sheer number of citations, though, is his overall character as an interpreter. Terrence Kardong, in an introduction to Smaragdus's commentary, builds a composite picture of his interpretive activities that sounds strikingly similar to Cassiodorus:

> The very fact that Smaragdus wrote a systematic, verse-by-verse commentary on the whole of the *Rule* certainly says something about him as a personality. He believed in careful, persevering activity rather than mere flashes of brilliance. . . . One of Smaragdus' favorite methods of interpretation is etymology. Usually with the aid of Isidore of Seville's *Etymologies*, he attempts to unpack the significance of Benedict's legislation through an analysis of

the key words Benedict employed. Although some of these etymologies amount more to flights of fancy rather than philological facts, they nevertheless constitute a genuine tendency towards analysis. Moreover in itself imagination is by no means a foreign element in a good commentary. At times Smaragdus exercises a good deal of creative imagination in his treatment of a text. . . . Unfortunately, Smaragdus sometimes employs rhetorical devices that produce boredom rather than delight. At times, he indulges in a penchant for long rhetorical strings of synonyms that strike the modern reader as tedious and unnecessary. The same can be said for his use of biblical quotations, which at times he piles up in great mounds. Still, the contemporary reader must realize that some of this is the by-product of his monastic *lectio divina*. . . . Like most monastic writers, he had a predilection for the Book of Psalms. As regards the New Testament, he makes much use of Matthew and John, but his real favorite is Paul.[30]

Any of these things could be said of Cassiodorus; indeed, we have already said many of them of Cassiodorus. If the names were swapped, Kardong's description of Smaragdus's intellectual habits would fit Cassiodorus to a tee.

In addition to these factors, Kardong goes on to describe Smaragdus's relationship to his source material. Smaragdus relied heavily on the great yet unwieldy compendium of monastic legislation compiled by his associate Benedict of Aniane. Smaragdus judiciously edited it and applied it carefully and intelligently, creating, in Kardong's words, "an accessible form of the *Concordia Regularum*, a document that will probably never be translated. Moreover, Smaragdus makes judicious selections from the CR, which can itself be quite repetitious."[31] In short, Smaragdus performs on the *Concordia Regularum* the same kind of judicious editorial process that Cassiodorus employs on Augustine's work on the Psalms.

A final testimony that, to me, speaks volumes about the impact of Cassiodorus on the thought and method of Smaragdus comes from

---

[30] Terrence Kardong, "Smaragdus and His Work," in Smaragdus of Saint Mihiel, *Commentary on the Rule of Saint Benedict*, trans. David Barry, Cistercian Studies 212 (Kalamazoo, MI: Cistercian Publications, 2007), 1–7, esp. 3, 4, 5.

[31] Ibid., 6.

a poem that circulated with his commentary on the readings for the liturgical year. Kardong translates it thus:

> Here you will find that measure of gold which comes from heaven and which we have been accorded by the Holy Ghost himself. In this book, he relates the great deeds of the Patriarchs; in it the lyricism of the Psalms resounds. This little book is full of holy gifts; it contains Scripture and it is seasoned with grammar. Scripture teaches us to seek after the kingdom of God, to detach the self from the earth, to rise above the self. It promises the blessed these heavenly boons: to live with the Lord, to swell always with Him. Grammar, then, through the goodness of God, confers great benefits on those who read it with care.[32]

The union of Scripture, prayer, and the art of reading are exactly what Cassiodorus strived to communicate to his readers.

Summary

By many metrics, the *Explanation of the Psalms* was a success. The counts of surviving manuscripts indicate that the original stated goal of Cassiodorus—to create a shorter, more manageable version of Augustine's *Enarrations on the Psalms*—was accomplished: Cassiodorus's commentary survives in more copies than Augustine's. Furthermore, Cassiodorus's work was accepted by the tradition almost immediately. Not only was it copied and circulated in its own right, it was itself edited and digested and recompiled into a variety of works. The Durham Cassiodorus is simultaneously our earliest witness to the circulation of the work and the first example of an abridgement of it. Its repackaging alongside other patristic materials in the pseudonymous *Brevarium of Jerome* and the widely circulated commentary attributed to Bede further communicated its interpretive principles.

The adaptation of his discussion of the divisions of the psalms in the *tituli* Series VI preserved the unique structural approach of Cassiodorus in apportioning sections to different speakers within a psalm and transmitted them to later generations. The mining of the text of the *Explanation* proper, the *Brevarium*, and the Bedan edition for use

---

[32] Ibid., 4.

in marginal glosses kept his exegetical observations in circulation into the scholastic period and beyond.

Nevertheless, the truest mark of the success of Cassiodorus is found not in books but in people, in the pattern of the monastic culture that he and his book helped shape. The techniques of reading that he taught—grammar, rhetoric, dialectic, allegory, typology, etymology—offered tools for understanding that would be transformed into wings of prayer with which monks would ascend spiritually in their communal chanting of the Daily Office as well as in their private contemplation. The men whose words we possess—and undoubtedly too the women whose words have not come down to us—testify to his success and to his influence in the shaping and praying of the medieval monastic centuries.

Bibliography

Athanasius. "Letter to Marcellinus." Pages 97–119 in *On the Incarnation*. Translated by a religious of CSMV. Crestwood, NY: St. Vladimir's Seminary Press, 1996.

———. "Life of Antony." Pages 3–70 in *Early Christian Lives*. Translated and edited by Carolinne White. New York: Penguin, 1998.

Augustine. *Confessions*. Translated by R. S. Pine-Coffin. London: Penguin, 1961.

Bede. *A History of the English Church and People*. Translated by Leo Sherley-Price. Revised by R. E. Latham. New York: Penguin Books, 1968.

———. *Homilies on the Gospels: Book One Advent to Lent*. Translated by Lawrence T. Martin and David Hurst. Cistercian Studies 110. Kalamazoo, MI: Cistercian Publications, 1991.

Bjornlie, M. Shane. *Politics and Tradition Between Rome, Ravenna and Constantinople: A Study of Cassiodorus and the Variae, 527–554*. Cambridge: Cambridge University Press, 2013.

Boethius. *The Consolation of Philosophy*. Revised edition. Translated by Victor Watts. London: Penguin, 1999.

Boynton, Susan. "Training for the Liturgy as a Form of Monastic Education." Pages 7–20 in *The Practice of the Bible in the Middle Ages: Production, Reception, and Performance in Western Christianity*. Edited by Susan Boynton and Diane J. Reilly. New York: Columbia University Press, 2011.

Caesarea of Arles. "A Letter from Caesaria, Abbess of Arles (c. 550)." Epistolae project. Translated by Joan Ferrante. Accessed January 30, 2017. Online: https://epistolae.ccnmtl.columbia.edu/letter/915.html.

Carney, James. *Medieval Irish Lyrics*. Berkeley: University of California Press, 1967.

Courcelle, Pierre. *Late Latin Writers and Their Greek Sources.* Translated by Harry E. Wedeck. Cambridge, MA: Harvard University Press, 1969.

de Lubac, Henri. *Medieval Exegesis.* Vol. 1. Translated by Mark Sebanc. Grand Rapids, MI: Eerdmans, 1998.

Eusebius. *The History of the Church.* Translated by G. A. Williamson. Revised and edited by Andrew Lowth. New York: Penguin, 1989.

Flynn, William. *Medieval Music as Medieval Exegesis.* Studies in Liturgical Musicology 8. Lanham, MD: Scarecrow Press, 1999.

Fortunatus. "St. Radegund." Pages 70–86 in *Sainted Women of the Dark Ages.* Edited and translated by Jo Ann McNamara, John E. Halborg, with E. Gordon Whatley. Durham, NC: Duke University Press, 1992. Accessed June 26, 2017. Online: http://people.uwm.edu/carlin/venantius-fortunatus-life-of-st-radegund/.

Gamble, Harry Y. *Books and Readers in the Early Church: A History of Early Christian Texts.* New Haven, CT: Yale University Press, 1995.

Gameson, Richard. "The Royal 1. B. Vii Gospels and English Book Production in the Seventh and Eighth Centuries." Pages 24–52 in *The Early Medieval Bible: Its Production, Decoration, and Use.* Edited by Richard Gameson. Cambridge: Cambridge University Press, 1994.

Ganz, David. "Mass Production of Early Medieval Manuscripts: The Carolingian Bibles from Tours." Pages 53–62 in *The Early Medieval Bible: Its Production, Decoration, and Use.* Edited by Richard Gameson. Cambridge, UK: Cambridge University Press, 1994.

Gibson, Margaret. "Carolingian Glossed Psalters." Pages 78–100 in *The Early Medieval Bible: Its Production, Decoration, and Use.* Edited by Richard Gameson. Cambridge: Cambridge University Press, 1994.

Gorman, Michael. "The Oldest Epitome of Augustine's *Tractatus in Euangelium Ioannis* and Commentaries on the Gospel of John in the Early Middle Ages." *Revue des Études Augustiniennes* 43 (1997): 63–103.

Hill, Jonathan. *The History of Christian Thought.* Downers Grove, IL: IVP, 2003.

Hilner, Julia. "Monastic Imprisonment in Justinian's Novels." *Journal of Early Christian Studies* 15, no. 2 (Summer 2007): 205–37.

Hornby, Emma. *Medieval Liturgical Chant and Patristic Exegesis: Words and Music in the Second Mode Tracts.* Studies in Medieval and Renaissance Music 9. Woodbridge, UK: Boydell Press, 2009.

Jerome. *The Homilies of Saint Jerome*. Vol. 1. Translated by Marie Ligouri Ewald. Fathers of the Church 48. Washington, DC: The Catholic University of America Press, 1964.

———. *The Principal Works of St. Jerome*. Translated by W. H. Fremantle, G. Lewis, and W. G. Martley. NPNF[2]. Vol. 6. Edited by Philip Schaff and Henry Wace. Grand Rapids, MI: William B. Eerdmans, 1996.

Kardong, Terrence. "Smaragdus and His Work." Pages 1–7 in *Commentary on the Rule of Saint Benedict*, by Smaragdus of Saint Mihiel. Translated by David Barry. Cistercian Studies 212. Kalamazoo, MI: Cistercian Publications, 2007.

Kennedy, George A. *Classical Rhetoric and Its Christian and Secular Tradition from Ancient to Modern Times*. 2nd rev. ed. Chapel Hill: University of North Carolina Press, 1999.

Leclercq, Jean. *The Love of Learning and the Desire for God: A Study of Monastic Culture*. Translated by Catharine Misrahi. New York: Fordham University Press, 1982.

McKinnon, James. *The Advent Project: The Late Seventh-Century Creation of the Roman Mass Proper*. Berkeley: University of California Press, 2000.

McLarney, Gerard. *St. Augustine's Interpretation of the Psalms of Ascent*. Washington, DC: The Catholic University of America Press, 2014.

O'Donnell, James J. *Augustine: A New Biography*. New York: HarperCollins, 2006.

———. *Cassiodorus*. Berkeley: University of California Press, 1979.

———. "Eugippius." Pages 337–38 in *Augustine through the Ages: An Encyclopedia*. Edited by Allan D. Fitzgerald. Grand Rapids, MI: Eerdmans, 1999.

———. *The Ruin of the Roman Empire: A New History*. New York: Ecco, 2009.

O'Keefe, John J., and R. R. Reno. *Sanctified Vision: An Introduction to Early Christian Interpretation of the Bible*. Baltimore: Johns Hopkins University Press, 2005.

O'Loughlin, Thomas. "Individual Anonymity and Collective Identity: The Enigma of Early Medieval Latin Theologians." *Recherches de Theologie et Philosophie medievales* 64, no. 2 (1997): 291–314.

Quasten, Johannes. *Patrology*. 4 vols. Translated by Placid Solari. Notre Dame, IN: Christian Classics, 1986.

Salmon, Pierre. *Les 'Tituli Psalmorum' des Manuscripts Latin*. Collectanea Biblical Latina 12. Rome: Vatican Library, 1959.

Smaragdus of Saint Mihiel. *Commentary on the Rule of Saint Benedict.* Translated by David Barry. Cistercian Studies 212. Kalamazoo, MI: Cistercian Publications, 2007.

Tennyson, Alfred. "The Higher Pantheism." Accessed on June 26, 2017. Online: https://www.poetryfoundation.org/poems-and-poets/poems/detail/45323.

Thompson, Bard. *Liturgies of the Western Church.* Philadelphia: Fortress Press, 1961.

Toswell, M. J. *The Anglo-Saxon Psalter.* Medieval Church Studies 10. Turnhout: Brepols, 2014.

van Liere, Frans. *An Introduction to the Medieval Bible.* New York: Cambridge University Press, 2014.

Vitz, Evelyn Birge. "Liturgy as Education in the Middle Ages." Pages 20–34 in *Medieval Education.* Edited by Ronald Begley and Joseph Koterski. Fordham Series in Medieval Studies 4. New York: Fordham University Press, 2000.

Walford, Edward. *Epitome of the Ecclesiastical History of Philostorgius, Compiled by Photius, Patriarch of Constantinople.* London: Henry G. Bohn, 1855. Accessed on October 28, 2016. Online: www.tertulian.org/fathers/philostorgius.htm.

Young, Frances. *Biblical Exegesis and the Formation of Christian Culture.* Peabody, MA: Hendrickson, 1997.

Index

Adrian, 140, 141, 144
Agapetus (Pope), 81–82, 110
Alexandrian school 120, 121–32
Antiochene school, 121, 140–42
anti-Semitism/anti-Judaism, 179, 217–18, 252–55
Antony, 13–14
Athalaric, 69, 70, 73, 81, 212
Athanasius of Alexandria, 13–14, 15, 19–25, 26, 121, 143, 159, 175–77, 179
Augustine of Dacia, 194
Augustine of Hippo, 16, 17, 39, 40, 41, 43, 45, 60, 75, 79, 83, 87, 98, 108, 118, 119, 120, 121, 126, 132–40, 141, 143, 144, 146, 149, 152, 153, 154, 155, 156, 159, 163, 164, 169, 170, 174, 180, 181–94, 195–97, 199–201, 203, 204, 206, 207, 209, 210–11, 215, 217, 219, 220–31, 233, 236, 238, 244, 250, 255, 264, 265–68, 271, 272, 273, 276, 278–79, 283, 286, 287, 290, 291, 294, 301, 302
Augustine of Hippo, editing, 181–94

Baptism, 83, 99, 100, 106, 167, 200, 201, 205, 221, 225, 236, 244, 249, 259–60

Bede, The Venerable, 11, 117, 185, 224, 275–77, 280, 284, 297–99, 300, 302
Benedict Biscop, 275–76
Benedict of Aniane, 280, 300
Benedict of Nursia, 56, 86, 127, 151, 156, 160n10, 213, 263, 264, 293, 300, 301
Bibles, physical shape, 30–34
Birge Vitz, Evelyn, 17–19
Boethius, 62, 66–68, 74, 75, 88, 142, 150, 151
Boynton, Susan, 51, 53, 55

Caesaria II of Arles, 2–5, 7, 11, 25
Carney, James, 57
Cassian, John 14, 86, 120, 126–32, 146, 183, 195, 196, 197, 213, 280
Cassiodorus, Institutions, xi, 79, 80, 85–89, 90, 102, 110, 115, 136, 142–46, 147, 158, 183, 188, 191–92, 239, 242, 244, 274, 275, 276, 294, 295, 296–97, 299, 300
Cassiodorus, political career, 62–66, 68–74, 75–76; religious career, 78–89
Cassiodorus, Variae, xi, 62, 73, 74, 75, 83, 89, 102, 212, 253, 268, 296

Christology, 133, 170, 229–31, 233–38, 246–47, 259–60
Christology, political implications, 76–77
church fathers, 6, 9, 33, 50, 87, 99, 107, 108, 115, 117, 119–20, 126, 144, 152, 161, 171, 172, 173, 185, 195, 199, 203, 204, 207, 218, 227, 245, 253, 266, 273, 291, 297, 298, 299, 300
church mothers, 5–11
conclusion of the psalm, 107–8, 142, 171–72, 175, 178, 236, 237, 240, 242, 251–52, 267, 270, 281
Constantinople, 63, 65, 66, 70, 71, 72, 74–75, 76, 77–79, 81, 85, 90, 126n8, 140, 141, 184, 190, 220, 234, 251, 263
Courcelle, Pierre, 276–77

David, 25, 95–98, 99, 101, 103, 104, 111, 112, 141, 160, 162, 164, 167, 169, 175, 179, 205, 222, 223, 226, 228, 230, 269, 270, 271
David and Jesus, 96–98
de Lubac, Henri, 195
Desert Fathers, 14, 20, 26, 127, 131, 280
dialectic, 85, 88, 103, 106, 112, 115, 142, 148, 149, 150, 151, 154, 155, 156, 157, 158, 269, 288, 295, 303

emotions, 5, 18, 21, 25, 48, 116, 209, 247, 270
Eucherius of Lyon, 127, 138–39, 144, 210
Eugippius, 87, 117, 182, 183–84
Eustochium, 6, 7, 11, 42, 151, 152
Explanation of the Psalms, and monastic prayer, 159–61

Explanation of the Psalms, Christianizing classical learning, 154–59
Explanation of the Psalms, comparison with Prosper and Augustine, 192–94
Explanation of the Psalms, edited into Psalters and Bibles, 281–94
Explanation of the Psalms, editing Augustine, 186–94
Explanation of the Psalms, inductive character, 114–16
Explanation of the Psalms, manuscript circulation, 278–81
Explanation of the Psalms, manuscript experience, 92–113
Explanation of the Psalms, marginal signs, 101–3, 105–6, 110, 147–48, 154, 157–59
Explanation of the Psalms, original structure, 170–73
Explanation of the Psalms, preface, 147–80
Explanation of the Psalms, psalm groupings, 175–80
Explanation of the Psalms, transmission, 274–77
Explanation of the Psalms, visual apparatus, 109–10, 187–88

Fassler, Margot, 292
Flynn, William, 291–92

Gameson, Richard, 37
Ganz, David, 36–37
Gibson. Margaret, 285–88
Glossa Ordinaria, 280, 293–95
Gorman, Michael, 182, 185–86
gospels, x, 4, 5, 7, 9, 11, 13, 23, 26, 33, 36, 41, 42, 43, 46, 47, 48, 49,

56, 60, 86, 148, 207, 218, 245, 277, 292, 300
Gradual Psalms, 264–71
grammar, 19, 54, 85, 88, 102, 112, 115, 132, 142, 149, 150, 151, 154, 156, 157, 158, 216, 229, 242, 257, 263, 288, 290, 291, 292, 295, 299, 302
Guigo II, 213

Halporn, James W., 279, 281
hermeneutics of Athanasius, 19–25
hermeneutics of Augustine, 121, 135–40, 196–97, 199–201
hermeneutics of Cassiodorus, 101–13, 142–46, 196–219
hermeneutics of Hilary of Poitiers, 163–68, 174–75
hermeneutics of John Cassian, 126–32
hermeneutics of Origen, 121–26
Hilary of Poitiers, 9, 87, 108, 120, 121, 143, 155, 162–75, 199, 203, 215, 233, 238, 271, 273, 282, 283
Hornby, Emma, 290–91

incarnation, 25, 99, 100, 108, 163, 166, 169, 230, 235, 250–51, 257, 268, 270
Isidore of Seville, 181, 296–97

Jerome, 5–11, 12, 16, 26, 41–44, 87, 108, 118, 119, 120, 126, 127, 133, 134, 135, 143, 151, 152, 155, 162, 163, 164, 165, 169, 170, 203, 215, 220, 222, 225, 227, 228, 231, 238, 266, 273, 282, 283, 286, 287, 288, 289, 290, 302
Jesus, 4, 5, 6, 11, 16, 17, 25, 27, 28, 47, 48, 49, 95, 96, 97, 98, 141, 153, 163, 166, 169, 175, 199, 207, 217, 221, 222, 223, 224, 226, 227, 229, 230, 236, 237, 238, 244, 245, 246, 247, 250, 252, 253, 258, 259, 260, 290, 292
Jews, 125, 129, 177, 179, 208, 224, 249 (*see also* anti-Semitism/anti-Judaism)
Jolly, Karen, 45
Junillus Africanus, 140, 141, 144
Justinian, 66, 70–72, 73, 74, 75, 77, 80, 90, 126n8, 251

Kardong, Terrance, 300–302
Kennedy, George, 158
King, Jr., Martin Luther, 205

language, the challenges of, 29, 38–44
Leclercq, Jean, 290
literacy, 4, 7, 11, 24, 26, 27, 30, 44–47, 52, 53, 54, 55, 59, 60, 109, 148, 155, 191
liturgy, 256–64, 290–92
Liturgy of the Hours/Daily Office, 3, 5, 10, 14, 16, 17, 34–35, 47–48, 50–51, 55, 159–60, 161, 213, 258, 265, 298, 303
liturgy, solution to technological problems, 47–57

Mael Isu, 57–59, 288
manuscript production, 35–38
martyrs, 12, 13, 248, 261–62, 263, 275
Mass (or Eucharist), 5, 16–17, 18, 33, 34, 47, 48, 49, 49, 51, 55, 56, 77, 160, 168, 236, 244, 251, 261–63, 264, 291, 292, 298
master of offices, 64, 66, 67, 68, 89

McKinnon, James, 15, 19
memorization, 3, 8, 9, 10, 11, 24, 25, 26, 48, 50–56, 60, 109, 112, 113, 131, 132, 136, 142–43, 146, 150, 151, 213, 258, 293
monasticism, 7, 10, 11, 12–14, 15, 32, 34, 50–53, 55, 57, 60, 81, 84–86, 88, 120, 127, 160, 213, 263–64, 280
music, 16, 17, 24, 66, 85, 88, 112, 115, 148, 156, 157, 158, 159, 165, 169, 222, 258, 290–93

numerology, 108, 164–65, 236

O'Donnell, James, 72, 74, 81, 89, 134, 140, 187, 294
O'Keefe, John J. and R. R. Reno, 203–9
O'Loughlin, Thomas, 118–19
orality, 52, 109, 187–88
Origen of Alexandria, 77, 87, 120, 121–26, 127, 140, 146, 152, 162, 163, 164, 165, 166, 167–68, 169, 174, 195, 197, 199, 208, 215, 217, 233, 238, 251, 283

Paula (the elder) 6, 7, 10–11, 42
Peter of Tripoli, 184–85
plague, 1, 61, 71, 75, 85, 289
poem to a psalter, 57–59
praetorian prefect, 64, 67, 69, 70, 73, 75, 81, 83, 89, 212
Prosper of Aquitaine, 149, 182, 183, 192–94, 278
Psalm 1, interpretation of, 232–38
Psalm 6, interpretation of, 239–44
Psalm 18, interpretation of 94–108
Psalm 22, interpretation of, 244–55
Psalm 66, interpretation of, 256–64

Psalm 84, interpretation of, 265–68
Psalm 87, interpretation of 220–31
Psalm 131, interpretation of, 264, 268–71
psalm divisions, 98–100, 111, 222, 224, 233, 242, 245, 280
psalm headings, 95–98, 165, 111, 222
Psalms as microcosm of Scripture, 19–20, 48, 60
Psalms in public worship, 14–17

quadriga, the (four senses of Scripture), 194–96
quaestor, 64, 65, 68, 69, 73, 89

Radegund, 1–5, 7, 11, 12, 25, 26, 81
reading strategies, allegory, 120, 121, 125, 128, 129, 138, 140, 146, 149, 168, 178, 180, 194, 195, 196, 197, 199, 200, 203, 204, 205–11, 212, 214, 218, 237, 245, 249, 255, 288, 289, 291, 292, 297, 303
reading strategies, etymology, 79, 101, 102, 110, 112, 115, 138, 148, 157, 210, 273, 296, 300, 301, 303
reading strategies, figurative reading, 194–214
reading strategies, intensive reading, 204
reading strategies, legitimacy, 215–17
reading strategies, prayerful reading (lectio divina), 197, 212–15, 247, 252
reading strategies, typology, 138, 204–5, 207, 208, 292, 303
religious affections, 17–19
rhetoric, 39, 55, 83, 85, 88, 98, 112, 115, 132, 136, 141–42, 146–51,

154–59, 224, 228, 230, 239–40, 241, 244, 252, 272, 273, 288, 290, 291–92, 295, 299, 301, 303

sacrifice, 10, 15–17, 205, 250, 262, 263, 271, 283
Salmon, Pierre, 284
Septuagint (Greek Old Testament), 29, 38–39, 42, 43, 94, 95, 129n16, 210, 227, 228, 264
Smaragdus of Saint-Mihiel, 280, 300–302
speakers within a psalm, 98–99, 108, 111–12, 113, 141, 162, 174–75, 178, 180, 222–23, 283, 302
spread of the church, 27–30
Stegmüller, Friedrich, 278

Theodore of Mopsuestia, 121, 140–141

Theodoric the Great, 46, 63–69, 73, 74
Toswell, M. J., 289, 297, 299
traditioning, 116–20, 279
trivium (the classical arts of reading), 149–50
trivium, Christian scruples about, 151–52

van Liere, Frans, 45
veiled reading, 100–101, 105, 125, 130, 138, 164, 166–68, 198–217
Vivarium, 79, 80, 81, 82, 84–85, 89, 90, 170, 185, 192, 220, 224, 264, 274–75, 277, 297

Wiesenekker, Evert, 289

Young, Frances, 141

www.ingramcontent.com/pod-product-compliance
Lightning Source LLC
Chambersburg PA
CBHW051935290426
44110CB00015B/1985